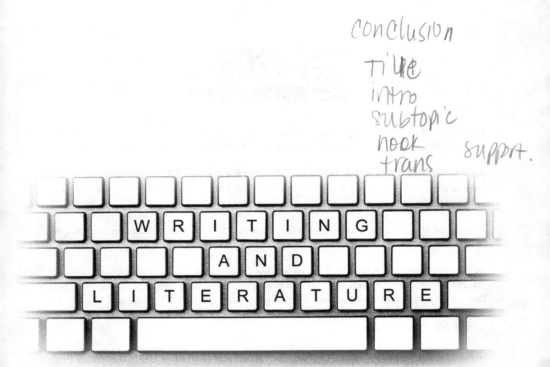

COMPOSITION AS INQUIRY, LEARNING, THINKING, AND COMMUNICATION

TANYA LONG BENNETT

D1547787

University System of Georgia
"Creating A More Educated Georgia"

UNG
UNIVERSITY of
NORTH GEORGIA™
UNIVERSITY PRESS

Blue Ridge | Cumming | Dahlonega | Gainesville | Oconee

Published by:
University of North Georgia Press
Dahlonega, Georgia

Cover Design by Corey Parson and Amy Beard

ISBN: 978-1-940771-23-6

Printed in the United States of America, 2017

For more information, please visit: http://ung.edu/university-press
Or email: ungpress@ung.edu

Table of Contents

Why Write About Literature?

The odds are high that even though you are using this textbook for a first year English composition class, you are not an English major. Probably, you are required to take this course as part of your first year of college coursework to sharpen your writing, research, argument, and thinking skills so that in future classes, and later in your life, these proficiencies will serve you well in accomplishing important tasks. A study of **rhetoric,** the art of persuasion, can help you refine your ability to influence others, through both writing and speaking. With these goals in mind, it may seem odd that this first year composition book is filled with poetry, short stories, and plays, and even includes discussion of literary devices, like rhyme and rhythm, metaphor, and point of view! Yet, many English instructors do, indeed, choose to teach at least one semester of first year composition in the context of literary studies.

Why do they do this? Do they enjoy watching you squirm as you struggle to find the meaning in a line of Shakespeare's poetry? Probably not. There are a couple of other important reasons that are much more pivotal to the content choice of your instructor—let's call him Dr. Lopez—than his desire to bedevil you.

Most likely, Dr. Lopez feels that literature is the best context for your writing this semester because

1. He is better able to evaluate the effectiveness of your compositions if they are written on a topic with which he has some expertise. If you wrote a paper arguing for the superiority of one cancer treatment over another, he would certainly be able to test the validity of your logic and the clarity of your

presentation. However, he might not feel comfortable judging whether current cancer research supports your stance. After following your research process all semester, he might become familiar with the sources you employed in your paper, but he would still lack knowledge of the general body of research on this subject. On the other hand, if you write your essay on how, in the poem "Do Not Go Gentle into That Good Night," Dylan Thomas illustrates his speaker's fear of his own death, Dr. Lopez is on much firmer ground. Since he is an expert on twentieth century British literature, and happens to have earned a master's degree in twentieth century world literature, not only can he see the gaps in your argument, but he can also guide you toward sources that could help fill in those gaps. The resulting student papers written as a product of Dr. Lopez's literature-focused class will likely be more valid than if he had chosen a topic less familiar to him.

2.   Further, he believes that no matter what content a professor uses for this course, students should be improving their understanding of how language makes meaning. What better context for pursuing this goal than a discipline in which words are the subject? In writing your paper on Thomas's poem, you will not only be practicing your skills in research, argument, organization, grammar, and documentation, but you will also be learning, from Thomas himself (among other authors), how words can be used rhetorically to persuade one's reader toward a particular perspective.

3.   Literature is a fruitful context in which to practice supporting an argument with textual evidence. Periodically, in one of my upper level English literature classes, I encounter a pre-law student who is required to take my class as part of her pre-law curriculum. If this policy at first seems odd, closer examination reveals its logic. In a court of law, attorneys spend much of their time referring to the language of particular laws and drawing the jury's attention to specific pieces of evidence—often from reports, letters, interview transcripts, and previous cases. The first time I served on a jury, I was fascinated to see how much the trial's structure—with the lawyers' opening remarks, their back-and-forth examination of evidence and witnesses, and their closing remarks—resembled that of an argumentative

essay. I was gratified to witness their constant references to written texts as evidence supporting their positions, either as prosecutor or defender.

4. In spite of all the poems, stories, and dramas on Dr. Lopez's syllabus, make no mistake—his purpose is to help you improve your writing. In particular, such a course focuses on the rhetorical skills that will aid you in making successful arguments based on convincing and well-presented evidence. Of course, here, the term argument does not necessarily mean heated debate, but rather refers to the case a writer makes in defending a specific perspective. If most readers have assumed that "Do Not Go Gentle into That Good Night" is a simple expression of the speaker's sorrow about his father's impending death, your essay might convince those readers that a better understanding of the poem comes with recognition of the speaker's anxiety about death in general, which includes the speaker's fear of his own demise. As you practice constructing a strong case for your interpretation of a literary work, you will be building skills that help produce effective writing in any context.

I hope that in the process of reading closely and critically, gathering evidence, working through various paths of thought, researching secondary sources, organizing ideas into logical arguments, and revising your writing for the greatest impact, you will also enjoy the literature you read in this class. When students write about something that truly interests them, the product is almost always better than if a writer has simply "jumped through the hoops." Look for works in this volume that explore issues and themes you care about. This should help make the semester an engaging and enjoyable one, for both you *and* Dr. Lopez!

Reading Like a Professional

Many college students who graduate at the top of their high school classes experience a rude awakening when, after reading an assignment for a college course, they fail a quiz over the assignment the next day in class. What happened? You know you read every page of the assignment, but when the professor asked you about a specific point in the reading, you blanked. Or even worse, even as you read, you were never quite sure just what the author's **central argument**, or **thesis**, was.

The reading assigned in college courses can be quite challenging. Authors often pursue their goals in complex and sophisticated ways, employing vocabulary, metaphors, and allusions that are unfamiliar to many readers. Authors of literature are no exception to these practices. Yet, avid fans of poetry, fiction, and drama often claim that the world is broadened incredibly by literature, if only one can determine how to navigate it.

You probably enjoy reading certain kinds of texts, such as internet articles on your pet interests or biographies of people you admire. You may even have literary favorites. You may have spent many happy hours immersed in the world of Middle Earth, in Tolkien's *Lord of the Rings*, or in Forks, Washington, trying to guess what will happen to Stephenie Meyer's Bella in the *Twilight* series. Still, you may feel a bit uncertain surmising the meaning of Nathaniel Hawthorne's allegorical short story "Young Goodman Brown" or interpreting Robert Frost's sonnet "Design."

Take heart! The more you learn about literature and the more you practice unraveling its meanings, the more adept you will become at understanding it. In fact, this is the case for all kinds of texts. Many students just beginning to study law, for instance, find the specialized language

4

and style of the field almost impossible to understand, but after a year or two of reading case documents, they undoubtedly find the task much less daunting. Similarly, students new to academic research articles and books often have difficulty plowing through them and then summarizing the authors' points. Yet, after some practice, this task becomes much less challenging and even—dare I say it?—intellectually stimulating!

So how does one improve comprehension of such texts? The following "active" reading process is recommended to boost you beyond common frustrations with challenging reading assignments. It may seem tedious at first, but if you practice it often enough, it will become second nature to you as you tackle tough readings.

1. Skim the text first. Get an idea of what sort of text you are dealing with. Is it an article based on primary research, such as experiments or participant interviews? Is it a critique of a previously published study? Is it a personal essay based on the author's life? Is it a sonnet or a one-act play? How is the piece structured? Can you find a statement or passage that seems to capture the text's central message?

2. Next, read the whole piece slowly and carefully. We cannot expect to understand dense, sophisticated texts through the same reading process by which we might read a newspaper article or a Facebook post. We must be willing to slow down to absorb subtleties and complexities.

3. Engage with the text. **Annotate** as you go. In other words, write on the page! If you cannot write directly on the page, use sticky notes or electronic note-taking strategies. Look up unfamiliar terms and jot down the definitions, highlight or underline key ideas, and write down questions and ideas that come to you as you read. Note patterns in the text that might be considered later to help unravel the meaning.

4. Reread the text as necessary. Seek to fill in gaps in your understanding that may remain after your first reading.

5. Gather outside information about the piece's context if it is helpful, though you should be careful not to "read into" the text's meaning too much. Any historical or biographical interpretation of a literary work must still be supported by the text itself.

6. React. Record your personal response to what you read. If you disagree with a statement, make a note of your reaction. You may change your mind as you proceed through the text, but moving beyond the role of a passive reader, who simply memorizes information, will generate a much deeper understanding. Your brain wants to fit this new perspective into the other ideas already stored there. Working through contradictions and/or exploring relationships between old information and new information will increase retention and understanding of the new material.

Using the guidelines above, let's consider this excerpt from a scholarly article by Jacob Michael Leland, "'Yes, That is a Roll of Bills in My Pocket': The Economy of Masculinity in *The Sun Also Rises.*"

> A great deal of critical attention has been paid to masculine agency and its displacement in Ernest Hemingway's fiction. The story is familiar by now: the Hemingway hero loses some version of his maleness to the first World War and he replaces it with a tool—in Upper Michigan, a fishing rod or a pocket knife; in Africa, a hunting rifle—a new object that emblematizes his mastery over his surroundings and whose status as a fetishized commodity and Freudian symbolic significance is something less than subtle. In *The Sun Also Rises*, this pattern repeats itself, but with important differences that arise from the novel's cosmopolitan European setting. Mastery over the elements, here, has more to do with economic agency and control over social relationships than with nature and survival. The stakes are different, too; in the modern European city, the Hemingway hero recovers not only masculinity but also American identity in social and sexual interaction. (37)

In researching *The Sun Also Rises* for a project, Ling Ti found Leland's article. What follows is her annotated copy of the above excerpt:

Agency: the ability to assert one's will, as an agent

A great deal of critical attention has been paid to masculine <u>agency</u> and its <u>displacement</u> in Ernest Hemingway's fiction. The story is familiar by now: the Hemingway hero loses some version of his maleness to the first World War and he replaces it with a tool—in Upper Michigan, a fishing rod or a pocket knife; in Africa, a hunting rifle—a new object that <u>emblematizes</u> his mastery over his surroundings and whose status as a <u>fetishized</u> <u>commodity</u> and <u>Freudian symbolic</u> significance is something less than subtle. In *The Sun Also Rises*, this pattern repeats itself, but with important differences that arise from the novel's cosmopolitan European setting. Mastery over the elements, here, has more to do with economic agency and control over social relationships than with nature and survival. The stakes are different, too; in the modern European city, the Hemingway hero recovers not only masculinity but also American identity in social and sexual interaction.

Displacement: being pushed out of your position

Emblematizes: represents

Fetishized: obsessed over

Freudian symbol: something representing subconscious insecurity or desire – knife=penis=mastery?

Commodity: something to buy and sell

Economic power = masculinity = mastery?

If Leland is saying that the character uses economic mastery to feel like a man, what does this say about big spenders in general? About American consumers who think they have to have a certain kind of phone or car or jeans? Is spending really related to masculine identity? I'm not sure—I need to think about it. Maybe it's at least true for Jake in the 1920's Paris and Spain settings of the novel.

Upon her first reading of the article, Ling wasn't quite sure what Leland was saying, but after interacting with the text according to the above recommendations, she was able not only to understand his argument but also to consider *whether or not it is convincing.*

Exercise:

Try this process with The Gettysburg Address. After skimming, rereading, annotating, and reacting to the text, compare your notes on the speech's meaning with those of your classmates. Does this process of *active* reading give you a deeper understanding than a simple, passive reading would?

The Gettysburg Address

Four score and seven years ago our fathers brought forth on this continent, a new nation, conceived in Liberty, and dedicated to the proposition that all men are created equal.

Now we are engaged in a great civil war, testing whether that nation, or any nation so conceived and so dedicated, can long endure. We are met on a great battle-field of that war. We have come to dedicate a portion of that field, as a final resting place for those who here gave their lives that that nation might live. It is altogether fitting and proper that we should do this.

But, in a larger sense, we can not dedicate—we can not consecrate—we can not hallow—this ground. The brave men, living and dead, who struggled here, have consecrated it, far above our poor power to add or detract. The world will little note, nor long remember what we say here, but it can never forget what they did here. It is for us the living, rather, to be dedicated here to the unfinished work which they who fought here have thus far so nobly advanced. It is rather for us to be here dedicated to the great task remaining before us—that from these honored dead we take increased devotion to that cause for which they gave the last full measure of devotion—that we here highly resolve that these dead shall not have died in vain—that this nation, under God, shall have a new birth of freedom—and that government of the people, by the people, for the people, shall not perish from the earth.

Abraham Lincoln
November 19, 1863

Regardless of the *type* of text you are confronted with, this engaged reading process should serve to deepen your understanding of it. An important assumption of this book is that as your reading skills become more sophisticated, so will your writing. As you practice these methods of active reading, you will likely begin to regard your own writing in the same way that you do the other texts you read. You will learn that the strategies used by well-regarded authors are available to you as a writer, and you will begin to imagine your audience's reaction to your writing more effectively than you have done in the past. You will start to recognize that reading and writing are inextricably related to one another.

Forming a Perspective on the Subject

2.1 Discovering and Honoring Your Passions and Values

After reading a work carefully, annotating it, and reacting to it, the next step is to determine how it fits into your perspective on the world. For example, how do you *feel* about Abraham Lincoln's Gettysburg Address? Do you appreciate Lincoln's assertion that in order to honor what these dead sacrificed, we should work hard to keep our democratic nation together? Or does it irritate you that in reminding his audience that in this nation, "all men were created equal," Lincoln neglects to acknowledge the terrible wrongs done to Native Americans as the nation was formed? Did you tend to focus less on the theme of the speech and more on Lincoln's rhetorical strategy and poetic language? Forming your own conclusions about a literary work, or a topic of any kind, is the first step to shaping an argument and, ultimately, making a case for your perspective through a persuasive essay.

To practice the process of forming a perspective on a topic, consider Theodore Roethke's poem "My Papa's Waltz," at http://www.poetryfoundation.org/poem/172103. In an initial reading of the poem, you may have already noticed that some elements of "My Papa's Waltz" seem to suggest that the father is abusive toward his son, while to the contrary, other lines imply that the son wants to continue this waltz. Seeking the "truth" of this poem, readers often debate over which interpretation is being developed by Roethke. After careful analysis of this text, first-year composition student Marion Velis decided that in spite of the poem's seemingly violent undertones, it is the son's *love* for his father that leaves the strongest impression. What follows is the essay she produced to develop this argument.

10

Marion Velis
English 1102

Clinging to Love: Theodore Roethke's "My Papa's Waltz"

At first glance, Theodore Roethke's poem "My Papa's Waltz" may seem like a poem about a boy's fear of his controlling, abusive, alcoholic father. But the poem goes much deeper than that. Roethke uses specific rhythm, word choice, and a controlling metaphor to give the poem a reminiscent tone that looks back on the father in love.

One of the most noticeable elements of the poem is its waltz rhythm. Each line in the poem is made up of three iambs, which create the six-count beat of a waltz. When Roethke combines this rhythm with specific words, the reader gets a spinning sensation. This is clearly shown in the first stanza of the poem, when Roethke writes, "The whiskey on your breath / Could make a small boy dizzy; / But I hung on like death: / Such waltzing was not easy" (1-4). Roethke uses this waltzing rhythm in conjunction with his description of a drinking father to convey the spinning, drunk feeling generated by this dance. When the poet says, "We romped until the pans / Slid from the kitchen shelf" (5-6), the reader can imagine the father spinning in his drunkenness and making a mess of the house. The speaker's mother seems ashamed in lines 7-8, where the poet writes, "My mother's countenance / Could not unfrown itself." The boy, on the other hand, says, "But I hung on like death" (3), as if he wanted to continue to love his father, despite his obvious flaws.

This is why the speaker's point of view is important. Whether the speaker is supposed to be Roethke or not is not relevant. What is important is that Roethke chose to speak here as a man looking back on his childhood. This perspective suggests an innocence about the "small boy" (2) as if he couldn't fully understand what was going on, but now that he is a man, he can look back objectively. Yet, still, Roethke portrays the same love towards the father.

This lovingness towards the speaker's father is conveyed through the controlling metaphor in the poem, along with specific diction. The poet compares the young boy's life with his father to a waltz and uses that comparison to lighten the image of his father. When Roethke writes that the boy's father "waltzed [him] off to bed / Still clinging to [his] shirt" (15-6), the reader sees the playfulness between father and son, like that implied by the playful rhythm of the poem. The reader also sees that in spite of "steps" the father "missed" (11) that caused the father's belt buckle to "scrape" the boy's ear (12), the boy "hung on like death" (3), "clinging" (16) to his father with an unconditional love. The diction used here is both disconcerting and urgent. One doesn't usually get "scraped" when dancing—even the sound of this word creates a disturbing tone. But words like "missed," "scraped," and "death" are offset by words like "hung on" and "clinging." In the portrayal of this dance, the speaker reveals a yearning toward his father, rough though he was, and the time they spent together.

The message of unconditional, eternal love is a repeated theme throughout the poem. Roethke uses each element of the poem to deliver that message, and when the poem is looked at as a whole, it forwards that theme in a marvelous way.

Instructions for effective writing usually emphasize clarity of purpose, sound logic, convincing evidence, effective structure, and impressive style, all crucial elements certainly. Yet, it is difficult to compose a truly persuasive argument if you, yourself, do not *care about the subject*. As you can see from Marion's essay, powerful writing can arise from a writer's desire to share her passion about the topic. So, what if you are given an assignment you are *not* initially interested in? You may not feel that poetry is your "thing." Or maybe you feel like a "fish out of water" when required to write about history or business. However, for the best results, I strongly encourage you to find an angle of the topic that connects with what you care about.

For example, when art major Wesley Hardesty was assigned to write a paper about an aspect of World War I, he found himself struggling to get interested in the topic. For the first essay of the course, his professor had required a literary analysis paper over Ernest Hemingway's novel, *The Sun Also Rises*. With some difficulty, Wesley had completed that assignment, supporting his interpretation of the novel with key passages of the text as evidence. For Essay 2, however, which required students to research an aspect of the novel's World War I context and formulate an argument on that topic, Wesley was having trouble choosing a specific area of focus. He procrastinated on the research, because each time he sat down at his computer to search for books and articles, his thoughts would wander and he would become bored. He could not seem to pinpoint any aspect of World War I on which he would be motivated to take a position and build an argument.

Finally, he met with his professor and told her about his difficulty deciding on a topic for his paper. During their conversation, she asked about his major, his future career plans, and what he liked to do in his spare time. In response to her last question, he answered that he enjoyed playing video games with his friends. She asked if he ever played *Call of Duty*. Soon, they were discussing whether the *Call of Duty* games authentically recreate the experience of fighting as a soldier, the trauma of which Hemingway explores in *The Sun Also Rises*. They agreed that even though the *Call of Duty* games focus on World War II rather than World War I, this topic might be a fruitful one for Wesley's research essay.

When Wesley got back to his dorm room and tried, once again, researching for the paper, he found that this time, he was much more engaged in the task. Later, when he reviewed his notes on the games themselves, as well as the psychology and history articles he had gathered on the subject, he concluded that although the games do simulate actual warfare in a number of ways, they cannot reproduce the same fear, uncertainty, and trauma that many soldiers experience during real wars. Below is the product of Wesley's research and writing:

Wesley Hardesty
Composition II

Call of Duty: Short of Reality

Video games are often made to represent historical war time events in a stronger sense than any other form of media. They immerse you as a participant in past historical events, but how well and in depth do they recreate the actual historical event to make it your reality? A generation of military gamers who spend hours and hours playing *Call of Duty* think they understand and know modern warfare, but do they really? Soldiers who have actually served in a time of war might beg to differ. Just as there is evidence that shows there are some similarities in gaming and the real life combat that took place in World War II, there is also evidence to show that what takes place in a video game such as *Call of Duty* can be quite different from what takes place in an actual combat mission during a time of war. There are many bases for comparison and contrast between actual war and *Call of Duty*, such as the attitudes and feelings of a real soldier versus that of a gamer during times of combat, the skill level and training of an actual soldier versus that of a gamer, and the actual real time combat events taking place during battle and that of a mission's story line in the game *Call of Duty*.

Just as the attitude of a real soldier can be quite different from the attitude of a gamer during a combat mission, it can also be quite similar. Most "video games combine the moral and narrative associations of the war with the physical activity of shooting, creating a sense of mastery and control" (Allison 183), all of which strongly affects the attitude of the player. After viewing many combat videos captured on helmet mounted cameras of actual soldiers during a time of war—showing things like bombings, firefights, and airstrikes—Luke Plunkett argues that a soldier's attitudes and emotional reactions to these things are "not too different to what you might hear over a headset on Xbox Live" during a *Call of Duty* online match. The reactions and emotional outbursts to such events are quite similar. In my own experience and observations as a gamer, the outbursts consist of a mix of excitement, fear, and adrenaline. They also involve a great deal of screaming and yelling in addition to desperate calls for help. The soldier is calling to his fellow squad members for help or back up, where a gamer is usually calling for another gamer for back up. The level of excitement is much the same, as most gamers become fully immersed in the game.

However, in many of these videos the soldiers are also wounded and in distress. This is where the attitudes are quite different. In a game of *Call of Duty*, if the gamer is injured there is always another life and the game moves on. There are never the calls of desperation and absolute panic that are seen and heard in helmet-cam videos of actual soldiers. The *Call of Duty* video game tends to glorify war and the gamer cannot possibly relate to or comprehend the consequences of real violence or death in the way that the soldier experiences it in real life combat. No game or video can possibly be as realistic as actual life events. Rejack says that "clicks of a mouse or movements of a joystick do not provide a pathway to historical identification through the body in the way that running across the battlefield might" (413). In addition, soldiers who are deployed overseas during a time of war are fully engrossed in a lifestyle of combat and fear. They live every day not knowing whether or not they will make it home to their family or loved ones. *Call of Duty* is just a form of entertainment. Although many spend hours and hours engrossed in the game and fully immersed in the virtual combat, they can never actually comprehend what it is like to live in the situations that a soldier is living in daily. The gamer can choose to simply turn the game off.

Further, the skills needed to participate in actual combat compared to the skills needed to participate in an online match of *Call of Duty* strongly differ, though there are similarities. A "combination of tactical elements and intense battle scenes is one reason why the game has proved to be so popular" (Rejack 414). During World War I and World War II, men were drafted into war and were sent into combat with hardly any training or experience, so many entered war with the skill level of a player new to *Call of Duty*. In the video game world "users are invited to take part in history from their living rooms, replicating the museum from a video game console" (Hess 341). Thus, today's gamers might be under the illusion that they could easily take on the same warfare challenges in real life with the same success that they enjoy playing *Call of Duty*. However, in contrast, soldiers now have to go through intense physical, mental, weapon, and strategy training just to survive out in the field. The military provides cutting-edge training throughout a soldier's military career—they do not just stop at boot camp. Currently the military requires advanced training for their assigned occupational fields. The military uses advanced modeling and simulations to provide very realistic training situations. Today's soldiers participate in realistic combat role-playing exercises that include real weapons, special effects and explosions to recreate physical combat settings before they are deployed. Our military is highly skilled before they are allowed to be deployed for combat. A gamer simply learns to press a few buttons on a handset or controller and he is prepared for virtual battle.

While the storylines and the combat scenarios that *Call of Duty* uses follow many actual events that took place in World War II, there are major gaps in these narratives, as well. The *Call of Duty* game series includes numerous games that specifically deal with the events of this particular war. In each game, the "intersection between the gameplay narrative and the historical narrative is underscored through mission objectives" (Hess 345). There are four games in the *Call of Duty* series that deal with World War II. These games include *Call of Duty, Call of Duty 2, Call of Duty 3* and *Call of Duty: World at War.* In each of these games, the player plays out numerous missions through an avatar-soldier of each United States alliance. *Call of Duty, Call of Duty 2* and *Call of Duty 3* all focus on the European conflict in which the gamer goes to combat with the Germans. *Call of Duty 2* focuses only on the North African Campaign, including Italy and Sicily. *Call of Duty: World at War* focuses on the United States Marine Corp fighting the Japanese in the Pacific, as well as the Red Army in the Eastern Region. In most cases "the digital interface of a video game mirrors the interface on dozens of computerized instruments and weapons currently being used by the American military" (Allison 191), which makes the games seem very realistic. However, although all of the games in this series are modeled after actual World War II conflicts or missions and follow history quite closely, games must allow for the individual experience of the gamer, while offering a likely chance of success for the player. As a result, *Call of Duty* does not attempt to play out the experiences of soldiers who actually fought in the war. In the games there are numerous objects to take cover behind to avoid being shot—in an actual war, these shielding objects are not always available. Also, in actual war, most of the time you do not see who you are shooting at or who is shooting at you. You rarely get close enough to shoot accurately. Real war is not like a video game where the enemy just pops up into your view. In comparison, the terrain may be the same and the mission may be the same, but the video game lacks the sensory perception of actually being there. In the game you do not experience the same smells, sights or feelings of actually being there. You can never feel your heart rate getting above 120 beats per minute while you lose control over your motor skills and cannot even reload your weapon. You cannot possibly understand or feel what it would be like to carry over 100 pounds of gear up a mountain during firefight with an enemy in temperatures above 100 degrees. As a gamer you get a glimpse into what war might be like, but your experience cannot substantially compare to actually being there in a real life battle as a soldier.

The *Call of Duty* video game series continues to make billions of dollars a year and keeps the developers at the top of their industry. Although gamers all over the world wait on pins and needles for the next game release, gamers should be fully aware that it is just a form of entertainment. Even though these video games are often made to represent historical events in a stronger sense than any other form of media, the gaming experience still lacks much compared to actual historical events. While somewhat accurate and realistic in comparison to modern war and the actual events of the World Wars, there is still an extreme contrast between playing the game and actually taking part as a real soldier at war.

Works Cited

Allison, Tanine. "The World War II Video Game, Adaptation, and Postmodern History." *Literature Film Quarterly*, vol. 38, no. 3, 2010, pp. 183-193.

Hess, Aaron. "'You Don't Play, You Volunteer': Narrative Public Memory Construction in *Medal of Honor: Rising Sun.*" *Critical Studies in Media Communication*, vol. 24, no. 4, 2007, pp. 339-356.

Plunkett, Luke. "Forget Call of Duty, This is What Real War Looks Like." Kotaku, 12 Sept. 2012, https://kotaku.com/5947161/forget-call-of-duty-this-is-what-real-war-looks-like/. Accessed 25 Mar. 2014.

Rejack, Brian. "Toward a Virtual Reenactment of History: Video Games and the Recreation of the Past." *Rethinking History*, vol. 11, no. 3, 2007, pp. 411-425.

To return to this chapter's emphasis on *forming a perspective on your topic*, Wesley determined, and supported with research and personal observations, that *Call of Duty* falls short of reproducing the full combat experience. Rather than attempting to base his thesis about soldiers' experience only on objective data, he interpreted the findings of his research at least partially by considering his own passion for and experience with video games. Why is his thesis important and valuable to his audience? He implies that it is important because although in contemporary American culture, gamers want the most authentic experience possible, the authenticity of games like *Call of Duty* worries some people. Could it cause psychological damage as war can? Could it persuade young gamers toward joining the military by providing an experience that seems both authentic and pleasurable? Because Wesley considered his passions as well as his *values* in approaching this essay, the essay connected with concerns his readers might share with him and was thus more effective than it might have been if he had just "jumped through the hoops" of the assignment.

Your composition professor might have important reasons for not allowing the same flexibility for paper topics that Wesley's professor did. Perhaps, as his instructor did in her Essay 1 assignment, your professor will insist that you engage in literary textual analysis in order to meet certain course outcomes, like *understanding how literary strategy can be used for rhetorical purposes* and *demonstrating the ability to use text as evidence to support an argument*. Regardless of the boundaries of your assignment, you are encouraged to find an angle that inspires you to real passion about your subject.

To recap this section's key ideas:

1. When forming a perspective on a text or other topic, do not ignore your own passions or values. Both Marion and Wesley drew on these aspects of themselves to produce provocative essays.

2. Be sure that your perspective (which will determine your argument) is supported by the evidence. If not, consider how your position needs to be adjusted in light of the evidence. What if Wesley's research had revealed that video games can indeed reproduce the full effect of war? How would his argument need to be revised? How might he respond personally to the knowledge that the video game experience is authentic after all? How might that knowledge be useful or significant to his audience?

2.2 Critical Perspectives

Forming your perspective on a poem, story, or play might be easier if you understand some of the approaches commonly taken toward interpreting literature's meaning. Literary studies have been around long enough that likeminded readers and scholars have gravitated toward basic common positions as they engage in dialogue with each other. As a result, there are a number of widely-recognized critical approaches to literature, from formalists (who focus on how an author employs strategies and devices for a particular effect) to psychoanalytical critics (who explore texts to better understand humans' psychological structure and their typical responses to particular experiences). As you consider a poem or story, you might choose one of these approaches as the general lens through which to examine that work. What follows is a list of some of the most common **critical perspectives**. Consider them and make a note of any that strikes you as particularly interesting. You may find that one or several of these reflect your own way of looking at the world.

Biographical Criticism:

This approach examines the life and attitudes of an author as the key to understanding the writer's work. You should probably avoid heavy dependence on this approach, however, as you write essays for this class. Commonly used in the late eighteenth and nineteenth centuries, it has now been largely discounted as a reliable way to understand the meaning of a text.

Formalism (also referred to as "New Criticism"):

Rising to prominence in the 1920s, this approach considers a literary work as an entity separate from its author and its historical context. The formalist explores a poem as a mechanic would explore an engine. The mechanic would assume that the engine's parts and function can be studied without any understanding of the maker's life and/or the history of the period in which the engine exists. Similarly, to assess a poem's impact and understand its meaning, a scholar might "take it apart," considering its separate elements—the form, line length, rhythm, rhyme scheme, figurative language, and diction—and how those pieces make up the effect of and shape the meaning of the whole.

Psychoanalytical Criticism:

Based on the theories of Freud and others, this approach examines a text for signs and symbols of the subconscious processes, both of the characters and of humans in general. Revelatory symbols in a work might include water (the womb or the subconscious), a phallus (patriarchal power or sexual desire), a vessel such as a vase or pitcher (the vagina or sexual desire), and dark passageways (the feared subconscious where we store our unacceptable impulses and desires, and in which we are afraid we might get lost from the ordered, visible world).

Archetypal Criticism:

Springing from psychoanalytical criticism, this approach focuses on common figures and story-lines that reveal patterns in human behavior and psychology. Well-known archetypal characters are the hero, the scapegoat, the Earth mother, the temptress, the mentor, and the devil figure. Some common archetypal storylines are the journey, the quest, the fall, and death and rebirth. Carl Jung and Joseph Campbell, key figures in the development of this approach, found that in the many stories they collected from cultures all over the world, these figures and storylines emerged over and over again. Their conclusion was that these figures and storylines are etched into the human psyche (or subconscious), and as we recreate them in our stories, our audiences recognize them as symbolic of their own experience.

Feminist Criticism:

Using this approach, one examines a literary work for insight into why and how women are subjected to oppression and, sometimes, how they subvert the forces that oppress them.

Gender Theory:

Expanding on feminist criticism, gender studies explore literature for increased understanding of socially defined gender identity and behavior and its impact on the individual and on society. It includes study of sexual orientation and how non-heterosexual identities are treated by mainstream ideology, a dynamic sometimes reflected in, sometimes critiqued by, literary works.

Marxist Criticism:

This approach to literature examines how class and economic forces shape human dynamics. It is important to note that Marxist criticism is not a promotion of socialist government, but rather a close study of how invisible economic forces underpin, and often undermine, authentic human relationships.

Historical Criticism:

This approach seeks to illuminate a text's original meaning by uncovering details of the text's historical context.

New Historicism:

Modifying the historical approach described above, the new historicist assumes that material factors interact with each other, thus while this approach seeks to understand a text through its cultural context, it also attempts to discover through the literary work insight into intellectual history. For example, a new historicist might consider Frederick Douglass's *Narrative of the Life of Frederick Douglass* as a product shaped not only by Douglass's experience as a U.S. slave, but also by Douglass's challenge of finding a publisher (most of whom were white), and by his primarily Christian readership. These factors, according to the new historicist, would interact to shape the text and its meanings.

In finding a perspective that interests you, consider these common ways of approaching literary study and interpretation and how those approaches might intersect with your own passions and values. Scholarly study should be objective, in that academic arguments should be supported by credible and substantial evidence, but scholarly argument is valuable when it aids us in better understanding our world and realizing our goals as humans, communities, and societies. Connecting to these objectives as a writer will help you find your reason for writing and the most effective rhetorical methods for reaching your goals.

Effective Argument

3.1 Logos, Ethos, and Pathos

In order to persuade a particular audience of a particular point, a writer makes decisions about how best to convince the reader. Aristotle recognized three basic appeals that a writer (or orator) should consider when presenting an argument: *logos*, *ethos*, and *pathos*.

3.1.1 Logos

Consider this hypothetical plea from Zach to his father: "Dad, could you loan me money for gas until I get my paycheck at the end of the week? If you do, I'll be able to haul your junk pile to the dump as well as drive myself back and forth to work. I'll pay you back as soon as I get my check!"

Logos, a Latin term referring to logic, appeals to the reader's intellect. As readers, we test arguments for their soundness. Does the writer make false assumptions? Are there gaps in the argument? Does the writer leap to conclusions without sufficient evidence to back up his claims? As writers, it is our job to build a solid, well-explained, sufficiently supported argument. In academic texts, logos is usually considered the most important appeal since scholarly research is supposed to be objective and thus more dependent on logic than on emotion (pathos) or on the reputation of the scholar (ethos). What about Zach's argument above? Essentially, he asserts that a loan from his father would benefit both Zach and his dad. Does the argument seem sound? We do not know why Zach is short on cash this week—his father may be aware that Zach spent most of last week's check on the newest iPhone, so he does not have enough to cover his gas this week. Thus, there may be factors that undermine Zach's implication that his request is motivated by responsibility. However, he does offer evidence that the loan will allow him to fulfill his obligations.

Logic is based on either *inductive* or *deductive reasoning*. Understanding these types of logic can help us test the soundness of arguments, both our own and those of others.

Inductive Reasoning

You likely use inductive reasoning every day. By this kind of logic, we form conclusions based on samples. Lab experiments, for example, must be repeatable in order for scientists to gather a convincing amount of data to prove a hypothesis. If a scientist hypothesizes that addiction to a particular drug causes a certain, predictable behavior, the experiment must be carefully controlled, and must be repeated hundreds of times in order to prove that the behavior is consistently associated with the addiction and that other possible causes of that behavior have been ruled out. If we observe enough examples of an event occurring under similar circumstances, we can employ inductive reasoning to draw a conclusion about the pattern. For example, if we pay less each time we buy apples at Supermart than when we purchase apples at Pete's Grocery, we will likely conclude, inductively, that apples are less expensive at Supermart.

Literary argument is often based on inductive reasoning. Here are two illustrations of such reasoning:

1. In Robert Frost's sonnet "Design," the color white is used ironically to suggest that only a devious designer would clothe the universe's evil in so much beauty. The "dimpled spider, fat and white"; the "white heal-all" flower that "hold[s] up" the moth for the spider's feast; and the rhyming of "blight" with "white" and "right" work together to generate the poem's disturbing sense that the innocence implied in the whiteness of the natural scene is deceptive.

2. As powerful evidence of the irreversible destruction of war, Hemingway's *The Sun Also Rises* presents Jake Barnes's struggles to overcome the damage incurred during his service as a soldier in World War I. Jake's difficulty coping with his injury, his tendency to self-medicate with alcohol, his inability to pray, and his failure to sustain an intimate relationship with another person all exemplify the terrible destruction inflicted on him by the war.

When writing a literary analysis essay, such as the paper that might develop from the second argument above, you will need to provide enough examples to support your assertion that the pattern you observed in the text does, indeed, exist.

Deductive Reasoning

Deductive reasoning, on the other hand, is drawing a conclusion based on a *logical equation*. It can be argued that we see deduction in its purest form in the context of scientific or mathematical reasoning. A logical equation of this sort is based on a *proven* assumption and/or clearly and inflexibly-defined terms. Commonly manifesting these conditions, computer programs accomplish tasks through deductive logic. For example, *Mary, an art major who has completed 24 credit hours, cannot register for English 4500*. This statement is true because the university course enrollment system is governed by the following logic: Only English majors with 30 or more credit hours may register for English 4500. Students who have not officially declared as English majors and/or whose records do not exhibit completion of credit hours equal to or greater than 30 will be automatically prevented from registering for English 4500. Similarly, the following statement is based on deductive logic: *Glyptol paint cannot be cleaned up with water only*. This conclusion is based on the fact that Glyptol contains alkyds, which are not water soluble. Therefore, clean-up of any paint containing alkyds will require turpentine or another petroleum-based solvent.

Having examined deductive reasoning in its pure form, however, we can see that argument will rarely be required in such a context. Investigation may be required in order to determine the characteristic and/or definition of a material, but once the facts are ascertained, scientists will not need to debate whether or not alkyds are water-soluble. *Persuasion* becomes relevant when the issue moves beyond proven facts. As we explore issues of ethics and values, logical reasoning can seem a bit mushy, yet rather than throw up their hands in abandonment of deductive reasoning, humanities scholars generally work hard to establish valid assumptions, or generally agreed-upon notions, that can be used to help humans move closer to reasonable, or logical, social and political beliefs and behaviors.

Sir Arthur Conan Doyle's famous fictional detective Sherlock Holmes is famous for employing deductive reasoning to solve mysteries. In "Five Orange Pips," Holmes uses deductive reasoning to work as far as possible toward solving John Openshaw's case, based on the facts Holmes and Watson have been given:

Now let us consider the situation and see what may be deduced from it. In the first place, we may start with a strong presumption that Colonel Openshaw had some very strong reason for leaving America. Men at his time of life do not change all their habits and exchange willingly the charming climate of Florida for the lonely life of an English provincial town. His extreme love of solitude in England suggests the idea that he was in fear of someone or something, so we may assume as a working hypothesis that it was fear of someone or something which drove him from America. As to what it was he feared, we can only deduce that by considering the formidable letters which were received by himself and his successors. Did you remark the postmarks of those letters?

Equations such as the ones being forwarded by Holmes, when seen in their complete form, comprise a three part logical statement called a **syllogism**.

The statement includes
1. A **general statement**, or **major premise**: Middle-aged men do not readily embrace change.
2. A **minor premise**: Colonel Openshaw is a middle-aged man.
3. And a **conclusion**: Colonel Openshaw would not have changed his circumstances without a strong impetus.

Although some might argue that Holmes came to the major premise through inductive reasoning (observing the behavior of many, many middle-aged men), in the above passage, he asserts the major premise as the basis for his deductive logical equation proving that Colonel Openshaw must have had a strong impetus for leaving America. If we agree with Holmes's *premise*, we are likely to trust his *conclusion*.

Here is a more questionable logical equation, considered by the characters of Stephen Crane's short story "The Open Boat":

If I am going to be drowned—if I am going to be drowned—if I am going to be drowned, why, in the name of the seven mad gods who rule the sea, was I allowed to come thus far and contemplate sand and trees? Was

I brought here merely to have my nose dragged away as I was about to nibble the sacred cheese of life? It is preposterous. If this old ninny-woman, Fate, cannot do better than this, she should be deprived of the management of men's fortunes. She is an old hen who knows not her intention. If she has decided to drown me, why did she not do it in the beginning and save me all this trouble. The whole affair is absurd.... But, no, she cannot mean to drown me. She dare not drown me. She cannot drown me. Not after all this work.

The following syllogism reflects the men's attitude:

1. Major premise: The world is just and reasonable.
2. Minor premise: All of the men in the life-boat are good men and are working hard to survive.
3. Conclusion: All of the men should survive.

You can see in the latter example that sometimes syllogisms are flawed, or illogical. Most of us doubt, at least some of the time, that the universe is indeed just and reasonable, at least by human standards. If it is not just, then the men's conclusion that they ought to survive may be incorrect.

The occurrence of flawed logic is most problematic when we find an equation in its incomplete form: an **enthymeme**. If we consider the major premise as the *underlying assumption*, and recognize that this premise often goes *unstated*, we see that the enthymeme is a type of elliptical statement that sometimes "leaps" to its conclusion unreasonably. Consider the following examples:

Sample 1
- Enthymeme: Sarah, don't eat that beef; it came from Bob's Café.
- Major premise: All food from Bob's Café is bad.
- Minor premise: That beef came from Bob's Café.
- Conclusion: That beef is bad.

Sample 2
- Enthymeme: Lisa Harmon would be a good hire for our company; she has a degree from Harvard University.

- Major premise: Anyone with a degree from Harvard University would be a good employee for our company.
- Minor premise: Lisa has a degree from Harvard University.
- Conclusion: Lisa would be a good employee for our company.

Sample 3
- Enthymeme: *Kill Bill* is a chick flick.
- Major premise: Any movie that features a female protagonist is a chick flick.
- Minor premise: *Kill Bill* features a female protagonist.
- Conclusion: *Kill Bill* is a chick flick.

As you test the major premises above, how do they fare? Are they true? If a writer asserted the above enthymemes, would you, as the reader, agree with the major premise of each? Why or why not? What is the danger of reading (or hearing) only the enthymeme and not testing the underlying (unspoken) assumption which would complete the syllogism?

Logical Fallacies:
Whether an assertion is based on inductive or deductive reasoning, when we test a claim, it helps to know about the following logical fallacies commonly found in weak arguments:

Bandwagon Argument:
This claim encourages us to agree with a particular opinion because "everyone else agrees with it." *Frost's "Design" implies an evil creator; several important critics agree that this is Frost's message.* Does the text *itself* support this theory?

Single Cause:
This kind of argument suggests that a problem results from one particular cause when the causes may actually be complex and multiple: *In* The Great Gatsby, *it is Gatsby's decision to pursue a decadent woman like Daisy that leads to his downfall.* Are there any other factors that might lay the groundwork for the tragic events of the novel?

Either/Or:

This type of statement implies that there are only two options: *Roethke's poem "My Papa's Waltz" either points to abuse,* or *it emphasizes the love between father and son.* Is it possible for *both* to be true?

Slippery Slope:

In this kind of argument, the writer warns that one step in the "wrong" direction will result in complete destruction: *If the instructor curves the grade for this assignment, students will expect a curve on all assignments, and they will lose their motivation to work hard toward their own learning.* Is the compromised course grade *inevitable* as the result of one curved assignment grade? A similar argument is the following: *If the government gives welfare to poor citizens, those citizens will become permanently dependent on "handouts" and will lose their motivation to work for a living.*

Straw Man:

In this approach, the writer holds up an *extreme* and usually easy-to-defeat example of the opposition as the general representative of that opposition instead of considering the opposition's most reasonable arguments. *Senator Jill Campbell was convicted of bribery, confirming that politicians can't be trusted.* Are there *any* ethical politicians? If so, this conclusion is logically flawed.

False Cause:

Here, the writer offers a cause that *seems* linked to the problem but does not actually establish the causal relationship. *The university cut three class days due to snow, and now I'm failing history; therefore, the university should have added three extra days to the semester.*

As you listen to and read arguments forwarded by others, test the claims carefully to ensure that you are not accepting an illogical line of thinking. Also, carefully review your own arguments to avoid forwarding faulty logic yourself!

3.1.2 Ethos

Ethos, an appeal based on the credibility of the author, can affect a reader's willingness to trust the writer. This credibility is often generated by the author's apparent ethics. If the reader perceives that she shares important values with the writer, the door of communication opens wider than if the writer and reader seem to lack common values. Reflecting back to Zach's request for a loan from his father, Zach does remind his father subtly that the loan will allow him to work, both at his job and at home. This respect for work is likely a value held by Zach's father, so it becomes important common ground for the argument.

Consider again the previously presented thesis about Hemingway's *The Sun Also Rises*:

> As powerful evidence of the irreversible destruction of war, Hemingway's *The Sun Also Rises* presents Jake Barnes's struggles to overcome the damage incurred during his service as a soldier in World War I. Jake's difficulty coping with his injury, his tendency to self-medicate with alcohol, his inability to pray, and his failure to sustain an intimate relationship with another person all exemplify the terrible destruction inflicted on him by the war.

Hopefully, the writer, let's call him Bill, will go on to support, with evidence from the text, the claim that the portrayal of Jake's struggles promotes anti-war sentiment. Beyond the logical soundness of the argument, however, the reader will inevitably react on a personal level to the values underlying the statement. Bill, in his decision to focus on this aspect of the text, seems to appreciate the anti-war stance he observes in the novel. If the reader is sympathetic to this position, she may be more open to Bill's argument as a whole.

Aside from the writer's ethics, ethos can also be generated by the author's credibility, which is usually based on (1) the ability to forward a logical argument (hence, ethos can be affected by logos!), (2) thoroughness of significant research, and (3) credentials proving the writer's expertise. If Bill is not an expert in the field of literary studies yet, but is a sophomore English Major, he may have no recognizable credentials to persuade the reader in his favor. But if he has been careful and thorough in his presentation of evidence (passages and examples from the text itself) and has considered (and possibly integrated) material from scholarly articles and books to help define and support his argument, his ethos is likely to be strong.

3.1.3 Pathos

What about **pathos**, or the appeal to the reader's emotions? Certainly, Zach's father will be affected by his feelings for his son Zach as he considers whether to loan Zach the money for gas, but what about in a more academic or professional context? Even though the goal of an academic writer is to approach a research topic as objectively as possible, even scholars are people, and people are emotional creatures. Bill's awareness of this fact leads him to choose some particularly poignant passages from Hemingway's novel to support his point:

> The damage caused by Jake's war experience is not only physical but also psychological. For example, after looking in the mirror at the scar from his wound, he lies in bed unable to sleep:
>
>> I lay awake thinking and my mind jumping around. Then I couldn't keep away from it, and I started to think about Brett and all the rest of it went away. I was thinking about Brett and my mind stopped jumping around and started to go in sort of smooth waves. Then all of a sudden I started to cry. Then after a while it was better and I lay in bed and listened to the heavy trams go by and way down the street, and then I went to sleep. (Hemingway 31)
>
> Although Jake makes a convincing show in public of dealing with his trauma, this passage reveals the challenge he faces in trying to cope.

Although Bill's readers will critically consider whether this passage logically supports Bill's claim, it is likely that they will also react emotionally to Jake's anguish, thus reinforcing the persuasive effectiveness of Bill's argument.

3.2 Audience Awareness

For success in any project, a writer must be aware of and carefully consider his audience. Zach seems to know his audience pretty well—the evidence he presents that a loan would benefit both Zach and his father shows that Zach understands his father's values, and chances are good that Zach considers his filial status as an advantage with this audience. After all, he did ask his father, rather than a stranger, for the loan.

On the other hand, an academic audience can be a tough one since scholars are trained to consider claims critically, rigorously questioning and testing their validity. Your professors are in this camp, and you and your peers are quickly joining these ranks as well. While this audience is not a highly sympathetic one, its critical rigor is not intended for intimidation but for establishing and maintaining high standards of thought and research. Academia's purpose is to maintain and improve the quality of our world, so you are encouraged to consider this audience as a factor as you work to produce increasingly significant and well-written texts.

3.3 Evidence

3.3.1 Primary Sources

Primary Evidence is the *thing* we study. In academic writing, this kind of evidence differs according to discipline. In biology and chemistry, primary evidence can be an experiment's results. In the field of history, it might be a letter written by a World War I soldier, a memo issued by a U.S. president, a Civil War bullet, or cave drawings. In sociology, it can be the data gathered from participant surveys (quantitative) or information arising from a case study (qualitative).

In the field of English literature, primary evidence comes from the poem, novel, short story, play, or memoir you are studying. Bill, for example, presents direct quotes from the novel *The Sun Also Rises* supporting specific claims he forwards in his argument, as well as **summarized** and **paraphrased** passages in which he describes, in his own words, key occurrences in the novel. Below, he *summarizes* a conversation between Jake and Robert Cohn, condensing a lengthy passage of dialogue into one sentence:

> In an early conversation between Jake and Robert Cohn, Jake warns his friend that Cohn desires to go to South America only because he has been reading sentimental literature.

Later, *paraphrasing* the novel's description of Jake's and his friends' response to a bullfight, Bill translates Hemingway's words into his own in about the same number of words as the original passage:

> Jake observes Brett for any signs of serious disturbance as she watches the matador kill the bull, but Brett is not upset by the scene. Instead she expresses her appreciation for the matador's extraordinary grace.

These examples from the primary text support Bill's argument, but how does Bill decide when to quote, summarize, or paraphrase?

These decisions are important ones for effectively incorporating primary evidence into an essay. Here are a few guidelines as you consider these options in your own writing:

Quotes:

Use the shortest quote possible to generate (a) the evidence needed and (b) the effect you seek. Be careful to *avoid* long quotes unless they serve a significant purpose in forwarding your argument. *Do* use quotes to "liven up" your argument, to bring the voice of the literary text into your academic prose.

Summary:

Use summary to provide a broad-scoped piece of evidence (a long passage from the novel, for example) to the reader. That "Jake and Brett have multiple tension-filled encounters" (Bill's summary) is evidence that they still care for each other even though they cannot overcome Jake's impotence to settle into a committed relationship. There may be no need in this section of Bill's essay to focus more closely on particular tension-filled exchanges.

Paraphrase:

Employ paraphrase when the content of a scene or passage is pertinent but does not require the original language itself. Bill's description of Jake's and Brett's behavior during the bullfight is a helpful example of effective paraphrase use.

3.3.2 Secondary Sources

Although the proof that Jake's struggles reveal the destructive potential of war must come from the novel itself, the primary source, Bill can use **secondary sources** to (a) help explain his perspective on the novel, and (b) indicate how his argument fits into the ongoing scholarly dialogue about the novel. Plenty of people have contributed to the conversation on the meaning of *The Sun Also Rises*. Bill's goal is to say something *new*, to bring the reader fresh insight about the novel, to contribute something *original* to the conversation. To clarify the significance of his argument, he can integrate material from carefully selected **scholarly articles and books**.

How does one find and use secondary sources? Chapter 8 elaborates on these processes. But to get started, we can discuss some of the basics here. First, let's distinguish between **popular** and **scholarly**, or **peer-reviewed**,

sources. There is a vast amount of information available on a vast number of topics, both in print and on the internet. Most digital and print publications these days are written for a popular, or mass, audience. Since the average reader is not writing a research project on the topic he is interested in, most texts are written for the non-expert. Such a reader, having just finished *The Sun Also Rises*, might seek some basic general information on Hemingway or on World War I, which could easily be found on sites such as Wikipedia or the Poetry Foundation website (poetryfoundation.org).

However, the scholar who is working on her own research project needs more in-depth analysis than is provided in these popular sources. Thus, she must gather academic or scholarly resources. These are written for an expert audience, assuming that this reader already has a more sophisticated knowledge and understanding of the subject and is researching a specific aspect of the topic rather than looking for general information. These sources are often more difficult to find and obtain. They are rarely free and must usually be accessed through a university library system.

The differences between the purposes and production processes of popular and scholarly sources result in their having distinct characteristics. Here is a chart to help you visualize the differences:

	Popular sources	Scholarly sources
Example	*Time Magazine*, Spark Notes, or Shmoop article	An article from *The Hemingway Review*
Location	Newsstand or internet (accessible through a Google search)	Subscribed to by universities and libraries. Usually accessible only to members of those institutions
Target reader	Non-expert, lay reader	Experts/professionals in a particular area of study
Appearance	Glossy visuals, eye-catching layout, strategies to attract buyers/readers	Plain text; generally not marketed at all since experts are professionally motivated to seek out this kind of resource

Production process	• Written not by experts in the field but by journalists and other professional writers • Fact-checked and edited by publishing and editing professionals (or sometimes not at all) • Published every month, every week, or sometimes even daily	• Written by experts in the field • Reviewed by the expert's peers and accepted or rejected by their recommendation • Edited by journal or press editor • As a result of the research and peer-review process, these journals are usually published only 1-4 times annually
Features	Short articles, meant to be read in one sitting; no bibliography; short, clear paragraphs and sentences; vocabulary meant for middle to high school reading level; usually published for profit	Long articles, sometimes based on a year or more of research/ analysis; include substantial bibliography of other peer-reviewed sources used in research; vocabulary often specialized, reasoning often complex, targeting readers familiar with the field; published by academic journals or not-for-profit university presses

3.4 Articulating an Effective Thesis

The understanding of pathos, logos and ethos is crucial to formulating a significant and arguable thesis, which should capture the essence of *your perspective* on a text. The argument itself will require much more than a sentence or two, but the **thesis**, or the statement of the central argument, is an important tool in presenting a persuasive case. It should relay to your reader the *specific point* around which the rest of the argument revolves and *why that point is so important.*

You are encouraged to compose, early in your writing process, a **working thesis**. At this point, the thesis is not yet set in stone, but it will help guide your research and your logic as you formulate your case. Once you have analyzed the text, read the research on your topic, and determined your perspective and purpose, you will need to revise and refine your thesis to ensure that it sets up and controls your argument with real impact.

Experiencing the Power of Poetry

4.1 Analyzing Poetry

Our exploration of literary genres brings us first to poetry, with good reason: Because many people are intimidated by poetry, especially "old" poetry, facing our fears is the first step toward prowess and confidence as scholars and writers. Furthermore, this brave plunge into poetry comes with a bonus: Once we manage to "open up" a poem, we can experience its power and beauty, as well as its insights into human life. We begin with John Keats's 1819 "Ode on a Grecian Urn."

> Thou still unravish'd bride of quietness,
>   Thou foster-child of Silence and slow Time,
> Sylvan historian, who canst thus express
>   A flowery tale more sweetly than our rhyme:
> What leaf-fringed legend haunts about thy shape   5
>   Of deities or mortals, or of both,
>   In Tempe or the dales of Arcady?
>   What men or gods are these? what maidens loth?
> What mad pursuit? What struggle to escape?
>   What pipes and timbrels? What wild ecstasy?   10
>
> Heard melodies are sweet, but those unheard
>   Are sweeter; therefore, ye soft pipes, play on;
> Not to the sensual ear, but, more endear'd,
>   Pipe to the spirit ditties of no tone:
> Fair youth, beneath the trees, thou canst not leave   15
>   Thy song, nor ever can those trees be bare;
>   Bold lover, never, never canst thou kiss,

Though winning near the goal—yet, do not grieve;
  She cannot fade, though thou hast not thy bliss,
    For ever wilt thou love, and she be fair!   20

Ah, happy, happy boughs! that cannot shed
  Your leaves, nor ever bid the Spring adieu;
And, happy melodist, unwearied,
  For ever piping songs for ever new;
More happy love! more happy, happy love!   25
  For ever warm and still to be enjoy'd,
    For ever panting, and for ever young;
All breathing human passion far above,
  That leaves a heart high-sorrowful and cloy'd,
    A burning forehead, and a parching tongue.   30

Who are these coming to the sacrifice?
  To what green altar, O mysterious priest,
Lead'st thou that heifer lowing at the skies,
  And all her silken flanks with garlands drest?
What little town by river or sea shore,   35
  Or mountain-built with peaceful citadel,
    Is emptied of this folk, this pious morn?
And, little town, thy streets for evermore
  Will silent be; and not a soul to tell
    Why thou art desolate, can e'er return.   40

O Attic shape! Fair attitude! with brede
  Of marble men and maidens overwrought,
With forest branches and the trodden weed;
  Thou, silent form, dost tease us out of thought
As doth eternity: Cold pastoral!   45
  When old age shall this generation waste,
    Thou shalt remain, in midst of other woe
Than ours, a friend to man, to whom thou say'st,
  'Beauty is truth, truth beauty'—that is all
    Ye know on earth, and all ye need to know.   50

(1819)

    Upon a first reading of this British Romantic poem, not only does the
language elude us, but even much of the imagery may be unfamiliar. If

we have ever seen an urn, it probably contained the ashes of a relative and was likely not decorated with scenes like those described in the poem. So how do we conquer our fears and dive in to unravel the poem's meaning?

Here are some pointers for getting started:

1. Read full sentences (if they exist in the poem) without stopping at the end of the line.

2. Look up words you do not know and write their definitions on the page.

3. Note recurring ideas or images—color code these with highlighters for visual recognition as you look at the poem on the page.

4. Determine formal patterns. Is there a regular rhythm? How would you describe it? Can it be characterized by the number of syllables in each line? If not, do you note a certain number of beats (moments where your voice emphasizes the sound) in the line? Are there rhyming sounds? Where do they occur?

5. What is the overarching effect of all these elements taken together? What do you think is the message conveyed by the poem?

Here is a copy of the poem after first year composition student Judy Smith reviewed it carefully and annotated it with notes and highlights:

Ode: a poem paying tribute to someone or something

Sylvan: associated with the woods

Tempe: a valley in Greece where Apollo and the Muses could often be found

Ode on a Grecian Urn

Thou still unravish'd bride of quietness,
    Thou foster-child of Silence and slow Time,
Sylvan historian, who canst thus express
    A flowery tale more sweetly than our rhyme:
What leaf-fringed legend haunts about thy shape
    Of deities or mortals, or of both,
      In Tempe or the dales of Arcady?
    What men or gods are these? What maidens loth?
What mad pursuit? What struggle to escape?
    What pipes and timbrels? What wild ecstasy?

Heard melodies are sweet, but those unheard
    Are sweeter; therefore, ye soft pipes, play on;
Not to the sensual ear, but, more endear'd,

Urn: a decorative vase

Unravish'd: uninitiated, sexually?

Arcadia: Beautiful and wild region of Greece; home of Pan

Yellow: negative words and phrases—about frustrated desires

Blue: positive words suggesting youth, spring, happiness

Green: consider the urn is like thinking about eternity

Pipe to the spirit ditties of no tone:
Fair youth, beneath the trees, thou canst not leave
   Thy song, nor ever can those trees be bare;
      Bold Lover, never, never canst thou kiss,
Though winning near the goal—yet, do not grieve;
   She cannot fade, though thou hast not thy bliss,
      For ever wilt thou love, and she be fair!

Ah, happy, happy boughs! that cannot shed
   Your leaves, nor ever bid the Spring adieu;
And, happy melodist, unwearièd,
   For ever piping songs for ever new;
More happy love! more happy, happy love!
   For ever warm and still to be enjoy'd
      For ever panting, and for ever young;
All breathing human passion far above,
   That leaves a heart high-sorrowful and cloy'd,
      A burning forehead, and a parching tongue.

Cloyed: sick with excess sweetness

Who are these coming to the sacrifice?
   To what green altar, O mysterious priest,
Lead'st thou that heifer lowing at the skies,
   And all her silken flanks with garlands drest?
What little town by river or sea-shore,
   Or mountain-built with peaceful citadel,
      Is emptied of its folk, this pious morn?
And, little town, thy streets for evermore
   Will silent be; and not a soul, to tell
      Why thou art desolate, can e'er return.

Google search—refers to Attica, region where Athens, Greece is located

Beauty and truth are the same things; how so? This is the urn's final message to humanity.

The urn will outlast the poet.

O Attic shape! fair attitude! with brede
   Of marble men and maidens overwrought,
With forest branches and the trodden weed;
   Thou, silent form! dost tease us out of thought
As doth eternity: Cold Pastoral!
   When old age shall this generation waste,
      Thou shalt remain, in midst of other woe
Than ours, a friend to man, to whom thou say'st
'Beauty is truth, truth beauty,—that is all
   Ye know on earth, and all ye need to know.'

Brede: embroidery

Considering the poem's meaning in light of her annotations, Judy makes a few additional observations in her notes:

1. The rhythm of each line includes ten syllables, with the accent on the second syllable of each pair.

2. The rhymes are almost regular: The first stanza end-sounds follow the pattern of A, B, A, B, C, D, E, C, E, D. The next stanza is close, but varies a bit: A, B, A, B, C, D, E, C, D, E. Stanzas three and four follow the same pattern as two, but the final stanza reflects the switched sounds of the final two lines that we saw in stanza one. So the poem is very formal, generally, but it does feature this one odd shift. Why?

3. The positive and negative words and phrases seem to pull against each other. In some ways it might be terrible to be "stuck" in time—the youth wants to kiss his lover, but he'll never be able to. The figures on the urn can't leave to go on with their lives. But the urn's creator has captured a moment where everything is ripe—the tree is full and green and will never lose its leaves. Maybe the feeling of desire the youth feels for the girl is even better than the actual kiss will be.

4. In the second stanza, "Heard melodies are sweet, but those unheard" seems to mean that we can't hear the "heard melodies." I can't make sense of that. But if I read the whole sentence, including a bit of the stanza's second line, it starts to make sense: "Heard melodies are sweet, but those unheard / are sweeter." So the melody played by the urn's pipers is sweeter than if we could actually hear it! Not sure why yet, but it's an interesting claim.

5. The urn won't change like the real world will—is this a good thing or not? The speaker says the urn helps us see beyond our ordinary "thought," maybe to see real beauty, which is rare? And beauty is truth, so the beauty in the urn reveals a kind of truth? What is that truth? It sounds like Keats does have a high regard for art's place in the world, though I'm not sure being "stuck" in the perfect moment is what we really want.

The process in which Judy has engaged fulfills the process of annotating a text to better understand it, discussed in Chapter 1, refining that process to fit the conventions of poetry. To go a step further, Judy might use these notes to form a *perspective* on the poem and compose an essay arguing for that perspective.

Keats is an example of a poet who employs traditional elements of poetry to great effect. But what about a poem that seems to *resist* some of the conventions traditionally associated with poetry? Consider Langston Hughes's 1926 poem, "The Weary Blues," located at http://www.poetryfoundation.org/poem/176785. Try using the process outlined above for unpacking the poem and then spend a few minutes making observations about the poem's meaning and effects. What do you think the poem might be saying to us?

Questions for Consideration:

1. You may have noticed that instead of the traditional iambic pentameter used by Keats in "Ode on a Grecian Urn," Hughes's form here sounds more contemporary. Reading it aloud reveals its blues rhythms—its own syncopation, for example, like that the speaker describes in the old blues singer's song. Why might Hughes have chosen this form instead of the iambic pentameter rhythm in "Ode on a Grecian Urn"?

2. The speaker seems to enjoy the performance of the blues singer, but he notes that the singer finishes, goes to bed, and sleeps "like a rock or a man that's dead" (line 35). What emotions are usually associated with the blues? Why do people sing the blues? Why do people go to clubs to hear someone else sing the blues and maybe even dance to the songs? With these issues in mind, what do you think the poem's last line means?

3. How does Hughes convey the dialect of the singer? Are these dialect features important to the overall effect of the poem? How so?

4.2 Considering the Writer's Life

Readers are often tempted to look for insight into a poem by reading about the *poet*. Many professors will discourage students from integrating the poet's biographical background into a paper as evidence of the students' interpretation of the poem. After all, look how much we gained from analyzing the poem *itself*. As mentioned earlier, **formalism**, an approach to literary criticism that came about in the 1920s and remains well-regarded by many today, holds that artwork (including literature) should be considered as an object separate from the author. Formalists feel that a text *means* on its own. The practice of analyzing a poem's effects apart from the poet's biography is an important one. If we interpret the poem with preformed ideas about the message a poet *would probably* want to convey, we might miss elements in the poem that are staring us right in the face. We know from our *own* observations of Hughes's poem that "The Weary Blues" challenges traditional poetic forms, so we are already curious about *why* he might have chosen this form. However, after performing our own analysis, it can be intriguing and sometimes helpful to consider the author's life. An African American, Hughes wrote during the Harlem Renaissance, the first large-scale African American artistic movement. Although he had read the poetry of many well-regarded British and American poets, he determined to raise the status of African American folk forms, challenging the idea that great art must follow the traditions of European forms. Adding this biographical and historical component to our study increases our understanding of the importance of Hughes's contribution to the improvement of African American lives and his celebration of African Americans' part in shaping U.S. culture.

4.3 Literary Terminology

When you enter the dialogue of an unfamiliar discipline, you are often confronted with unfamiliar vocabulary. If you have ever read a legal document, you understand this challenge of venturing into the territory of an unfamiliar professional dialogue. You may hesitate to sign this document until you have had a chance to look up the meanings of key words in order to ensure that you really agree with the terms you're signing off on. Similarly, in the fields of biology, political science, and education, we may run into specialized vocabulary that we must master in order to enter the dialogue of the field. Your academic essays in various disciplines represent your forays into these dialogues.

Literary studies can be frustrating for students because many already enjoy reading literature and talking about their favorite books with their friends. So, when a professor insists that students use specific literary terms to express their views on a work, students are sometimes forced to review their understanding of the terms themselves before they can write an English paper. "Why can't I just explain in my own way why the novel is so powerful?" a student might ask.

To find the answer to this seemingly reasonable question, consider a parallel situation. If your car was running badly, you could go to the mechanic and tell her your impression of the problem: "It's been making a weird sound. Instead of the usual hum of the engine, it sounds more like 'mm-pachuk, mm-pachuk.' I've also noticed my gas mileage is lower than normal." The mechanic might be able to look under the hood, drive the car, and figure out the issue, but some car-owners worry that if they present the problem to the mechanic this way, not only will it take longer for the mechanic to diagnose the problem and fix it, but she might even take advantage of their ignorance and complete expensive additional "repairs" that are not immediately necessary.

Your *ethos*, or credibility, is weak in such an exchange, and that weakness may cost you extra time and money. However, if you were to tell the mechanic that you believe the car needs a new spark plug, your ethos would be stronger. The mechanic would recognize your relative expertise and might be more likely to call and ask for your approval before addressing other issues. In this case, simply using common professional terminology would have improved your position. Similarly, scientists using the accepted terms of their disciplines will be listened to with more respect than those using unconventional vocabulary ("the blobby-looking organism"). Your expertise is evidenced, in some part, by your ability to employ accepted terminology.

What terms are important to our study of literature? Some terms overlap among genres, but we will begin with the terms useful to the study of poetry. The term **genre** distinguishes one type of literature from another. The major genres are *poetry*, *fiction*, *drama*, and *creative nonfiction*. However, genre can also be used to refer to subcategories of each; for example, fiction can be broken down into *novel* and *short story*, and the novel can itself be broken into genres such as the *mystery* novel, the *romance* novel and the *science fiction* novel. Sometimes the word **form** is used almost interchangeably with *genre*. This overlap is not entirely surprising since we often consider the *form* of a work as a clue to its *genre*. To illustrate, consider the difference between the visual appearance of a *poem* on the page as compared with that of a short story. In this case, we can *see* the differences in *form*. However, though their meanings overlap, *form* does have a meaning distinct from that of *genre*. The term **form** can be used to indicate very specific features of a work. A **sonnet** is a *poetic form* that traditionally employs fourteen lines in iambic pentameter (see *iambic pentameter* below). A **villanelle**, on the other hand, is a poetic form requiring nineteen lines, distributed into five tercets and a quatrain, and also requiring that the first and third line of the first stanza be repeated alternately in the last lines of the stanzas that follow it. In the final quatrain, the two repeated lines conclude the poem. Thus, we could describe Shakespeare's Sonnet 130 as being a different *form* than Dylan Thomas's "Do Not Go Gentle into That Good Night."

Theme is another term common to discussion of literature. Though *theme* is similar to *message* or *argument*, it is not necessarily an *assertion* like the other two terms are. In connecting to a work's meaning, a *theme* can refer to *key topics* of a work. Thus, while we might say "Ode on a Grecian Urn" *argues* that the state of desire should be appreciated beyond the moment of satisfaction, we might state that the *themes* of the poem are *becoming versus being, the role of timeless art in a time-dependent world,* and *the relationship between beauty and truth.*

The **tone** of a work is crucial to its meaning and effect. The tone of a poem, often generated by *diction, rhythm,* and *rhyme,* can be, for example, sad, angry, celebratory, ironic, respectful, and/or yearning. Most effective poems exhibit **tension**. The *tone* can help to generate that tension. Tension itself can be generated in a variety of ways, but one common method is the juxtaposition of two seemingly opposing forces against one another. In "Ode on a Grecian Urn," the two forces that seem to pull against each other are *time* and *timelessness.* To develop that tension, Keats employs carefully crafted **diction,** or word choice. To generate an awareness of time, he uses words like "historian," "legend," and "old age." This awareness, however, is challenged by words associated with the vase's "frozen" timeless scene: "for ever new," "for ever young," and "eternity." Diction can be used to generate *tension* and to set a poem's *tone,* as well as to establish significant themes in a work. Consider Hughes's use in "The Weary Blues" of "drowsy," "mellow," "dull pallor," "lazy," and "melancholy." These words not only reflect the "drowsy" sound of blues, but they also suggest the melancholy *mood* of that music.

It is important, in understanding a poem's meaning, to consider its **point of view**. Remember, we must not assume that the poem's **speaker** is the *poet.* The speaker is constructed by the poet to provide point of view for the poem. In "The Weary Blues," the speaker is actually on Lenox Avenue listening to the blues singer and imagining, later, the singer's life when he leaves the club. We might ask ourselves why the speaker's thoughts follow the blues singer home in this way. What does the speaker's point of view tell us about him or her? Why does Hughes describe the event from this perspective? In some poems, the point of view is not first person (in other words, we don't hear of the main character as *I*). Instead, the **persona** (or main character) is referred to in third person (*he* or *she*).

Irony is an idea turned back upon itself; in an ironic passage, the words mean something different than their literal definitions would suggest. Consider Marianne Moore's "Poetry" located at http://www.poets.org/poetsorg/poem/poetry.

Following the title, the first line seems to state *that the speaker does not like poetry* ("it"). In the next line, she even seems to cast aspersion on poetry by calling it "fiddle." One irony, then, is that the speaker seems to be insulting poetry in a…well, in a *poem*. So, from this moment, the reader understands that Moore is presenting the reader with a puzzle. As the poem develops, however, it becomes clear that it is a certain *kind* of poem that the speaker doesn't like—a poem that spurs "high-sounding interpretation" (9) but contains no "useful" substance (12), nothing "genuine" (40). After building a gradual argument that "it" is actually not poetry at all, Moore brings us logically to the concluding line, that if what we dislike is "poetry" that we can't understand—"poetry" that presents complicated emptiness, if we demand the *genuine*—it is likely that we "are interested in poetry" after all (40). Moore's use of irony here yields a wonderful twist, driving home her point, and giving her own poem great impact.

While we may think of **setting** as an element more relevant to fiction, it is often an important feature of poetry, as well. The setting of Lenox Avenue for "The Weary Blues," for example, provides historical context and authenticity to the blues song. Lenox Avenue is a famous street in Harlem in which African American culture (particularly jazz, blues, and soul food) thrived during the Harlem Renaissance.

Finally, let's examine a few literary elements associated more specifically with poetry. **Rhyme** is produced when two words *ending in the same vowel sound* are juxtaposed with one another. In "The Weary Blues," "tune" and "croon" produce a rhyme, along with "night" and "light," "sway" and "play," and "key" and "melody." These rhymes give the poem a lyrical, or musical, quality. Although the term **lyric poem** refers to classical poetry following specific rhythms and rhyme schemes, these poems were often accompanied by music, and "The Weary Blues" does conjure the sounds of blues music. Hughes's purposeful use of blues **rhythm** in this poem is a departure from traditional European rhythms, the most common of which are *iambic pentameter* and *ballad meter*. An iamb is a two syllable *foot* (we measure poetic rhythmic units in *feet*), with the accent on the second syllable. "Thou still unravish'd bride of quietness," the first line of "Ode on a Grecian Urn," is written in iambic pentameter. "Thou still" reflects the two syllable foot with the accent on the second syllable. In this line, there are five feet, a line-length which we describe as *pentameter* (*penta* meaning five). Many poems have been composed in this meter over the centuries, often with each pair of lines rhyming. Pairs like this are called **couplets**. Consider the rhyme and rhythm of Shakespeare's "My Mistress' Eyes" (Sonnet 130):

My mistress' eyes are nothing like the sun;
Coral is far more red than her lips' red;
If snow be white, why then her breasts are dun;
If hairs be wires, black wires grow on her head.
I have seen roses damasked, red and white,　　　　　　　5
But no such roses see I in her cheeks;
And in some perfumes is there more delight
Than in the breath that from my mistress reeks.
I love to hear her speak, yet well I know
That music hath a far more pleasing sound;　　　　　　　10
I grant I never saw a goddess go;
My mistress when she walks treads on the ground.
　　And yet, by heaven, I think my love as rare
　　As any she belied with false compare.

(1623)

With its conventional fourteen lines, this sonnet exhibits all the rules of the form we now call the Shakespearean sonnet. Each line is written in iambic pentameter, and the rhyme scheme of the poem follows this pattern: ABAB CDCD EFEF GG. Concluding with a couplet, the Shakespearean sonnet resolves the conflict or problem in the final two lines, and the GG rhyme enhances this feeling of completion.

The **ballad stanza** (the poetic version of a paragraph) is a *quatrain* (a four-line stanza), and the rhythm alternates iambic *tetrameter* lines (featuring four iambs) with iambic *trimeter* lines (with three iambs each). While there is no rhyme with line one or line three of the stanza, line two rhymes with line four. The "sing-song" quality produced by the ballad's rhythm and rhyme has generally been more popular among common folks than has iambic pentameter, which is usually associated with "high art." There are many examples of ballad meter, even in our culture today. Many Christian hymns follow this form, such as "Amazing Grace" and "It Came Upon a Midnight Clear." In addition, the oeuvre of Emily Dickinson's poems is written in ballad form. See if you can trace the ballad rhythm and rhyme scheme in this one:

I heard a Fly buzz - when I died -
The Stillness in the Room
Was like the Stillness in the Air -
Between the Heaves of Storm -

The Eyes around - had wrung them dry -   5
And Breaths were gathering firm
For that last Onset - when the King
Be witnessed - in the Room -

I willed my Keepsakes - Signed away
What portion of me be   10
Assignable - and then it was
There interposed a Fly -

With Blue - uncertain - stumbling Buzz -
Between the light - and me -
And then the Windows failed - and then   15
I could not see to see -

                                                            (1890)

Can you see Dickinson's structure at work? Why would she use this "sing-song" form to explore the serious subject of death? Perhaps her focus on the fly offers a clue.

There are many forms that restrict the poet to a particular rhythm and rhyme. One of strictest poetic forms is the traditional villanelle. It might not be so difficult to write a poem that meets the formal requirements of the villanelle, but to write one that makes sense and conveys an important idea is quite a challenge. Read Dylan Thomas's 1952 "Do Not Go Gentle into That Good Night," one of the most famous villanelles in English literature, at http://www.poets.org/poetsorg/poem/do-not-go-gentle-good-night.

Questions for Consideration:

1. Why would Thomas choose such a restrictive form in which to express the son's urgent response to his father's impending death?

2. What is the effect of the repeated lines?

3. Besides the repeated lines, what other elements help to create the emotional tone?

Many poems reject the strict forms that dictate rhyme and rhythm. **Blank verse**, itself relatively traditional, uses an iambic pentameter line but without rhyme. Much of Shakespeare's drama is written in such verse. **Slant rhyme** also veers away from our expectations, presenting an "almost rhyme" that causes us to pause, either with words that look like they should rhyme but don't (like "be" and "Fly" in lines 10 and 12 of Dickinson's poem above) or with words whose sounds are similar but not exactly the same (such as "Room" and "Storm" in lines 2 and 4 of Dickinson's poem). Further, many contemporary poets take their freedom a step further to produce **free verse**, which is not governed by any common rules. This is not to say that contemporary poetry does not generate the musical effect we expect of the genre—it simply finds new ways to do so. Consider Galway Kinnell's 1980 "Blackberry Eating" at https://www.poetrysociety.org/psa/poetry/poetry_in_motion/atlas/chicago/blackberry_eating/.

Of course, a central element of poetry is its use of **figurative language**, which, as opposed to *literal language*, suggests meaning beyond a word's denotation. We expect poetry to compress language in ways that other genres do not. In a fourteen-line sonnet, there is a limited amount of space (even a limited number of syllables) in which to express an idea. Thus, poetry often employs metaphors and similes which pack much meaning into only a word or phrase. A **metaphor** is a comparison of two generally *unlike* things in order to emphasize a particular quality that they do share. Marianne Moore compares powerful poetry to "[h]ands that can grasp" (6), for instance, emphasizing its ability to move beyond the abstract and affect the reader's real and concrete experience. Shakespeare's speaker, in describing his mistress, asserts that "black wires grow on her head" (4). Hair and wire are two distinct materials, but in this comparison, he emphasizes the hair's lack of often-desired softness and suppleness, conveying his point about this woman's failure to meet conventional standards of beauty. Kinnell's poem compares words to blackberries in an **extended** or **controlling metaphor**, which carries the central metaphor all the way through the poem. A **simile** is a similar type of comparison, but uses the words *like* or *as* to link the two items. In "I Heard a Fly Buzz - When I Died," Dickinson writes that "The Stillness in the Room / Was like the Stillness in the Air - / Between the Heaves of Storm" (2-4). What effect does this comparison generate? How is the stillness of a dead body in an (almost) empty room like the still pause between "Heaves of a storm"? If death is a still moment, what are the "heaves" on either side of it?

Students sometimes find it difficult to distinguish between a symbol and a metaphor. While a metaphor is a comparison between two unlike things to emphasize their similarity, such as a blackberry and a word, blackberries don't *usually* refer to words. That's what makes Kinnell's poem so surprising. A **symbol**, on the other hand, is a link—one thing's representation of another—which many readers recognize. The representational "thing" has become a symbol by long-term association with what it represents. For example, the United States flag is a recognized symbol of American patriotism. For many, the flag represents the freedoms guaranteed in the U.S. Constitution. Similarly, in Western culture, the red rose historically symbolizes love and beauty. Shakespeare's use of this symbol in "My Mistress' Eyes" effectively reminds us of traditional notions of female beauty.

Two other poetic elements often used to great effect are alliteration and enjambment. **Alliteration** is the placement of same or similar sounds near each other to draw our attention, sometimes to the sound, sometimes to meanings of the words being linked to each other by the sounds, and sometimes both. In "Blackberry Eating," Kinnell conveys the message of the near physical quality of words through the "s" alliteration in the words "strengths," "squinched," "syllabled," "squeeze," "squinch," and "splurge," words that capture surprisingly well the experience of the tongue when we bite into a blackberry!

Enjambment carries one poetic line into the following one, yielding *two* meanings—one generated by the first line alone, and the other produced by taking the finished phrase or clause as it is completed in the next line. As discussed previously, in the first stanza of Keats's "Ode on a Grecian Urn," he creates one impression with line 11 on its own: "Heard melodies are sweet, but those unheard." But when we read on to finish the clause, we read instead, "Heard melodies are sweet, but those unheard / Are sweeter" (11-12). Line 11 might create a sad tone, suggesting that we cannot hear the urn-piper's melody, but taken together, lines 11 and 12 convey that the urn-piper's unheard song is *even sweeter* than a heard melody. Our momentary misconception boosts the effect of the real message.

As you read poems like those we have discussed in this chapter, as well as those that follow, consider how the above elements function to generate effect and power. You may choose one of these to write about, and as you develop your perspective on the meaning and relevance of the poem, these terms will no doubt help express your point to your audience.

4.4 Additional Poems

Dover Beach

By Matthew Arnold

The sea is calm tonight.
The tide is full, the moon lies fair
Upon the straits; on the French coast the light

Gleams and is gone; the cliffs of England stand,
Glimmering and vast, out in the tranquil bay.   5
Come to the window, sweet is the night-air!
Only, from the long line of spray
Where the sea meets the moon-blanched land,
Listen! you hear the grating roar
Of pebbles which the waves draw back, and fling,   10
At their return, up the high strand,
Begin, and cease, and then again begin,
With tremulous cadence slow, and bring
The eternal note of sadness in.

Sophocles long ago   15
Heard it on the Ægean, and it brought
Into his mind the turbid ebb and flow
Of human misery; we
Find also in the sound a thought,
Hearing it by this distant northern sea.   20

The Sea of Faith
Was once, too, at the full, and round earth's shore
Lay like the folds of a bright girdle furled.
But now I only hear
Its melancholy, long, withdrawing roar,   25
Retreating, to the breath
Of the night-wind, down the vast edges drear
And naked shingles of the world.

Ah, love, let us be true
To one another! for the world, which seems   30
To lie before us like a land of dreams,
So various, so beautiful, so new,
Hath really neither joy, nor love, nor light,
Nor certitude, nor peace, nor help for pain;
And we are here as on a darkling plain   35
Swept with confused alarms of struggle and flight,
Where ignorant armies clash by night.

(1867)

Annabel Lee
By Edgar Allan Poe

It was many and many a year ago,
   In a kingdom by the sea,
That a maiden there lived whom you may know
   By the name of Annabel Lee;
And this maiden she lived with no other thought   5
   Than to love and be loved by me.

I was a child and *she* was a child,
   In this kingdom by the sea,
But we loved with a love that was more than love—
   I and my Annabel Lee—   10
With a love that the wingèd seraphs of Heaven
   Coveted her and me.

And this was the reason that, long ago,
   In this kingdom by the sea,
A wind blew out of a cloud, chilling   15
   My beautiful Annabel Lee;
So that her highborn kinsmen came
   And bore her away from me,
To shut her up in a sepulchre
   In this kingdom by the sea.   20

The angels, not half so happy in Heaven,
   Went envying her and me—
Yes!—that was the reason (as all men know,
   In this kingdom by the sea)
That the wind came out of the cloud by night,   25
   Chilling and killing my Annabel Lee.

But our love it was stronger by far than the love
   Of those who were older than we—
   Of many far wiser than we—
And neither the angels in Heaven above   30
   Nor the demons down under the sea
Can ever dissever my soul from the soul
   Of the beautiful Annabel Lee;

For the moon never beams, without bringing me dreams
    Of the beautiful Annabel Lee;   35
And the stars never rise, but I feel the bright eyes
    Of the beautiful Annabel Lee;
And so, all the night-tide, I lie down by the side
    Of my darling—my darling—my life and my bride,
In her sepulchre there by the sea—   40
In her tomb by the sounding sea.

                                      (1849)

Frederick Douglass
By Paul Laurence Dunbar

Ah, Douglass, we have fall'n on evil days,
Such days as thou, not even thou didst know,
When thee, the eyes of that harsh long ago
Saw, salient, at the cross of devious ways,
And all the country heard thee with amaze.   5
Not ended then, the passionate ebb and flow,
The awful tide that battled to and fro;
We ride amid a tempest of dispraise.

Now, when the waves of swift dissension swarm,
And Honour, the strong pilot, lieth stark,   10
Oh, for thy voice high-sounding o'er the storm,
For thy strong arm to guide the shivering bark,
The blast-defying power of thy form,
To give us comfort through the lonely dark.

                                      (1895)

The Hunting of the Hare
By Margaret Cavendish

Betwixt two Ridges of Plowd-land, lay Wat
Pressing his Body close to Earth lay squat.
His Nose upon his two Fore-feet close lies
Glaring obliquely with his great gray Eyes.
His Head he alwaies sets against the Wind;   5
If turne his Taile, his Haires blow up behind:
Which he too cold will grow, but he is wise,

And keeps his Coat still downe, so warm he lies.
Thus resting all the day, till Sun doth set
Then riseth up, his Reliefe for to get.   10
Walking about untill the Sun doth rise
Then back returnes, down in his Forme he lyes.
At last, Poore Wat was found, as he there lay
By Hunts-men, with their Dogs which came that way.
Seeing, gets up, and fast begins to run,   15
Hoping some waies the Cruell Dogs to shun.
But they by Nature have so quick a Sent,
That by their Nose they race, what way he went.
And with their deep, wide Mouths set forth a Cry,
Which answer'd was by Ecchoes in the Skie.   20
Then Wat was struck with Terrour, and with Feare,
Thinkes every Shadow still the Dogs they were.
And running out some distance from the noise,
To hide himselfe, his Thoughts he new employs.

Under a Clod of Earth in Sand-pit wide,   25
Poore Wat sat close, hoping himselfe to hide.
There long he had not sat, but strait his Eares
The Winding Hornes, and crying Dogs he heares:
Starting with Feare, up leapes, then doth he run,
And with such speed, the Ground scarce treades upon.   30
Into a great thick Wood he strait way gets,
Where underneath a broken Bough he sits.
At every Leafe that with the wind did shake,
Did bring such Terrour, made his Heart to ake.
That Place he left, to Champion Plaines he went,   35
Winding about, for to deceive their Sent.
And while they snuffling were, to find his Track,
Poore Wat, being weary, his swift pace did slack.
On his two hinder legs for ease did sit,
His Fore-feet rub'd his Face from Dust, and Sweat.   40
Licking his Feet, he wip'd his Eares so cleane,
That none could tell that Wat had hunted been.
But casting round about his faire great Eyes,
The Hounds in full Careere he neere him 'pies:
To Wat it was so terrible a Sight,   45
Feare gave him Wings, and made his Body light.

Though weary was before, by running long,
Yet now his Breath he never felt more strong.
 Like those that dying are, think Health returns,
When tis but a faint Blast, which Life out burnes.   50
 For Spirits seek to guard the Heart about,
Striving with Death, but Death doth quench them out.
Thus they so fast came on, with such loud Cries,
That he no hopes hath left, no help espies.
With that the Winds did pity poore Wats case,   55
And with their Breath the Sent blew from the Place.
Then every Nose is busily imployed,
And every Nostrill is set open, wide:
And every Head doth seek a severall way,
To find what Grasse, or Track, the Sent on lay.   60
Thus quick Industry, that is not slack,
Is like to Witchery, brings lost things back.
For though the Wind had tied the Sent up close,
A Busie Dog thrust in his Snuffling Nose:
And drew it out, with it did foremost run,   65
Then Hornes blew loud, for the rest to follow on.
The great slow-Hounds, their throats did set a Base,
The Fleet swift Hounds, as Tenours next in place;
The little Beagles they a Trebble sing,
And through the Aire their Voice a round did ring.   70
Which made a Consort, as they ran along;
If they but words could speak, might sing a Song,
The Hornes kept time, the Hunters shout for Joy,
And valiant seeme, poore Wat for to destroy:
Spurring their Horses to a full Careere,   75
Swim Rivers deep, leap Ditches without feare;
Indanger Life, and Limbes, so fast will ride,
Onely to see how patiently Wat died.
For why, the Dogs so neere his Heeles did get,
That they their sharp Teeth in his Breech did set.   80
Then tumbling downe, did fall with weeping Eyes,
Gives up his Ghost, and thus poore Wat he dies.
Men hooping loud, such Acclamations make,
As if the Devill they did Prisoner take.
When they do but a shiftlesse Creature kill;   85
To hunt, there need no Valiant Souldiers skill.

But Man doth think that Exercise, and Toile,
To keep their Health, is best, which makes most spoile.
Thinking that Food, and Nourishment so good,
And Appetite, that feeds on Flesh, and blood.   90
When they do Lions, Wolves, Beares, Tigers see,
To kill poore Sheep, strait say, they cruell be.
But for themselves all Creatures think too few,
 For Luxury, with God would make them new.
As if that God made Creatures for Mans meat,   95
To give them Life, and Sense, for Man to eat;
Or else for Sport, or Recreations sake,
Destroy those Lives that God saw good to make:
Making their Stomacks, Graves, which full they fill
With Murther'd Bodies, that in sport they kill.   100
Yet Man doth think himselfe so gentle, mild,
When he of Creatures is most cruell wild.
And is so Proud, thinks onely he shall live,
That God a God-like Nature did him give.
And that all Creatures for his sake alone,   105
Was made for him, to Tyrannize upon.

(1653)

Also for Consideration:
 • "Those Winter Sundays," by Robert Hayden, 1962:
 http://www.poets.org/poetsorg/poem/those-winter-sundays

 • "Still I Rise," by Maya Angelou, 1978:
 http://www.poets.org/poetsorg/poem/still-i-rise

The Truths of Fiction

5.1 Fiction as a Genre

While definitions of fiction often emphasize its fabricated nature as opposed to historical or other "factual" genres, most readers understand that truth can arise from fiction in its own special way. Think of your favorite short story or novel—what does it reveal to you about yourself? How does it illuminate the human condition? While stories can convey a variety of "truths," which to some extent depend on each reader's identity and experience, we still seek in these narratives connections with characters and other readers. Up through the first part of the twentieth century, scholars often referred to these connections as "universal truths." This term refers to experiences, feelings, and insights that are common to *all* people. Yet, events of the 1950s and 1960s raised questions about whether *any* experience was truly universal. With the Civil Rights Movement came the understanding that people's experiences can vary wildly due to factors such as gender, class, ethnicity, and culture. Much to the surprise of many scholars (the vast majority of whom were, at the time, white, middle class, and male), not everyone could completely identify with Mark Twain's young protagonist Huckleberry Finn. For example, because of rigid social codes and physical risks unique to U.S. women, a young American female reader might not have the option of experiencing a physical journey like Huck's. In fact, it might be difficult for her even to *imagine* taking such a trip down the Mississippi River, since there is little to no evidence in history of a woman ever having done so. Even Huck's friend Jim, an escaped slave, is vulnerable in ways that Huck is not, as the two travel together. Readers of color might identify less with Huck's circumstances and more with Jim's. Even so, most readers can connect with Huck's *inner conflict* as he struggles between his obligation to follow the social rules taught to him as absolute morals and his own conscience, which tells him that Jim should not be subjected to slavery.

As you form your perspective on a story and then develop that perspective in an essay, your own readers will still seek an insight that is relevant to them. Thus, while we must be sensitive to the differences among individuals' experiences as we form an argument about a short story or novel, it is still important to forward a case based on *common ground* between our readers and ourselves. Consider the difference between these two assertions:

1. To mature as a moral creature, Huck must separate himself from society for a time and explore the world beyond his own narrow-minded hamlet.
2. Huck's journey away from his own narrow-minded hamlet and its teachings enables his moral maturation.

Note the first assertion's implication that if one *cannot* leave one's hamlet and separate him or herself from his or her restrictive environment, one cannot mature morally. A reader who cannot take such a journey because of economic or social factors (such as having to stay at home and care for a child or work to support a family) might respond to such a pronouncement by (a) feeling condemned to stunted personal growth and inferiority, as a person excluded from this experience, or (b) becoming defensive at such a claim. On the other hand, the second assertion will likely ring true both for those who *can* take the journey and those who *cannot*. It does not suggest that the *only* way of achieving moral growth is to take a physical journey like Huck's. Thus, even considering the sometimes stark differences among readers' lives, if interpretation of literature is handled well, it can reveal our common experiences.

As a place where we can connect with one another as well as learn about ourselves, fiction indeed offers us a special brand of truth. Although history and philosophy pursue these goals as well, **fiction** is a narrative that is *not* bound to either historical events or scientific facts. The writer takes liberties with a fictional story, using his imagination to craft a plot that achieves the desired effect and meaning. The term **narrative** refers to the sequence of events in a story, often suggesting a *cause and effect* relationship among these events. A term that captures this concept more specifically, **plot** is defined as the sequence of events that develops the conflict and shapes the story. Rather than tell everything that might possibly happen to a character in certain circumstances, the writer carefully selects the details that will develop the plot, the characters, and the story's *themes* and *messages*. The writer engages in character development in order to develop the plot and the meaning of the story, paying special attention to the **protagonist**, or main character. In a conventional story, the protagonist grows and/or changes as a result of having to negotiate the story's central **conflict**. A character might be developed through **exposition**, in which the narrator simply tells us about this person. But more often, the character is developed through **dialogue, point of view,** and **description** of this person's expressions and actions.

The traditional shape of a story is based on common conventions of Greek drama:

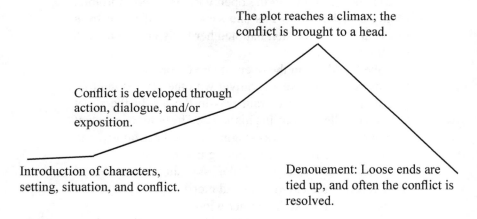

The plot reaches a climax; the conflict is brought to a head.

Conflict is developed through action, dialogue, and/or exposition.

Introduction of characters, setting, situation, and conflict.

Denouement: Loose ends are tied up, and often the conflict is resolved.

5.2 Writing about Short Stories

To examine how plot, character development, dialogue, setting, exposition, and action can be brought together to produce a specific effect and particular themes, let's consider an exceptionally brief 1894 short story by Kate Chopin.

The Story of an Hour

Knowing that Mrs. Mallard was afflicted with a heart trouble, great care was taken to break to her as gently as possible the news of her husband's death.

It was her sister Josephine who told her, in broken sentences; veiled hints that revealed in half concealing.

Her husband's friend Richards was there, too, near her. It was he who had been in the newspaper office when intelligence of the railroad disaster was received, with Brently Mallard's name leading the list of "killed." He had only taken the time to assure himself of its truth by a second telegram, and had hastened to forestall any less careful, less tender friend in bearing the sad message.

She did not hear the story as many women have heard the same, with a paralyzed inability to accept its significance. She wept at once, with sudden, wild abandonment, in her sister's arms. When the storm of grief had spent itself she went away to her room alone. She would have no one follow her.

There stood, facing the open window, a comfortable, roomy armchair. Into this she sank, pressed down by a physical exhaustion that haunted her body and seemed to reach into her soul.

She could see in the open square before her house the tops of trees that were all aquiver with the new spring life. The delicious breath of rain was in the air. In the street below a peddler was crying his wares. The notes of a distant song which some one was singing reached her faintly, and countless sparrows were twittering in the eaves.

There were patches of blue sky showing here and there through the clouds that had met and piled one above the other in the west facing her window.

She sat with her head thrown back upon the cushion of the chair, quite motionless, except when a sob came up into her throat and shook her, as a child who has cried itself to sleep continues to sob in its dreams.

She was young, with a fair, calm face, whose lines bespoke repression and even a certain strength. But now there was a dull stare in her eyes, whose gaze was fixed away off yonder on one of those patches of blue sky. It was not a glance of reflection, but rather indicated a suspension of intelligent thought.

There was something coming to her and she was waiting for it, fearfully. What was it? She did not know; it was too subtle and elusive to name. But she felt it, creeping out of the sky, reaching toward her through the sounds, the scents, the color that filled the air.

Now her bosom rose and fell tumultuously. She was beginning to recognize this thing that was approaching to possess her, and she was striving to beat it back with her will—as powerless as her two white slender hands would have been. When she abandoned herself a little whispered word escaped her slightly parted lips. She said it over and over under her breath: "free, free, free!" The vacant stare and the look of terror that had followed it went from her eyes. They stayed keen and bright. Her pulses beat fast, and the coursing blood warmed and relaxed every inch of her body.

She did not stop to ask if it were or were not a monstrous joy that held her. A clear and exalted perception enabled her to dismiss the suggestion as trivial. She knew that she would weep again when she saw the kind, tender hands folded in death; the face that had never looked save with love upon her, fixed and gray and dead. But she saw beyond that bitter moment a long procession of years to come that would belong to her absolutely. And she opened and spread her arms out to them in welcome.

There would be no one to live for during those coming years; she would live for herself. There would be no powerful will bending hers in that blind persistence with which men and women believe they have a right to impose a private will upon a fellow-creature. A kind intention or a cruel intention made the act seem no less a crime as she looked upon it in that brief moment of illumination.

And yet she had loved him—sometimes. Often she had not. What did it matter! What could love, the unsolved mystery, count for in the face of this possession of self-assertion which she suddenly recognized as the strongest impulse of her being!

"Free! Body and soul free!" she kept whispering.

Josephine was kneeling before the closed door with her lips to the keyhold, imploring for admission. "Louise, open the door! I beg; open the door—you will make yourself ill. What are you doing, Louise? For heaven's sake open the door."

"Go away. I am not making myself ill." No; she was drinking in a very elixir of life through that open window.

Her fancy was running riot along those days ahead of her. Spring days, and summer days, and all sorts of days that would be her own. She breathed a quick prayer that life might be long. It was only yesterday she had thought with a shudder that life might be long.

She arose at length and opened the door to her sister's importunities. There was a feverish triumph in her eyes, and she carried herself unwittingly like a goddess of Victory. She clasped her sister's waist, and together they descended the stairs. Richards stood waiting for them at the bottom.

Some one was opening the front door with a latchkey. It was Brently Mallard who entered, a little travel-stained, composedly carrying his grip-sack and umbrella. He had been far from the scene of the accident, and did not even know there had been one. He stood amazed at Josephine's piercing cry; at Richards' quick motion to screen him from the view of his wife.

When the doctors came they said she had died of heart disease—of the joy that kills.

(1894)

Questions for Consideration:

1. How is Mrs. Mallard's character developed? Do you see examples of exposition, where the narrator simply tells us information about the protagonist? In addition, does Chopin portray particular emotional responses, thoughts, and actions to reveal Mrs. Mallard's character? If so, how so? How does she employ point of view in this story?

2. What is your impression of Brently Mallard? What elements of the story generate this impression?

3. How is setting (both the historical period and the physical atmosphere of the story) used to contribute to the story's meaning?

4. What is Mrs. Mallard's social class? What clues lead you to this conclusion?

5. What is the story's central conflict? Does Mrs. Mallard change, as we might expect a protagonist to do?

6. What are the important themes of this story?

As in poetry, fiction often utilizes **diction** and **figurative language** to convey important ideas. In this story, the words "aquiver," "spring," "delicious breath," and "twittering" suggest a kind of rebirth occurring for Mrs. Mallard. In further development of this notion, how does Chopin use the "patches of blue sky showing through the clouds" as a **metaphor** of Mrs. Mallard's potential transformation?

Of course, even in this brief work, Chopin reveals the story to be a complicated one. Why does Mrs. Mallard try to "beat...back with her will" this "thing" that is overtaking her? What is it? The plot of this story provides an unexpected twist at the conclusion. What is the effect of this surprise ending? Is there a **denouement**—in other words, are the "loose ends tied up"? Is the conflict resolved?

Consider the two following short stories to determine key elements that generate each work's impact and how they do so.

The Open Boat
By Stephen Crane

A Tale intended to be after the fact.

Being the experience of four men sunk from the steamer Commodore.

I

None of them knew the color of the sky. Their eyes glanced level, and were fastened upon the waves that swept toward them. These waves were of the hue of slate, save for the tops, which were of foaming white, and all of the men knew the colors of the sea. The horizon narrowed and widened, and dipped and rose, and at all times its edge was jagged with waves that seemed thrust up in points like rocks.

Many a man ought to have a bath-tub larger than the boat which here rode upon the sea. These waves were most wrongfully and barbarously abrupt and tall, and each froth-top was a problem in small boat navigation.

The cook squatted in the bottom and looked with both eyes at the six inches of gunwale which separated him from the ocean. His sleeves were rolled over his fat forearms, and the two flaps of his unbuttoned vest dangled as he bent to bail out the boat. Often he said: "Gawd! That was a narrow clip." As he remarked it he invariably gazed eastward over the broken sea.

The oiler, steering with one of the two oars in the boat, sometimes raised himself suddenly to keep clear of water that swirled in over the stern. It was a thin little oar and it seemed often ready to snap.

The correspondent, pulling at the other oar, watched the waves and wondered why he was there.

The injured captain, lying in the bow, was at this time buried in that profound dejection and indifference which comes, temporarily at least, to even the bravest and most enduring when, willy nilly, the firm fails, the army loses, the ship goes down. The mind of the master of a vessel is rooted deep in the timbers of her, though he command for a day or a decade, and this captain had on him the stern impression of a scene in the grays of dawn of seven turned faces, and later a stump of a top-mast with a white ball on it that slashed to and fro at the waves, went low and lower, and down. Thereafter there was something strange in his voice. Although steady, it was deep with mourning, and of a quality beyond oration or tears.

"Keep'er a little more south, Billie," said he.

"'A little more south,' sir," said the oiler in the stern.

A seat in this boat was not unlike a seat upon a bucking broncho, and, by the same token, a broncho is not much smaller. The craft pranced and reared, and plunged like an animal. As each wave came, and she rose for it, she seemed like a horse making at a fence outrageously high. The manner of her scramble over these walls of water is a mystic thing, and, moreover, at the top of them were ordinarily these problems in white water, the foam racing down from the summit of each wave, requiring a new leap, and a leap from the air. Then, after scornfully bumping a crest, she would slide, and race, and splash down a long incline and arrive bobbing and nodding in front of the next menace.

A singular disadvantage of the sea lies in the fact that after successfully surmounting one wave you discover that there is another behind it just as important and just as nervously anxious to do something effective in the way of swamping boats. In a ten-foot dingey one can get an idea of the resources of the sea in the line of waves that is not probable to the average experience, which is never at sea in a dingey. As each slaty wall of water approached, it shut all else from the view of the men in the boat, and it was not difficult to imagine that this particular wave was the final outburst of the ocean, the last effort of the grim water. There was a terrible grace in the move of the waves, and they came in silence, save for the snarling of the crests.

In the wan light, the faces of the men must have been gray. Their eyes must have glinted in strange ways as they gazed steadily astern. Viewed from a balcony, the whole thing would doubtlessly have been weirdly picturesque. But the men in the boat had no time to see it, and if they had had leisure there were other things to occupy their minds. The sun swung steadily up the sky, and they knew it was broad day because the color of the sea changed from slate to emerald-green, streaked with amber lights, and the foam was like tumbling snow. The process of the breaking day was unknown to them. They were aware only of this effect upon the color of the waves that rolled toward them.

In disjointed sentences the cook and the correspondent argued as to the difference between a life-saving station and a house of refuge. The cook had said: "There's a house of refuge just north of the Mosquito Inlet Light, and as soon as they see us, they'll come off in their boat and pick us up."

"As soon as who see us?" said the correspondent.

"The crew," said the cook.

"Houses of refuge don't have crews," said the correspondent. "As I understand them, they are only places where clothes and grub are stored for the benefit of shipwrecked people. They don't carry crews."

"Oh, yes, they do," said the cook.

"No, they don't," said the correspondent.

"Well, we're not there yet, anyhow," said the oiler, in the stern.

"Well," said the cook, "perhaps it's not a house of refuge that I'm thinking of as being near Mosquito Inlet Light. Perhaps it's a life-saving station."

"We're not there yet," said the oiler, in the stern.

II

As the boat bounced from the top of each wave, the wind tore through the hair of the hatless men, and as the craft plopped her stern down again the spray slashed past them. The crest of each of these waves was a hill, from the top of which the men surveyed, for a moment, a broad tumultuous expanse; shining and wind-riven. It was probably splendid. It was probably glorious, this play of the free sea, wild with lights of emerald and white and amber.

"Bully good thing it's an on-shore wind," said the cook. "If not, where would we be? Wouldn't have a show."

"That's right," said the correspondent.

The busy oiler nodded his assent.

Then the captain, in the bow, chuckled in a way that expressed humor, contempt, tragedy, all in one. "Do you think we've got much of a show, now, boys?" said he.

Whereupon the three were silent, save for a trifle of hemming and hawing. To express any particular optimism at this time they felt to be childish and stupid, but they all doubtless possessed this sense of the situation in their mind. A young man thinks doggedly at such times. On the other hand, the ethics of their condition was decidedly against any open suggestion of hopelessness. So they were silent.

"Oh, well," said the captain, soothing his children, "we'll get ashore all right."

But there was that in his tone which made them think, so the oiler quoth: "Yes! If this wind holds!"

The cook was bailing: "Yes! If we don't catch hell in the surf."

Canton flannel gulls flew near and far. Sometimes they sat down on the sea, near patches of brown sea-weed that rolled over the waves with a movement like carpets on line in a gale. The birds sat comfortably in groups, and they were envied by some in the dingey, for the wrath of the sea was no more to them than it was to a covey of prairie chickens a thousand miles inland. Often they came very close and stared at the men with black bead-like eyes. At these times they were uncanny and sinister in their unblinking scrutiny, and the men hooted angrily at them, telling them to be gone. One came, and evidently decided to alight on the top of the captain's head. The bird flew parallel to the boat and did not circle, but made short sidelong jumps in the air in chicken-fashion. His black eyes were wistfully fixed upon the captain's head. "Ugly brute," said the oiler to the bird. "You look as if you were made with a jack-knife." The cook and the correspondent swore darkly at the creature. The captain naturally wished to knock it away with the end of the heavy painter, but he did not dare do it, because anything resembling an emphatic gesture would have capsized this freighted boat, and so with his open hand, the captain gently and carefully waved the gull away. After it had been discouraged from the pursuit the captain breathed easier on account of his hair, and others breathed easier because the bird struck their minds at this time as being somehow grewsome and ominous.

In the meantime the oiler and the correspondent rowed. And also they rowed.

They sat together in the same seat, and each rowed an oar. Then the oiler took both oars; then the correspondent took both oars; then the oiler; then the correspondent. They rowed and they rowed. The very ticklish part of the business was when the time came for the reclining one in the stern to take his turn at the oars. By the very last star of truth, it is easier to steal eggs from under a hen than it was to change seats in the dingey. First the man in the stern slid his hand along the thwart and moved with care, as if he were of Sevres. Then the man in the rowing seat slid his hand along the other thwart. It was all done with the most extraordinary care. As the two sidled past each other, the whole party kept watchful eyes on the coming wave, and the captain cried: "Look out now! Steady there!"

The brown mats of sea-weed that appeared from time to time were like islands, bits of earth. They were travelling, apparently, neither one way nor the other. They were, to all intents stationary. They informed the men in the boat that it was making progress slowly toward the land.

The captain, rearing cautiously in the bow, after the dingey soared on a great swell, said that he had seen the lighthouse at Mosquito Inlet. Presently the cook remarked that he had seen it. The correspondent was at the oars, then, and for some reason he too wished to look at the lighthouse, but his back was toward the far shore and the waves were important, and for some time he could not seize an opportunity to turn his head. But at last there came a wave more gentle than the others, and when at the crest of it he swiftly scoured the western horizon.

"See it?" said the captain.

"No," said the correspondent, slowly, "I didn't see anything."

"Look again," said the captain. He pointed. "It's exactly in that direction."

At the top of another wave, the correspondent did as he was bid, and this time his eyes chanced on a small still thing on the edge of the swaying horizon. It was precisely like the point of a pin. It took an anxious eye to find a lighthouse so tiny.

"Think we'll make it, captain?"

"If this wind holds and the boat don't swamp, we can't do much else," said the captain.

The little boat, lifted by each towering sea, and splashed viciously by the crests, made progress that in the absence of sea-weed was not apparent to those in her. She seemed just a wee thing wallowing, miraculously, top-up, at the mercy of five oceans. Occasionally, a great spread of water, like white flames, swarmed into her.

"Bail her, cook," said the captain, serenely.

"All right, captain," said the cheerful cook.

III

It would be difficult to describe the subtle brotherhood of men that was here established on the seas. No one said that it was so. No one mentioned it. But it dwelt in the boat, and each man felt it warm him. They were a captain, an oiler, a cook, and a correspondent, and they were friends, friends in a more curiously iron-bound degree than may be common. The hurt captain, lying against the water-jar in the bow, spoke always in a low voice and calmly, but he could never command a more ready and swiftly obedient crew than the motley three of the dingey. It was more than a mere recognition of what was best for the common safety. There was surely in it a quality that was personal and heartfelt. And after this devotion to the commander of the boat there was this comradeship that the correspondent, for instance, who had been taught to be cynical of men, knew even at the time was the best experience of his life. But no one said that it was so. No one mentioned it.

"I wish we had a sail," remarked the captain. "We might try my overcoat on the end of an oar and give you two boys a chance to rest." So the cook and the correspondent held the mast and spread wide the overcoat. The oiler steered, and the little boat made good way with her new rig. Sometimes the oiler had to scull sharply to keep a sea from breaking into the boat, but otherwise sailing was a success.

Meanwhile the light-house had been growing slowly larger. It had now almost assumed color, and appeared like a little gray shadow on the sky. The man at the oars could not be prevented from turning his head rather often to try for a glimpse of this little gray shadow.

At last, from the top of each wave the men in the tossing boat could see land. Even as the light-house was an upright shadow on the sky, this land seemed but a long black shadow on the sea. It certainly was thinner than paper. "We must be about opposite New Smyrna," said the cook, who had coasted this shore often in schooners. "Captain, by the way, I believe they abandoned that life-saving station there about a year ago."

"Did they?" said the captain.

The wind slowly died away. The cook and the correspondent were not now obliged to slave in order to hold high the oar. But the waves continued their old impetuous swooping at the dingey, and the little craft, no longer under way, struggled woundily over them. The oiler or the correspondent took the oars again.

Shipwrecks are apropos of nothing. If men could only train for them and have them occur when the men had reached pink condition, there would be less drowning at sea. Of the four in the dingey none had slept any time worth mentioning for two days and two nights previous to embarking in the dingey, and in the excitement of clambering about the deck of a foundering ship they had also forgotten to eat heartily.

For these reasons, and for others, neither the oiler nor the correspondent was fond of rowing at this time. The correspondent wondered ingenuously how in the name of all that was sane could there be people who thought it amusing to row a boat. It was not an amusement; it was a diabolical punishment, and even a genius of mental aberrations could never conclude that it was anything but a horror to the muscles and a crime against the back. He mentioned to the boat in general how the amusement of rowing struck him, and the weary-faced oiler smiled in full sympathy. Previously to the foundering, by the way, the oiler had worked double-watch in the engine-room of the ship.

"Take her easy, now, boys," said the captain. "Don't spend yourselves. If we have to run a surf you'll need all your strength, because we'll sure have to swim for it. Take your time."

Slowly the land arose from the sea. From a black line it became a line of black and a line of white, trees, and sand. Finally, the captain said that he could make out a house on the shore. "That's the house of refuge, sure," said the cook. "They'll see us before long, and come out after us."

The distant light-house reared high. "The keeper ought to be able to make us out now, if he's looking through a glass," said the captain. "He'll notify the life-saving people."

"None of those other boats could have got ashore to give word of the wreck," said the oiler, in a low voice. "Else the life-boat would be out hunting us."

Slowly and beautifully the land loomed out of the sea. The wind came again. It had veered from the northeast to the southeast. Finally, a new sound struck the ears of the men in the boat. It was the low thunder of the surf on the shore. "We'll never be able to make the light-house now," said the captain. "Swing her head a little more north, Billie," said the captain.

"'A little more north,' sir," said the oiler.

Whereupon the little boat turned her nose once more down the wind, and all but the oarsman watched the shore grow. Under the influence of this expansion doubt and direful apprehension was leaving the minds of the men. The management of the boat was still most absorbing, but it could not prevent a quiet cheerfulness. In an hour, perhaps, they would be ashore.

Their back-bones had become thoroughly used to balancing in the boat and they now rode this wild colt of a dingey like circus men. The correspondent thought that he had been drenched to the skin, but happening to feel in the top pocket of his coat, he found therein eight cigars. Four of them were soaked with sea-water; four were perfectly scatheless. After a search, somebody produced three dry matches, and thereupon the four waifs rode in their little boat, and with an assurance of an impending rescue shining in their eyes, puffed at the big cigars and judged well and ill of all men. Everybody took a drink of water.

IV

"Cook," remarked the captain, "there don't seem to be any signs of life about your house of refuge."

"No," replied the cook. "Funny they don't see us!"

A broad stretch of lowly coast lay before the eyes of the men. It was of low dunes topped with dark vegetation. The roar of the surf was plain, and sometimes they could see the white lip of a wave as it spun up the beach. A tiny house was blocked out black upon the sky. Southward, the slim light-house lifted its little gray length.

Tide, wind, and waves were swinging the dingey northward. "Funny they don't see us," said the men.

The surf's roar was here dulled, but its tone was, nevertheless, thunderous and mighty. As the boat swam over the great rollers, the men sat listening to this roar. "We'll swamp sure," said everybody.

It is fair to say here that there was not a life-saving station within twenty miles in either direction, but the men did not know this fact and in consequence they made dark and opprobrious remarks concerning the eyesight of the nation's life-savers. Four scowling men sat in the dingey and surpassed records in the invention of epithets.

"Funny they don't see us."

The light-heartedness of a former time had completely faded. To their sharpened minds it was easy to conjure pictures of all kinds of incompetency and blindness and indeed, cowardice. There was the shore of the populous land, and it was bitter and bitter to them that from it came no sign.

"Well," said the captain, ultimately, "I suppose we'll have to make a try for ourselves. If we stay out here too long, we'll none of us have strength left to swim after the boat swamps."

And so the oiler, who was at the oars, turned the boat straight for the shore. There was a sudden tightening of muscles. There was some thinking.

"If we don't all get ashore—" said the captain. "If we don't all get ashore, I suppose you fellows know where to send news of my finish?"

They then briefly exchanged some addresses and admonitions. As for the reflections of the men, there was a great deal of rage in them. Perchance they might be formulated thus: "If I am going to be drowned—if I am going to be drowned—if I am going to be drowned, why, in the name of the seven mad gods who rule the sea, was I allowed to come thus far and contemplate sand and trees? Was I brought here merely to have my nose dragged away as I was about to nibble the sacred cheese of life? It is preposterous. If this old ninny-woman, Fate, cannot do better than this, she should be deprived of the management of men's fortunes. She is an old hen who knows not her intention. If she has decided to drown me, why did she not do it in the beginning and save me all this trouble. The whole affair is absurd...But, no, she cannot mean to drown me. She dare not drown me. She cannot drown me. Not after all this work." Afterward the man might have had an impulse to shake his fist at the clouds: "Just you drown me, now, and then hear what I call you!"

The billows that came at this time were more formidable. They seemed always just about to break and roll over the little boat in a turmoil of foam. There was a preparatory and long growl in the speech of them. No mind unused to the sea would have concluded that the dingey could ascend these sheer heights in time. The shore was still afar. The oiler was a wily surfman. "Boys," he said, swiftly, "she won't live three minutes more and we're too far out to swim. Shall I take her to sea again, captain?"

"Yes! Go ahead!" said the captain.

This oiler, by a series of quick miracles, and fast and steady oarsmanship, turned the boat in the middle of the surf and took her safely to sea again.

There was a considerable silence as the boat bumped over the furrowed sea to deeper water. Then somebody in gloom spoke. "Well, anyhow, they must have seen us from the shore by now."

The gulls went in slanting flight up the wind toward the gray desolate east. A squall, marked by dingy clouds, and clouds brick-red, like smoke from a burning building, appeared from the southeast.

"What do you think of those life-saving people? Ain't they peaches?"

"Funny they haven't seen us."

"Maybe they think we're out here for sport! Maybe they think we're fishin'. Maybe they think we're damned fools."

It was a long afternoon. A changed tide tried to force them southward, but wind and wave said northward. Far ahead, where coast-line, sea, and sky formed their mighty angle, there were little dots which seemed to indicate a city on the shore.

"St. Augustine?"

The captain shook his head. "Too near Mosquito Inlet."

And the oiler rowed, and then the correspondent rowed. Then the oiler rowed. It was a weary business. The human back can become the seat of more aches and pains than are registered in books for the composite anatomy of a regiment. It is a limited area, but it can become the theatre of innumerable muscular conflicts, tangles, wrenches, knots, and other comforts.

"Did you ever like to row, Billie?" asked the correspondent.

"No," said the oiler. "Hang it."

When one exchanged the rowing-seat for a place in the bottom of the boat, he suffered a bodily depression that caused him to be careless of everything save an obligation to wiggle one finger. There was cold sea-water swashing to and fro in the boat, and he lay in it. His head, pillowed on a thwart, was within an inch of the swirl of a wave crest, and sometimes a particularly obstreperous sea came in-board and drenched him once more. But these matters did not annoy him. It is almost certain that if the boat had capsized he would have tumbled comfortably out upon the ocean as if he felt sure it was a great soft mattress.

"Look! There's a man on the shore!"

"Where?"

"There! See 'im? See 'im?"

"Yes, sure! He's walking along."

"Now he's stopped. Look! He's facing us!"

"He's waving at us!"

"So he is! By thunder!"

"Ah, now, we're all right! Now we're all right! There'll be a boat out here for us in half an hour."

"He's going on. He's running. He's going up to that house there."

The remote beach seemed lower than the sea, and it required a searching glance to discern the little black figure. The captain saw a floating stick and they rowed to it. A bath-towel was by some weird chance in the boat, and, tying this on the stick, the captain waved it. The oarsman did not dare turn his head, so he was obliged to ask questions.

"What's he doing now?"

"He's standing still again. He's looking, I think...There he goes again. Toward the house...Now he's stopped again."

"Is he waving at us?"

"No, not now! he was, though."

"Look! There comes another man!"

"He's running."

"Look at him go, would you."

"Why, he's on a bicycle. Now he's met the other man. They're both waving at us. Look!"

"There comes something up the beach."

"What the devil is that thing?"

"Why, it looks like a boat."

"Why, certainly it's a boat."

"No, it's on wheels."

"Yes, so it is. Well, that must be the life-boat. They drag them along shore on a wagon."

"That's the life-boat, sure."

"No, by——, it's—it's an omnibus."

"I tell you it's a life-boat."

"It is not! It's an omnibus. I can see it plain. See? One of these big hotel omnibuses."

"By thunder, you're right. It's an omnibus, sure as fate. What do you suppose they are doing with an omnibus? Maybe they are going around collecting the life-crew, hey?"

"That's it, likely. Look! There's a fellow waving a little black flag. He's standing on the steps of the omnibus. There come those other two fellows. Now they're all talking together. Look at the fellow with the flag. Maybe he ain't waving it."

"That ain't a flag, is it? That's his coat. Why, certainly, that's his coat."

"So it is. It's his coat. He's taken it off and is waving it around his head. But would you look at him swing it."

"Oh, say, there isn't any life-saving station there. That's just a winter resort hotel omnibus that has brought over some of the boarders to see us drown."

"What's that idiot with the coat mean? What's he signaling, anyhow?"

"It looks as if he were trying to tell us to go north. There must be a life-saving station up there."

"No! He thinks we're fishing. Just giving us a merry hand. See? Ah, there, Willie."

"Well, I wish I could make something out of those signals. What do you suppose he means?"

"He don't mean anything. He's just playing."

"Well, if he'd just signal us to try the surf again, or to go to sea and wait, or go north, or go south, or go to hell—there would be some reason in it. But look at him. He just stands there and keeps his coat revolving like a wheel. The ass!"

"There come more people."

"Now there's quite a mob. Look! Isn't that a boat?"

"Where? Oh, I see where you mean. No, that's no boat."

"That fellow is still waving his coat."

"He must think we like to see him do that. Why don't he quit it. It don't mean anything."

"I don't know. I think he is trying to make us go north. It must be that there's a life-saving station there somewhere."

"Say, he ain't tired yet. Look at 'im wave."

"Wonder how long he can keep that up. He's been revolving his coat ever since he caught sight of us. He's an idiot. Why aren't they getting men to bring a boat out. A fishing boat—one of those big yawls—could come out here all right. Why don't he do something?"

"Oh, it's all right, now."

"They'll have a boat out here for us in less than no time, now that they've seen us."

A faint yellow tone came into the sky over the low land. The shadows on the sea slowly deepened. The wind bore coldness with it, and the men began to shiver.

"Holy smoke!" said one, allowing his voice to express his impious mood, "if we keep on monkeying out here! If we've got to flounder out here all night!"

"Oh, we'll never have to stay here all night! Don't you worry. They've seen us now, and it won't be long before they'll come chasing out after us."

The shore grew dusky. The man waving a coat blended gradually into this gloom, and it swallowed in the same manner the omnibus and the group of people. The spray, when it dashed uproariously over the side, made the voyagers shrink and swear like men who were being branded.

"I'd like to catch the chump who waved the coat. I feel like soaking him one, just for luck."

"Why? What did he do?"

"Oh, nothing, but then he seemed so damned cheerful."

In the meantime the oiler rowed, and then the correspondent rowed, and then the oiler rowed. Gray-faced and bowed forward, they mechanically, turn by turn, plied the leaden oars. The form of the light-house had vanished from the southern horizon, but finally a pale star appeared, just lifting from the sea. The streaked saffron in the west passed before the all-merging darkness, and the sea to the east was black. The land had vanished, and was expressed only by the low and drear thunder of the surf.

"If I am going to be drowned—if I am going to be drowned—if I am going to be drowned, why, in the name of the seven mad gods, who rule the sea, was I allowed to come thus far and contemplate sand and trees? Was I brought here merely to have my nose dragged away as I was about to nibble the sacred cheese of life?"

The patient captain, drooped over the water-jar, was sometimes obliged to speak to the oarsman.

"Keep her head up! Keep her head up!"

"'Keep her head up,' sir." The voices were weary and low.

This was surely a quiet evening. All save the oarsman lay heavily and listlessly in the boat's bottom. As for him, his eyes were just capable of noting the tall black waves that swept forward in a most sinister silence, save for an occasional subdued growl of a crest.

The cook's head was on a thwart, and he looked without interest at the water under his nose. He was deep in other scenes. Finally he spoke. "Billie," he murmured, dreamfully, "what kind of pie do you like best?"

V

"Pie," said the oiler and the correspondent, agitatedly. "Don't talk about those things, blast you!"

"Well," said the cook, "I was just thinking about ham sandwiches, and—"

A night on the sea in an open boat is a long night. As darkness settled finally, the shine of the light, lifting from the sea in the south, changed to full gold. On the northern horizon a new light appeared, a small bluish gleam on the edge of the waters. These two lights were the furniture of the world. Otherwise there was nothing but waves.

Two men huddled in the stern, and distances were so magnificent in the dingey that the rower was enabled to keep his feet partly warmed by thrusting them under his companions. Their legs indeed extended far under the rowing-seat until they touched the feet of the captain forward. Sometimes, despite the efforts of the tired oarsman, a wave came piling into the boat, an icy wave of the night, and the chilling water soaked them anew. They would twist their bodies for a moment and groan, and sleep the dead sleep once more, while the water in the boat gurgled about them as the craft rocked.

The plan of the oiler and the correspondent was for one to row until he lost the ability, and then arouse the other from his sea-water couch in the bottom of the boat.

The oiler plied the oars until his head drooped forward, and the overpowering sleep blinded him. And he rowed yet afterward. Then he touched a man in the bottom of the boat, and called his name. "Will you spell me for a little while?" he said, meekly.

"Sure, Billie," said the correspondent, awakening and dragging himself to a sitting position. They exchanged places carefully, and the oiler, cuddling down to the sea-water at the cook's side, seemed to go to sleep instantly.

The particular violence of the sea had ceased. The waves came without snarling. The obligation of the man at the oars was to keep the boat headed so that the tilt of the rollers would not capsize her, and to preserve her from filling when the crests rushed past. The black waves were silent and hard to be seen in the darkness. Often one was almost upon the boat before the oarsman was aware.

In a low voice the correspondent addressed the captain. He was not sure that the captain was awake, although this iron man seemed to be always awake. "Captain, shall I keep her making for that light north, sir?"

The same steady voice answered him. "Yes. Keep it about two points off the port bow."

The cook had tied a life-belt around himself in order to get even the warmth which this clumsy cork contrivance could donate, and he seemed almost stove-like when a rower, whose teeth invariably chattered wildly as soon as he ceased his labor, dropped down to sleep.

The correspondent, as he rowed, looked down at the two men sleeping under foot. The cook's arm was around the oiler's shoulders, and, with their fragmentary clothing and haggard faces, they were the babes of the sea, a grotesque rendering of the old babes in the wood.

Later he must have grown stupid at his work, for suddenly there was a growling of water, and a crest came with a roar and a swash into the boat, and it was a wonder that it did not set the cook afloat in his life-belt. The cook continued to sleep, but the oiler sat up, blinking his eyes and shaking with the new cold.

"Oh, I'm awful sorry, Billie," said the correspondent, contritely.

"That's all right, old boy," said the oiler, and lay down again and was asleep.

Presently it seemed that even the captain dozed, and the correspondent thought that he was the one man afloat on all the oceans. The wind had a voice as it came over the waves, and it was sadder than the end.

There was a long, loud swishing astern of the boat, and a gleaming trail of phosphorescence, like blue flame, was furrowed on the black waters. It might have been made by a monstrous knife.

Then there came a stillness, while the correspondent breathed with the open mouth and looked at the sea.

Suddenly there was another swish and another long flash of bluish light, and this time it was alongside the boat, and might almost have been reached with an oar. The correspondent saw an enormous fin speed like a shadow through the water, hurling the crystalline spray and leaving the long glowing trail.

The correspondent looked over his shoulder at the captain. His face was hidden, and he seemed to be asleep. He looked at the babes of the sea. They certainly were asleep. So, being bereft of sympathy, he leaned a little way to one side and swore softly into the sea.

But the thing did not then leave the vicinity of the boat. Ahead or astern, on one side or the other, at intervals long or short, fled the long sparkling streak, and there was to be heard the whirroo of the dark fin. The speed and power of the thing was greatly to be admired. It cut the water like a gigantic and keen projectile.

The presence of this biding thing did not affect the man with the same horror that it would if he had been a picnicker. He simply looked at the sea dully and swore in an undertone.

Nevertheless, it is true that he did not wish to be alone with the thing. He wished one of his companions to awaken by chance and keep him company with it. But the captain hung motionless over the water-jar and the oiler and the cook in the bottom of the boat were plunged in slumber.

VI

"If I am going to be drowned—if I am going to be drowned—if I am going to be drowned, why, in the name of the seven mad gods, who rule the sea, was I allowed to come thus far and contemplate sand and trees?"

During this dismal night, it may be remarked that a man would conclude that it was really the intention of the seven mad gods to drown him, despite the abominable injustice of it. For it was certainly an abominable injustice to drown a man who had worked so hard, so hard. The man felt it would be a crime most unnatural. Other people had drowned at sea since galleys swarmed with painted sails, but still —

When it occurs to a man that nature does not regard him as important, and that she feels she would not maim the universe by disposing of him, he at first wishes to throw bricks at the temple, and he hates deeply the fact that there are no bricks and no temples. Any visible expression of nature would surely be pelleted with his jeers.

Then, if there be no tangible thing to hoot he feels, perhaps, the desire to confront a personification and indulge in pleas, bowed to one knee, and with hands supplicant, saying: "Yes, but I love myself."

A high cold star on a winter's night is the word he feels that she says to him. Thereafter he knows the pathos of his situation.

The men in the dingey had not discussed these matters, but each had, no doubt, reflected upon them in silence and according to his mind. There was seldom any expression upon their faces save the general one of complete weariness. Speech was devoted to the business of the boat.

To chime the notes of his emotion, a verse mysteriously entered the correspondent's head. He had even forgotten that he had forgotten this verse, but it suddenly was in his mind.

A soldier of the Legion lay dying in Algiers; There was lack of woman's nursing, there was dearth of woman's tears; But a comrade stood beside him, and he took that comrade's hand And he said: "I shall never see my own, my native land."

In his childhood, the correspondent had been made acquainted with the fact that a soldier of the Legion lay dying in Algiers, but he had never regarded the fact as important. Myriads of his school-fellows had informed him of the soldier's plight, but the dinning had naturally ended by making him perfectly indifferent. He had never considered it his affair that a soldier of the Legion lay dying in Algiers, nor had it appeared to him as a matter for sorrow. It was less to him than breaking of a pencil's point.

Now, however, it quaintly came to him as a human, living thing. It was no longer merely a picture of a few throes in the breast of a poet, meanwhile drinking tea and warming his feet at the grate; it was an actuality—stern, mournful, and fine.

The correspondent plainly saw the soldier. He lay on the sand with his feet out straight and still. While his pale left hand was upon his chest in an attempt to thwart the going of his life, the blood came between his fingers. In the far Algerian distance, a city of low square forms was set against a sky that was faint with the last sunset hues. The correspondent, plying the oars and dreaming of the slow and slower movements of the lips of the soldier, was moved by a profound and perfectly impersonal comprehension. He was sorry for the soldier of the Legion who lay dying in Algiers.

The thing which had followed the boat and waited had evidently grown bored at the delay. There was no longer to be heard the slash of the cut-water, and there was no longer the flame of the long trail. The light in the north still glimmered, but it was apparently no nearer to the boat. Sometimes the boom of the surf rang in the correspondent's ears, and he turned the craft seaward then and rowed harder. Southward, someone had evidently built a watch-fire on the beach. It was too low and too far to be seen, but it made a shimmering, roseate reflection upon the bluff back of it, and this could be discerned from the boat. The wind came stronger, and sometimes a wave suddenly raged out like a mountain-cat and there was to be seen the sheen and sparkle of a broken crest.

The captain, in the bow, moved on his water-jar and sat erect. "Pretty long night," he observed to the correspondent. He looked at the shore. "Those life-saving people take their time."

"Did you see that shark playing around?"

"Yes, I saw him. He was a big fellow, all right."

"Wish I had known you were awake."

Later the correspondent spoke into the bottom of the boat.

"Billie!" There was a slow and gradual disentanglement. "Billie, will you spell me?"

"Sure," said the oiler.

As soon as the correspondent touched the cold comfortable sea-water in the bottom of the boat, and had huddled close to the cook's life-belt he was deep in sleep, despite the fact that his teeth played all the popular airs. This sleep was so good to him that it was but a moment before he heard a voice call his name in a tone that demonstrated the last stages of exhaustion. "Will you spell me?"

"Sure, Billie."

The light in the north had mysteriously vanished, but the correspondent took his course from the wide-awake captain.

Later in the night they took the boat farther out to sea, and the captain directed the cook to take one oar at the stern and keep the boat facing the seas. He was to call out if he should hear the thunder of the surf. This plan enabled the oiler and the correspondent to get respite together. "We'll give those boys a chance to get into shape again," said the captain. They curled down and, after a few preliminary chatterings and trembles, slept once more the dead sleep. Neither knew they had bequeathed to the cook the company of another shark, or perhaps the same shark.

As the boat caroused on the waves, spray occasionally bumped over the side and gave them a fresh soaking, but this had no power to break their repose. The ominous slash of the wind and the water affected them as it would have affected mummies.

"Boys," said the cook, with the notes of every reluctance in his voice, "she's drifted in pretty close. I guess one of you had better take her to sea again." The correspondent, aroused, heard the crash of the toppled crests.

As he was rowing, the captain gave him some whiskey and water, and this steadied the chills out of him. "If I ever get ashore and anybody shows me even a photograph of an oar—"

At last there was a short conversation.

"Billie...Billie, will you spell me?"

"Sure," said the oiler.

VII

When the correspondent again opened his eyes, the sea and the sky were each of the gray hue of the dawning. Later, carmine and gold was painted upon the waters. The morning appeared finally, in its splendor with a sky of pure blue, and the sunlight flamed on the tips of the waves.

On the distant dunes were set many little black cottages, and a tall white wind-mill reared above them. No man, nor dog, nor bicycle appeared on the beach. The cottages might have formed a deserted village.

The voyagers scanned the shore. A conference was held in the boat. "Well," said the captain, "if no help is coming, we might better try a run through the surf right away. If we stay out here much longer we will be too weak to do anything for ourselves at all." The others silently acquiesced in this reasoning. The boat was headed for the beach. The correspondent wondered if none ever ascended the tall wind-tower, and if then they never looked seaward. This tower was a giant, standing with its back to the plight of the ants. It represented in a degree, to the correspondent, the serenity of nature amid the struggles of the individual—nature in the wind, and nature in the vision of men. She did not seem cruel to him, nor beneficent, nor treacherous, nor wise. But she was indifferent, flatly indifferent. It is, perhaps, plausible that a man in this situation, impressed with the unconcern of the universe, should see the innumerable flaws of his life and have them taste wickedly in his mind and wish for another chance. A distinction between right and wrong seems absurdly clear to him, then, in this new ignorance of the grave-edge, and he understands that if he were given another opportunity he would mend his conduct and his words, and be better and brighter during an introduction, or at a tea.

"Now, boys," said the captain, "she is going to swamp sure. All we can do is to work her in as far as possible, and then when she swamps, pile out and scramble for the beach. Keep cool now and don't jump until she swamps sure."

The oiler took the oars. Over his shoulders he scanned the surf. "Captain," he said, "I think I'd better bring her about, and keep her head-on to the seas and back her in."

"All right, Billie," said the captain. "Back her in." The oiler swung the boat then and, seated in the stern, the cook and the correspondent were obliged to look over their shoulders to contemplate the lonely and indifferent shore.

The monstrous inshore rollers heaved the boat high until the men were again enabled to see the white sheets of water scudding up the slanted beach. "We won't get in very close," said the captain. Each time a man could wrest his attention from the rollers, he turned his glance toward the shore, and in the expression of the eyes during this contemplation there was a singular quality. The correspondent, observing the others, knew that they were not afraid, but the full meaning of their glances was shrouded.

As for himself, he was too tired to grapple fundamentally with the fact. He tried to coerce his mind into thinking of it, but the mind was dominated at this time by the muscles, and the muscles said they did not care. It merely occurred to him that if he should drown it would be a shame.

There were no hurried words, no pallor, no plain agitation. The men simply looked at the shore. "Now, remember to get well clear of the boat when you jump," said the captain.

Seaward the crest of a roller suddenly fell with a thunderous crash, and the long white comber came roaring down upon the boat.

"Steady now," said the captain. The men were silent. They turned their eyes from the shore to the comber and waited. The boat slid up the incline, leaped at the furious top, bounced over it, and swung down the long back of the waves. Some water had been shipped and the cook bailed it out.

But the next crest crashed also. The tumbling boiling flood of white water caught the boat and whirled it almost perpendicular. Water swarmed in from all sides. The correspondent had his hands on the gunwale at this time, and when the water entered at that place he swiftly withdrew his fingers, as if he objected to wetting them.

The little boat, drunken with this weight of water, reeled and snuggled deeper into the sea.

"Bail her out, cook! Bail her out," said the captain.

"All right, captain," said the cook.

"Now, boys, the next one will do for us, sure," said the oiler. "Mind to jump clear of the boat."

The third wave moved forward, huge, furious, implacable. It fairly swallowed the dingey, and almost simultaneously the men tumbled into the sea. A piece of life-belt had lain in the bottom of the boat, and as the correspondent went overboard he held this to his chest with his left hand.

The January water was icy, and he reflected immediately that it was colder than he had expected to find it off the coast of Florida. This appeared to his dazed mind as a fact important enough to be noted at the time. The coldness of the water was sad; it was tragic. This fact was somehow mixed and confused with his opinion of his own situation that it seemed almost a proper reason for tears. The water was cold.

When he came to the surface he was conscious of little but the noisy water. Afterward he saw his companions in the sea. The oiler was ahead in the race. He was swimming strongly and rapidly. Off to the correspondent's left, the cook's great white and corked back bulged out of the water, and in the rear the captain was hanging with his one good hand to the keel of the overturned dingey.

There is a certain immovable quality to a shore, and the correspondent wondered at it amid the confusion of the sea.

It seemed also very attractive, but the correspondent knew that it was a long journey, and he paddled leisurely. The piece of life-preserver lay under him, and sometimes he whirled down the incline of a wave as if he were on a hand-sled.

But finally he arrived at a place in the sea where travel was beset with difficulty. He did not pause swimming to inquire what manner of current had caught him, but there his progress ceased. The shore was set before him like a bit of scenery on a stage, and he looked at it and understood with his eyes each detail of it.

As the cook passed, much farther to the left, the captain was calling to him, "Turn over on your back, cook! Turn over on your back and use the oar."

"All right, sir!" The cook turned on his back, and, paddling with an oar, went ahead as if he were a canoe.

Presently the boat also passed to the left of the correspondent with the captain clinging with one hand to the keel. He would have appeared like a man raising himself to look over a board fence, if it were not for the extraordinary gymnastics of the boat. The correspondent marvelled that the captain could still hold to it.

They passed on, nearer to shore—the oiler, the cook, the captain—and following them went the water-jar, bouncing gayly over the seas.

The correspondent remained in the grip of this strange new enemy—a current. The shore, with its white slope of sand and its green bluff, topped with little silent cottages, was spread like a picture before him. It was very near to him then, but he was impressed as one who in a gallery looks at a scene from Brittany or Algiers.

He thought: "I am going to drown? Can it be possible? Can it be possible? Can it be possible?" Perhaps an individual must consider his own death to be the final phenomenon of nature.

But later a wave perhaps whirled him out of this small

deadly current, for he found suddenly that he could again make progress toward the shore. Later still, he was aware that the captain, clinging with one hand to the keel of the dingey, had his face turned away from the shore and toward him, and was calling his name. "Come to the boat! Come to the boat!"

In his struggle to reach the captain and the boat, he reflected that when one gets properly wearied, drowning must really be a comfortable arrangement, a cessation of hostilities accompanied by a large degree of relief, and he was glad of it, for the main thing in his mind for some moments had been horror of the temporary agony. He did not wish to be hurt.

Presently he saw a man running along the shore. He was undressing with most remarkable speed. Coat, trousers, shirt, everything flew magically off him.

"Come to the boat," called the captain.

"All right, captain." As the correspondent paddled, he saw the captain let himself down to bottom and leave the boat. Then the correspondent performed his one little marvel of the voyage. A large wave caught him and flung him with ease and supreme speed completely over the boat and far beyond it. It struck him even then as an event in gymnastics, and a true miracle of the sea. An overturned boat in the surf is not a plaything to a swimming man.

The correspondent arrived in water that reached only to his waist, but his condition did not enable him to stand for more than a moment. Each wave knocked him into a heap, and the under-tow pulled at him.

Then he saw the man who had been running and undressing, and undressing and running, come bounding into the water. He dragged ashore the cook, and then waded toward the captain, but the captain waved him away, and sent him to the correspondent. He was naked, naked as a tree in winter, but a halo was about his head, and he shone like a saint. He gave a strong pull, and a long drag, and a bully heave at the correspondent's hand. The correspondent, schooled in the minor formulae, said: "Thanks, old man." But suddenly the man cried: "What's that?" He pointed a swift finger. The correspondent said: "Go."

In the shallows, face downward, lay the oiler. His forehead touched sand that was periodically, between each wave, clear of the sea.

The correspondent did not know all that transpired afterward. When he achieved safe ground he fell, striking the sand with each particular part of his body. It was as if he had dropped from a roof, but the thud was grateful to him.

It seems that instantly the beach was populated with men with blankets, clothes, and flasks, and women with coffee-pots and all the remedies sacred to their minds. The welcome of the land to the men from the sea was warm and generous, but a still and dripping shape was carried slowly up the beach, and the land's welcome for it could only be the different and sinister hospitality of the grave.

When it came night, the white waves paced to and fro in the moonlight, and the wind brought the sound of the great sea's voice to the men on shore, and they felt that they could then be interpreters.

(1897)

Questions for Consideration:

1. From whose point of view is this story told? How are the effects of the third person omniscient point of view different than if the story had been told in first person by one of the men?

2. How does Crane use setting to reveal the experience of the men? How does he use diction to set the tone of the story and to convey the story's meaning?

3. How do the men interpret certain events and items as signs of their fate? In what way is the man waving his shirt *ironic*?

4. What is the effect of repetition in the story?

5. What does a temple symbolize? How is this symbol used in the story?

6. Is there anything meaningful in the men's time together navigating the sea in a lifeboat?

7. What is the plot twist at the end of the story? Why do we consider this event unexpected? How does it affect the meaning of the story?

The Passing of Grandison
By Charles W. Chesnutt

I

When it is said that it was done to please a woman, there ought perhaps to be enough said to explain anything; for what a man will not do to please a woman is yet to be discovered. Nevertheless, it might be well to state a few preliminary facts to make it clear why young Dick Owens tried to run one of his father's negro men off to Canada.

In the early fifties, when the growth of anti-slavery sentiment and the constant drain of fugitive slaves into the North had so alarmed the slaveholders of the border States as to lead to the passage of the Fugitive Slave Law, a young white man from Ohio, moved by compassion for the sufferings of a certain bondman who happened to have a "hard master," essayed to help the slave to freedom. The attempt was discovered and frustrated; the abductor was tried and convicted for slave-stealing, and sentenced to a term of imprisonment in the penitentiary. His death, after the expiration of only a small part of the sentence, from cholera contracted while nursing stricken fellow prisoners, lent to the case a melancholy interest that made it famous in anti-slavery annals.

Dick Owens had attended the trial. He was a youth of about twenty-two, intelligent, handsome, and amiable, but extremely indolent, in a graceful and gentlemanly way; or, as old Judge Fenderson put it more than once, he was lazy as the Devil,—a mere figure of speech, of course, and not one that did justice to the Enemy of Mankind. When asked why he never did anything serious, Dick would good-naturedly reply, with a well-modulated drawl, that he didn't have to. His father was rich; there was but one other child, an unmarried daughter, who because of poor health would probably never marry, and Dick was therefore heir presumptive to a large estate. Wealth or social position he did not need to seek, for he was born to both. Charity Lomax had shamed him into studying law, but notwithstanding an hour or so a day spent at old Judge Fenderson's office, he did not make remarkable headway in his legal studies.

"What Dick needs," said the judge, who was fond of tropes, as became a scholar, and of horses, as was befitting a Kentuckian, "is the whip of necessity, or the spur of ambition. If he had either, he would soon need the snaffle to hold him back."

But all Dick required, in fact, to prompt him to the most remarkable thing he accomplished before he was twenty-five, was a mere suggestion from Charity Lomax. The story was never really known to but two persons until after the war, when it came out because it was a good story and there was no particular reason for its concealment.

Young Owens had attended the trial of this slave-stealer, or martyr,—either or both,—and, when it was over, had gone to call on Charity Lomax, and, while they sat on the veranda after sundown, had told her all about the trial. He was a good talker, as his career in later years disclosed, and described the proceedings very graphically.

"I confess," he admitted, "that while my principles were against the prisoner, my sympathies were on his side. It appeared that he was of good family, and that he had an old father and mother, respectable people, dependent upon him for support and comfort in their declining years. He had been led into the matter by pity for a negro whose master ought to have been run out of the county long ago for abusing his slaves. If it had been merely a question of old Sam Briggs's negro, nobody would have cared anything about it. But father and the rest of them stood on the principle of the thing, and told the judge so, and the fellow was sentenced to three years in the penitentiary."

Miss Lomax had listened with lively interest.

"I've always hated old Sam Briggs," she said emphatically, "ever since the time he broke a negro's leg with a piece of cordwood. When I hear of a cruel deed it makes the Quaker blood that came from my grandmother assert itself. Personally I wish that all Sam Briggs's negroes would run away. As for the young man, I regard him as a hero. He dared something for humanity. I could love a man who would take such chances for the sake of others."

"Could you love me, Charity, if I did something heroic?"

"You never will, Dick. You're too lazy for any use.

You'll never do anything harder than playing cards or fox-hunting."

"Oh, come now, sweetheart! I've been courting you for a year, and it's the hardest work imaginable. Are you never going to love me?" he pleaded.

His hand sought hers, but she drew it back beyond his reach.

"I'll never love you, Dick Owens, until you have done something. When that time comes, I'll think about it."

"But it takes so long to do anything worth mentioning, and I don't want to wait. One must read two years to become a lawyer, and work five more to make a reputation. We shall both be gray by then."

"Oh, I don't know," she rejoined. "It doesn't require a lifetime for a man to prove that he is a man. This one did something, or at least tried to."

"Well, I'm willing to attempt as much as any other man. What do you want me to do, sweetheart? Give me a test."

"Oh, dear me!" said Charity, "I don't care what you *do*, so you do *something*. Really, come to think of it, why should I care whether you do anything or not?"

"I'm sure I don't know why you should, Charity," rejoined Dick humbly, "for I'm aware that I'm not worthy of it."

"Except that I do hate," she added, relenting slightly, "to see a really clever man so utterly lazy and good for nothing."

"Thank you, my dear; a word of praise from you has sharpened my wits already. I have an idea! Will you love me if I run a negro off to Canada?"

"What nonsense!" said Charity scornfully. "You must be losing your wits. Steal another man's slave, indeed, while your father owns a hundred!"

"Oh, there'll be no trouble about that," responded Dick lightly; "I'll run off one of the old man's; we've got too many anyway. It may not be quite as difficult as the other man found it, but it will be just as unlawful, and will demonstrate what I am capable of."

"Seeing's believing," replied Charity. "Of course, what you are talking about now is merely absurd. I'm going away for three weeks, to visit my aunt in Tennessee.

If you're able to tell me, when I return, that you've done something to prove your quality, I'll—well, you may come and tell me about it."

II

Young Owens got up about nine o'clock next morning, and while making his toilet put some questions to his personal attendant, a rather bright looking young mulatto of about his own age.

"Tom," said Dick.

"Yas, Mars Dick," responded the servant.

"I'm going on a trip North. Would you like to go with me?"

Now, if there was anything that Tom would have liked to make, it was a trip North. It was something he had long contemplated in the abstract, but had never been able to muster up sufficient courage to attempt in the concrete. He was prudent enough, however, to dissemble his feelings.

"I wouldn't min' it, Mars Dick, ez long ez you'd take keer er me an' fetch me home all right."

Tom's eyes belied his words, however, and his young master felt well assured that Tom needed only a good opportunity to make him run away. Having a comfortable home, and a dismal prospect in case of failure, Tom was not likely to take any desperate chances; but young Owens was satisfied that in a free State but little persuasion would be required to lead Tom astray. With a very logical and characteristic desire to gain his end with the least necessary expenditure of effort, he decided to take Tom with him, if his father did not object.

Colonel Owens had left the house when Dick went to breakfast, so Dick did not see his father till luncheon.

"Father," he remarked casually to the colonel, over the fried chicken, "I'm feeling a trifle run down. I imagine my health would be improved somewhat by a little travel and change of scene."

"Why don't you take a trip North?" suggested his father. The colonel added to paternal affection a considerable respect for his son as the heir of a large estate. He himself had been "raised" in comparative poverty, and had laid the foundations of his fortune by hard work; and while he despised the ladder by which he had climbed, he could not entirely forget it, and unconsciously manifested, in his intercourse with his son, some of the poor man's deference toward the wealthy and well-born.

"I think I'll adopt your suggestion, sir," replied the son, "and run up to New York; and after I've been there awhile I may go on to Boston for a week or so. I've never been there, you know."

"There are some matters you can talk over with my factor in New York," rejoined the colonel, "and while you are up there among the Yankees, I hope you'll keep your eyes and ears open to find out what the rascally abolitionists are saying and doing. They're becoming altogether too active for our comfort, and entirely too many ungrateful niggers are running away. I hope the conviction of that fellow yesterday may discourage the rest of the breed. I'd just like to catch any one trying to run off one of my darkeys. He'd get short shrift; I don't think any Court would have a chance to try him."

"They are a pestiferous lot," assented Dick, "and dangerous to our institutions. But say, father, if I go North I shall want to take Tom with me."

Now, the colonel, while a very indulgent father, had pronounced views on the subject of negroes, having studied them, as he often said, for a great many years, and, as he asserted oftener still, understanding them perfectly. It is scarcely worth while to say, either, that he valued more highly than if he had inherited them the slaves he had toiled and schemed for.

"I don't think it safe to take Tom up North," he declared, with promptness and decision. "He's a good enough boy, but too smart to trust among those low-down abolitionists. I strongly suspect him of having learned to read, though I can't imagine how. I saw him with a newspaper the other day, and while he pretended to be looking at a woodcut, I'm almost sure he was reading the paper. I think it by no means safe to take him."

Dick did not insist, because he knew it was useless. The colonel would have obliged his son in any other matter, but his negroes were the outward and visible sign of his wealth and station, and therefore sacred to him.

"Whom do you think it safe to take?" asked Dick. "I suppose I'll have to have a body-servant."

"What's the matter with Grandison?" suggested the colonel. "He's handy enough, and I reckon we can trust him. He's too fond of good eating, to risk losing his regular meals; besides, he's sweet on your mother's maid, Betty, and I've promised to let 'em get married before long. I'll have Grandison up, and we'll talk to him. Here, you boy Jack," called the colonel to a yellow youth in the next room who was catching flies and pulling their wings off to pass the time, "go down to the barn and tell Grandison to come here."

"Grandison," said the colonel, when the negro stood before him, hat in hand.

"Yas, marster."

"Haven't I always treated you right?"

"Yas, marster."

"Haven't you always got all you wanted to eat?"

"Yas, marster."

"And as much whiskey and tobacco as was good for you, Grandison?"

"Y-a-s, marster."

"I should just like to know, Grandison, whether you don't think yourself a great deal better off than those poor free negroes down by the plank road, with no kind master to look after them and no mistress to give them medicine when they're sick and—and"——

"Well, I sh'd jes' reckon I is better off, suh, dan dem low-down free niggers, suh! Ef anybody ax 'em who dey b'long ter, dey has ter say nobody, er e'se lie erbout it. Anybody ax me who I b'longs ter, I ain' got no 'casion ter be shame' ter tell 'em, no, suh, 'deed I ain', suh!"

The colonel was beaming. This was true gratitude, and his feudal heart thrilled at such appreciative homage. What cold-blooded, heartless monsters they were who would break up this blissful relationship of kindly protection on the one hand, of wise subordination and loyal dependence on the other! The colonel always became indignant at the mere thought of such wickedness.

"Grandison," the colonel continued, "your young master Dick is going North for a few weeks, and I am thinking of letting him take you along. I shall send you on this trip, Grandison, in order that you may take care of your young master. He will need some one to wait on him, and no one can ever do it so well as one of the boys brought up with him on the old plantation. I am going to trust him in your hands, and I'm sure you'll do your duty faithfully, and bring him back home safe and sound—to old Kentucky."

Grandison grinned. "Oh yas, marster, I'll take keer er young Mars Dick."

"I want to warn you, though, Grandison," continued the colonel impressively, "against these cussed abolitionists, who try to entice servants from their comfortable homes and their indulgent masters, from the blue skies, the green fields, and the warm sunlight of their southern home, and send them away off yonder to Canada, a dreary country, where the woods are full of wildcats and wolves and bears, where the snow lies up to the eaves of the houses for six months of the year, and the cold is so severe that it freezes your breath and curdles your blood; and where, when runaway niggers get sick and can't work, they are turned out to starve and die, unloved and uncared for. I reckon, Grandison, that you have too much sense to permit yourself to be led astray by any such foolish and wicked people."

"'Deed, suh, I would n' low none er dem cussed, low-down abolitioners ter come nigh me, suh. I'd—I'd—would I be 'lowed ter hit 'em, suh?"

"Certainly, Grandison," replied the colonel, chuckling, "hit 'em as hard as you can. I reckon they'd rather like it. Begad, I believe they would! It would serve 'em right to be hit by a nigger!"

"Er ef I did n't hit 'em, suh," continued Grandison reflectively, "I'd tell Mars Dick, en *he'd* fix 'em. He'd smash de face off'n 'em, suh, I jes' knows he would."

"Oh yes, Grandison, your young master will protect you. You need fear no harm while he is near."

"Dey won't try ter steal me, will dey, marster?" asked the negro, with sudden alarm.

"I don't know, Grandison," replied the colonel, lighting a fresh cigar. "They're a desperate set of lunatics, and there's no telling what they may resort to. But if you stick close to your young master, and remember always that he is your best friend, and understands your real needs, and has your true interests at heart, and if you will be careful to avoid strangers who try to talk to you, you'll stand a fair chance of getting back to your home and your friends. And if you please your master Dick, he'll buy you a present, and a string of beads for Betty to wear when you and she get married in the fall."

"Thanky, marster, thanky, suh," replied Grandison, oozing gratitude at every pore; "you is a good marster, to be sho', suh; yas, 'deed you is. You kin jes' bet me and Mars Dick gwine git 'long jes' lack I wuz own boy ter Mars Dick. En it won't be my fault ef he don' want me fer his boy all de time, w'en we come back home ag'in."

"All right, Grandison, you may go now. You need n't work any more to-day, and here's a piece of tobacco for you off my own plug."

"Thanky, marster, thanky, marster! You is de bes' marster any nigger ever had in dis worl'." And Grandison bowed and scraped and disappeared round the corner, his jaws closing around a large section of the colonel's best tobacco.

"You may take Grandison," said the colonel to his son. "I allow he's abolitionist-proof."

III

Richard Owens, Esq., and servant, from Kentucky, registered at the fashionable New York hostelry for Southerners in those days, a hotel where an atmosphere congenial to Southern institutions was sedulously maintained. But there were negro waiters in the dining-room, and mulatto bell-boys, and Dick had no doubt that Grandison, with the native gregariousness and garrulousness of his race, would foregather and palaver with them sooner or later, and Dick hoped that they would speedily inoculate him with the virus of freedom. For it was not Dick's intention to say anything to his servant about his plan to free him, for obvious reasons. To mention one of them, if Grandison should go away, and by legal process be recaptured, his young master's part in the matter would doubtless become known, which would be embarrassing to Dick, to say the least. If, on the other hand, he should merely give Grandison sufficient latitude, he had no doubt he would eventually lose him. For while not exactly skeptical about Grandison's perfervid loyalty, Dick had been a somewhat keen observer of human nature, in his own indolent way, and based his expectations upon the force of the example and argument that his servant could scarcely fail to encounter. Grandison should have a fair chance to become free by his own initiative; if it should become necessary to adopt other measures to get rid of him, it would be time enough to act when the necessity arose; and Dick Owens was not the youth to take needless trouble.

The young master renewed some acquaintances and made others, and spent a week or two very pleasantly in the best society of the metropolis, easily accessible to a wealthy, well-bred young Southerner, with proper introductions. Young women smiled on him, and young men of convivial habits pressed their hospitalities; but the memory of Charity's sweet, strong face and clear blue eyes made him proof against the blandishments of the one sex and the persuasions of the other. Meanwhile he kept Grandison supplied with pocket-money, and left him mainly to his own devices. Every night when Dick came in he hoped he might have to wait upon himself, and every morning he looked forward with pleasure to the prospect of making his toilet unaided. His hopes, however, were doomed to disappointment, for every night when he came in Grandison was on hand with a bootjack, and a nightcap mixed for his young master as the colonel had taught him to mix it, and every morning Grandison appeared with his master's boots blacked and his clothes brushed, and laid his linen out for the day.

"Grandison," said Dick one morning, after finishing his toilet, "this is the chance of your life to go around among your own people and see how they live. Have you met any of them?"

"Yas, suh, I's seen some of 'em. But I don' keer nuffin fer 'em, suh. Dey're diffe'nt f'm de niggers down ou' way. Dey 'lows dey're free, but dey ain' got sense 'nuff ter know dey ain' half as well off as dey would be down Souf, whar dey'd be 'predated."

When two weeks had passed without any apparent effect of evil example upon Grandison, Dick resolved to go on to Boston, where he thought the atmosphere might prove more favorable to his ends. After he had been at the Revere House for a day or two without losing Grandison, he decided upon slightly different tactics.

Having ascertained from a city directory the addresses of several well-known abolitionists, he wrote them each a letter something like this:——

Dear Friend and Brother:——

A wicked slaveholder from Kentucky, stopping at the Revere House, has dared to insult the liberty-loving people of Boston by bringing his slave into their midst. Shall this be tolerated? Or shall steps be taken in the name of liberty to rescue a fellow-man from bondage? For obvious reasons I can only sign myself,

A Friend of Humanity.

That his letter might have an opportunity to prove effective, Dick made it a point to send Grandison away from the hotel on various errands. On one of these occasions Dick watched him for quite a distance down the street. Grandison had scarcely left the hotel when a long-haired, sharp-featured man came out behind him, followed him, soon overtook him, and kept along beside him until they turned the next corner. Dick's hopes were roused by this spectacle, but sank correspondingly when Grandison returned to the hotel. As Grandison said nothing about the encounter, Dick hoped there might be some self-consciousness behind this unexpected reticence, the results of which might develop later on.

But Grandison was on hand again when his master came back to the hotel at night, and was in attendance again in the morning, with hot water, to assist at his master's toilet. Dick sent him on further errands from day

to day, and upon one occasion came squarely up to him—
inadvertently of course—while Grandison was engaged
in conversation with a young white man in clerical garb.
When Grandison saw Dick approaching, he edged away
from the preacher and hastened toward his master, with a
very evident expression of relief upon his countenance.

"Mars Dick," he said, "dese yer abolitioners is jes'
pesterin' de life out er me tryin' ter git me ter run away. I
don' pay no 'tention ter 'em, but dey riles me so sometimes
dat I'm feared I'll hit some of 'em some er dese days, an'
dat mought git me inter trouble. I ain' said nuffin' ter you
'bout it, Mars Dick, fer I didn' wanter 'sturb yo' min'; but
I don' like it, suh; no, suh, I don'! Is we gwine back home
'fo' long, Mars Dick?"

"We'll be going back soon enough," replied Dick
somewhat shortly, while he inwardly cursed the stupidity
of a slave who could be free and would not, and registered
a secret vow that if he were unable to get rid of Grandison
without assassinating him, and were therefore compelled
to take him back to Kentucky, he would see that Grandison
got a taste of an article of slavery that would make him
regret his wasted opportunities. Meanwhile he determined
to tempt his servant yet more strongly.

"Grandison," he said next morning, "I'm going away
for a day or two, but I shall leave you here. I shall lock
up a hundred dollars in this drawer and give you the key.
If you need any of it, use it and enjoy yourself,—spend it
all if you like,—for this is probably the last chance you'll
have for some time to be in a free State, and you'd better
enjoy your liberty while you may."

When he came back a couple of days later and found
the faithful Grandison at his post, and the hundred dollars
intact, Dick felt seriously annoyed. His vexation was
increased by the fact that he could not express his feelings
adequately. He did not even scold Grandison; how could
he, indeed, find fault with one who so sensibly recognized
his true place in the economy of civilization, and kept it
with such touching fidelity?

"I can't say a thing to him," groaned Dick. "He
deserves a leather medal, made out of his own hide

tanned. I reckon I'll write to father and let him know what a model servant he has given me."

He wrote his father a letter which made the colonel swell with pride and pleasure. "I really think," the colonel observed to one of his friends, "that Dick ought to have the nigger interviewed by the Boston papers, so that they may see how contented and happy our darkeys really are."

Dick also wrote a long letter to Charity Lomax, in which he said, among many other things, that if she knew how hard he was working, and under what difficulties, to accomplish something serious for her sake, she would no longer keep him in suspense, but overwhelm him with love and admiration.

Having thus exhausted without result the more obvious methods of getting rid of Grandison, and diplomacy having also proved a failure, Dick was forced to consider more radical measures. Of course he might run away himself, and abandon Grandison, but this would be merely to leave him in the United States, where he was still a slave, and where, with his notions of loyalty, he would speedily be reclaimed. It was necessary, in order to accomplish the purpose of his trip to the North, to leave Grandison permanently in Canada, where he would be legally free.

"I might extend my trip to Canada," he reflected, "but that would be too palpable. I have it! I'll visit Niagara Falls on the way home, and lose him on the Canada side. When he once realizes that he is actually free, I'll warrant that he'll stay."

So the next day saw them westward bound, and in due course of time, by the somewhat slow conveyances of the period, they found themselves at Niagara. Dick walked and drove about the Falls for several days, taking Grandison along with him on most occasions. One morning they stood on the Canadian side, watching the wild whirl of the waters below them.

"Grandison," said Dick, raising his voice above the roar of the cataract, "do you know where you are now?"

"I's wid you, Mars Dick; dat's all I keers."

"You are now in Canada, Grandison, where your people go when they run away from their masters. If you wished, Grandison, you might walk away from me this very minute, and I could not lay my hand upon you to take you back."

Grandison looked around uneasily.

"Let's go back ober de ribber, Mars Dick. I's feared I'll lose you ovuh heah, an' den I won' hab no marster, an' won't nebber be able to git back home no mo'."

Discouraged, but not yet hopeless, Dick said, a few minutes later,———

"Grandison, I'm going up the road a bit, to the inn over yonder. You stay here until I return. I'll not be gone a great while."

Grandison's eyes opened wide and he looked somewhat fearful.

"Is dey any er dem dadblasted abolitioners roun' heah, Mars Dick?"

"I don't imagine that there are," replied his master, hoping there might be. "But I'm not afraid of *your* running away, Grandison. I only wish I were," he added to himself.

Dick walked leisurely down the road to where the whitewashed inn, built of stone, with true British solidity, loomed up through the trees by the roadside. Arrived there he ordered a glass of ale and a sandwich, and took a seat at a table by a window, from which he could see Grandison in the distance. For a while he hoped that the seed he had sown might have fallen on fertile ground, and that Grandison, relieved from the restraining power of a master's eye, and finding himself in a free country, might get up and walk away; but the hope was vain, for Grandison remained faithfully at his post, awaiting his master's return. He had seated himself on a broad flat stone, and, turning his eyes away from the grand and awe-inspiring spectacle that lay close at hand, was looking anxiously toward the inn where his master sat cursing his ill-timed fidelity.

By and by a girl came into the room to serve his order, and Dick very naturally glanced at her; and as she was young and pretty and remained in attendance, it was some minutes before he looked for Grandison. When he did so his faithful servant had disappeared.

To pay his reckoning and go away without the change was a matter quickly accomplished. Retracing his footsteps toward the Falls, he saw, to his great disgust, as he approached the spot where he had left Grandison, the familiar form of his servant stretched out on the ground, his face to the sun, his mouth open, sleeping the time away, oblivious alike to the grandeur of the scenery, the thunderous roar of the cataract, or the insidious voice of sentiment.

"Grandison," soliloquized his master, as he stood gazing down at his ebony encumbrance, "I do not deserve to be an American citizen; I ought not to have the advantages I possess over you; and I certainly am not worthy of Charity Lomax, if I am not smart enough to get rid of you. I have an idea! You shall yet be free, and I will be the instrument of your deliverance. Sleep on, faithful and affectionate servitor, and dream of the blue grass and the bright skies of old Kentucky, for it is only in your dreams that you will ever see them again!"

Dick retraced his footsteps towards the inn. The young woman chanced to look out of the window and saw the handsome young gentleman she had waited on a few minutes before, standing in the road a short distance away, apparently engaged in earnest conversation with a colored man employed as hostler for the inn. She thought she saw something pass from the white man to the other, but at that moment her duties called her away from the window, and when she looked out again the young gentleman had disappeared, and the hostler, with two other young men of the neighborhood, one white and one colored, were walking rapidly towards the Falls.

IV

Dick made the journey homeward alone, and as rapidly as the conveyances of the day would permit. As he drew near home his conduct in going back without Grandison took on a more serious aspect than it had borne at any previous time, and although he had prepared the colonel by a letter sent several days ahead, there was still the prospect of a bad quarter of an hour with him; not, indeed, that his father would upbraid him, but he was

100

likely to make searching inquiries. And notwithstanding the vein of quiet recklessness that had carried Dick through his preposterous scheme, he was a very poor liar, having rarely had occasion or inclination to tell anything but the truth. Any reluctance to meet his father was more than offset, however, by a stronger force drawing him homeward, for Charity Lomax must long since have returned from her visit to her aunt in Tennessee.

Dick got off easier than he had expected. He told a straight story, and a truthful one, so far as it went.

The colonel raged at first, but rage soon subsided into anger, and anger moderated into annoyance, and annoyance into a sort of garrulous sense of injury. The colonel thought he had been hardly used; he had trusted this negro, and he had broken faith. Yet, after all, he did not blame Grandison so much as he did the abolitionists, who were undoubtedly at the bottom of it.

As for Charity Lomax, Dick told her, privately of course, that he had run his father's man, Grandison, off to Canada, and left him there.

"Oh, Dick," she had said with shuddering alarm, "what have you done? If they knew it they'd send you to the penitentiary, like they did that Yankee."

"But they don't know it," he had replied seriously; adding, with an injured tone, "you don't seem to appreciate my heroism like you did that of the Yankee; perhaps it's because I wasn't caught and sent to the penitentiary. I thought you wanted me to do it."

"Why, Dick Owens!" she exclaimed. "You know I never dreamed of any such outrageous proceeding.

"But I presume I'll have to marry you," she concluded, after some insistence on Dick's part, "if only to take care of you. You are too reckless for anything; and a man who goes chasing all over the North, being entertained by New York and Boston society and having negroes to throw away, needs some one to look after him."

"It's a most remarkable thing," replied Dick fervently, "that your views correspond exactly with my profoundest convictions. It proves beyond question that we were made for one another."

* * * * *

They were married three weeks later. As each of them had just returned from a journey, they spent their honeymoon at home.

A week after the wedding they were seated, one afternoon, on the piazza of the colonel's house, where Dick had taken his bride, when a negro from the yard ran down the lane and threw open the big gate for the colonel's buggy to enter. The colonel was not alone. Beside him, ragged and travel-stained, bowed with weariness, and upon his face a haggard look that told of hardship and privation, sat the lost Grandison.

The colonel alighted at the steps.

"Take the lines, Tom," he said to the man who had opened the gate, "and drive round to the barn. Help Grandison down,—poor devil, he's so stiff he can hardly move!—and get a tub of water and wash him and rub him down, and feed him, and give him a big drink of whiskey, and then let him come round and see his young master and his new mistress."

The colonel's face wore an expression compounded of joy and indignation,—joy at the restoration of a valuable piece of property; indignation for reasons he proceeded to state.

"It's astounding, the depths of depravity the human heart is capable of! I was coming along the road three miles away, when I heard some one call me from the roadside. I pulled up the mare, and who should come out of the woods but Grandison. The poor nigger could hardly crawl along, with the help of a broken limb. I was never more astonished in my life. You could have knocked me down with a feather. He seemed pretty far gone,—he could hardly talk above a whisper,—and I had to give him a mouthful of whiskey to brace him up so he could tell his story. It's just as I thought from the beginning, Dick; Grandison had no notion of running away; he knew when he was well off, and where his friends were. All the persuasions of abolition liars and runaway niggers did not move him. But the desperation of those fanatics knew no bounds; their guilty consciences gave them no rest. They got the notion somehow that Grandison belonged to a nigger-catcher, and had been brought North as a spy to help capture ungrateful runaway servants. They actually kidnaped him—just think of it!—and gagged him and bound him and threw him rudely into a wagon, and carried him into the gloomy depths of a Canadian forest, and locked him in a lonely hut, and fed him on bread and water for three weeks. One of the scoundrels wanted to kill him, and persuaded the others that it ought to be done; but they got to quarreling about how they should do it, and before they had their minds made up Grandison escaped, and, keeping his back steadily to the North Star, made his way, after suffering incredible hardships, back to the old plantation, back to his master, his friends, and his home. Why, it's as good as one of Scott's novels! Mr. Simms or some other one of our Southern authors ought to write it up."

"Don't you think, sir," suggested Dick, who had calmly smoked his cigar throughout the colonel's animated recital, "that that kidnaping yarn sounds a little improbable? Isn't there some more likely explanation?"

"Nonsense, Dick; it's the gospel truth! Those infernal abolitionists are capable of anything—everything! Just think of their locking the poor, faithful nigger up, beating him, kicking him, depriving him of his liberty, keeping him on bread and water for three long, lonesome weeks, and he all the time pining for the old plantation!"

There were almost tears in the colonel's eyes at the picture of Grandison's sufferings that he conjured up. Dick still professed to be slightly skeptical, and met Charity's severely questioning eye with bland unconsciousness.

The colonel killed the fatted calf for Grandison, and for two or three weeks the returned wanderer's life was a slave's dream of pleasure. His fame spread throughout the county, and the colonel gave him a permanent place among the house servants, where he could always have him conveniently at hand to relate his adventures to admiring visitors.

* * * * *

About three weeks after Grandison's return the colonel's faith in sable humanity was rudely shaken, and its foundations almost broken up. He came near losing his belief in the fidelity of the negro to his master,—the servile virtue most highly prized and most sedulously cultivated by the colonel and his kind. One Monday morning Grandison was missing. And not only Grandison, but his wife, Betty the maid; his mother, aunt Eunice; his father, uncle Ike; his brothers, Tom and John, and his little sister Elsie, were likewise absent from the plantation; and a hurried search and inquiry in the neighborhood resulted in no information as to their whereabouts. So much valuable property could not be lost without an effort to recover it, and the wholesale nature of the transaction carried consternation to the hearts of those whose ledgers were chiefly bound in black. Extremely energetic measures were taken by the colonel and his friends. The fugitives were traced, and followed from point to point, on their northward run through Ohio. Several times the hunters were close upon their heels, but the magnitude of the escaping party begot unusual vigilance on the part of those who sympathized with the fugitives, and strangely enough, the underground railroad seemed to have had its tracks cleared and signals set for this particular train. Once, twice, the colonel thought he had them, but they slipped through his fingers.

One last glimpse he caught of his vanishing property, as he stood, accompanied by a United States marshal, on a wharf at a port on the south shore of Lake Erie. On the stern of a small steamboat which was receding rapidly from the wharf, with her nose pointing toward Canada, there stood a group of familiar dark faces, and the look they cast backward was not one of longing for the fleshpots of Egypt. The colonel saw Grandison point him out to one of the crew of the vessel, who waved his hand derisively toward the colonel. The latter shook his fist impotently—and the incident was closed.

(1899)

Questions for Consideration:

1. How does Chestnutt select and arrange plot details in this story so that the escape of Grandison and his family catches Colonel Owens, as well as the reader, by surprise? What assumptions does the colonel

hold that make it possible for him to be duped? Can you go back and find the moment when Grandison began planning his escape?

2. What is the import of Grandison's name? In what way does Colonel Owens's identity as a father depend on Grandison and the other slaves? In what way does it depend on Dick? Which "son" proves to be more worthy, according to Charity Lomax's standards?

3. What is the effect of the allusion to the Israelites when the narrator tells us that the expression of Grandison and his family as they looked back at the colonel "was not one of longing for the fleshpots of Egypt"?

4. How can this story's third-person narrator be characterized? Is he or she a character in the story? Does he or she view the events with omniscient knowledge (seeing and knowing all, including the characters' thoughts and feelings)? Is the perspective one of limited omniscience (seeing and knowing just one character's thoughts and feelings)? Or is the narrator omniscient at all? Does he or she relate only what an observer would know?

5.3 Writing about Novels

Short stories and novels often follow the hill-curve narrative shape illustrated earlier in this chapter. As you may observe in the above examples, short stories must develop their effect and/or meaning in a much more limited space than novels. As a result, the plot elements of short stories must be chosen and crafted for efficiency, thus producing a narrow effect. A novel, on the other hand, provides room for more fully developed characters, setting details, and plot, which can include multiple threads following multiple characters. Whether about a short story or a novel, a literary analysis essay that argues for a particular perspective demands **textual evidence**, specific examples from the primary text itself employed to illustrate/prove an assertion. Bill's argument on *The Sun Also Rises*, mentioned in Chapter 3, uses quotes from the novel, as well as summarized and paraphrased passages in order to illustrate particular points and, ultimately, to support Bill's argument that "In *The Sun Also Rises*, Hemingway presents Jake Barnes's struggles to overcome the damage incurred during his service as a soldier in World War I as powerful evidence of the irreversible destruction of war." To develop this argument, Bill could have explored Hemingway's use of effective *diction*, the work's unique *dialogue*, the *metaphor* of Jake's wound, and/or *point of view* (Jake's, first-person) to build the novel's impression of war's damage. He chose to examine the novel's use of metaphor.

Bill Day
English 1102

Does the Sun Rise? A Study of Metaphors in Ernest Hemingway's *The Sun Also Rises*

Although Hemingway's novel *The Sun Also Rises* begins with an epigraph from the biblical book of Ecclesiastes that suggests the constantly renewing cycles of the earth and of human generations, the author's use of metaphors in this story raises the question of whether we will always be able to recover from our own destructive behavior. If it is true that humans and the earth are resilient and that no force can disrupt the cycle of rebirth and regeneration, the novel should leave readers feeling optimistic. However, it does not end on a positive note. Instead, it ends with confirmation that even though Brett Ashley likes to imagine a happy life with protagonist Jake Barnes, they are too damaged to have one. Jake's cynical response to Brett's fantasy reminds us of this point: "Isn't it pretty to think so?" Jake's difficulty coping with his injury, his tendency to self-medicate with alcohol, his inability to pray, and his failure to sustain an intimate relationship with another person all exemplify the irreversible destruction inflicted by World War I. Specifically through the metaphors of Jake's wound and the tainted Pamplona fiesta, the novel conveys the possibility that if we are not careful, we can dangerously disrupt the cycle of renewal.

Jake's service as an American soldier in World War I has left him with an unusual wound: he took a hit to the groin and his sexual organs were damaged. Not only does this wound affect him physically, preventing him from being able to have sex and to reproduce, but it also affects him psychologically, robbing him of masculine confidence and of the chance for an intimate relationship with the woman he loves, Brett Ashley. Jake's response to the injury as he looks in the mirror reveals how powerfully the scar affects him: "I looked at myself in the mirror of the big armoire beside the bed....Of all the ways to be wounded. I suppose it was funny" (38). Although Jake tries to laugh off the injury, he suffers from the constant effort to cope with it and the general effects of his war experience: "I lay awake thinking and my mind jumping around. Then I couldn't keep away from it, and I started to think about Brett and all the rest of it went away. I was thinking about Brett and my mind stopped jumping around and started to go in sort of smooth waves. Then all of a sudden I started to cry" (39). The wound is a constant reminder to Jake that his life is different now.

Yet it also serves as a general metaphor for the psychological wounds he and all his friends are coping with. Like Jake's genital scar, his friends' pain is kept well-covered. They almost never speak of the war. When Robert Cohn asks Mike Campbell if he was in the war, Mike answers, "Was I not?" And then the subject shifts to a funny story about Mike's stealing medals earned by someone else so Mike could wear them to a formal dinner. Although he seems fun-loving, ready to laugh and party with his companions, Mike drinks and spends money indiscriminately in order to cope with his pain. We see the characters' dysfunctional behavior throughout the novel as the group constantly drinks and engages in distractions to cope with their own psychological wounds. The worst effects of these injuries are their inability to find hope in anything, even God, and to enjoy close and healthy relationships with each other.

Another metaphor employed effectively in the novel to suggest irreversible destruction is the ruined bull fights. Jake has been an *aficionado* of the bull fights for many years. He considers them almost sacred. He shares this feeling with his friend Montoya, at whose hotel he stays when he comes to Pamplona for the fiesta. "I had stopped at the Montoya for several years. We never talked for very long at a time. It was simply the pleasure of discovering what we each felt." (137). Even though Jake's mind wanders when he goes to church now, he has been able to maintain this special experience of the bull fights. The way he describes this "art" reveals that he sees something pure in it—a chance to confront one's fears with dignity, courage, and grace and then destroy those fears: "Romero's bull-fighting gave real emotion, because he kept the absolute purity of line in his movements and always quietly and calmly let the horns pass him close each time" (171). Since the events recur each year during fiesta, there is a sense of renewal associated with it.

However, when Brett initiates Romero into manhood through a brief sexual affair, it not only compromises Romero's innocence and purity as an artist, but it spoils the experience of fiesta for Jake. Montoya, his fellow *aficionado* blames Jake and his friends for not respecting Romero and the bull fight, and the loss of this friendship hurts Jake. Just before the group leaves town, Jake says, "We had lunch and paid the bill. Montoya did not come near us" (232). Montoya's previous regard for Jake will not likely be regained, since the aficion, or passion, they shared was very rare, and the affair has spoiled their bond. Like Jake and his friends' faith in anything transcending ordinary mundane life, Jake's experience of the bull fight has been tainted now by the dysfunctional actions of him and the rest of the group. This metaphor suggests that some kinds of destruction are permanent.

As the novel concludes, the reader wants to believe that Jake will survive and find some kind of happiness. Yet, the metaphors of Jake's wound and the tainted bull fights suggest that some kinds of damage cannot be undone. The novel implies that, as a result of one of the most destructive wars in human history, these characters will simply have to learn to live with their injuries and cope with their lost hopes. Their hardship serves as a warning that humans should think carefully before waging war against each other.

Work Cited

Hemingway, Ernest. *The Sun Also Rises*. Scribner, 1926.

In focusing on how a formal element—metaphor—develops the novel's message, Bill's essay employs a formalist perspective. Approaching this Hemingway novel from a feminist perspective, on the other hand, Katherine Jones produced the following researched essay. While she depends less on discussion of the novel's formal aspects, such as metaphor and point of view, she does gather examples directly from the text to support her assertions about one fruitful way to interpret Brett Ashley's character.

Katherine Jones
English 2140

"This Novel is About a Lady": Brett Ashley in *The Sun Also Rises*

While Ernest Hemingway's *The Sun Also Rises* is told from the viewpoint of one Jake Barnes, another prominent figure within the novel is Lady Brett Ashley. In fact, in Hemingway's original opening for the novel, he had written, "This novel is about a lady. Her name is Lady Ashley" (Qtd. in Martin 70). Brett, as she is developed in the novel, has been painted in different lights, depending on the interpreter, ranging from a sympathetic view to one of condemnation. The portrait of her that I will attempt to show is one of a human being, caught between the ideologies of two eras.

Brett Ashley is a woman living during an age of a new femininity and sexual freedom, during the end of the repressive Victorian era. Reflecting changing behaviors, she wears pants and has her hair cropped, and she is sexually uninhibited. Her experience may be analogous to the stereotypical college freshman who grew up in a strict household, one where the idea of drinking before twenty-one is demonized, so the freshman was not educated in safe practice. The newfound freedom is exhilarating, and the freshman is known to binge-drink, not thinking of his or her tolerance level and the consequences, such as an incapacitating hangover. The sexual promiscuity of Brett, and other women of her time period, may be viewed in the same light: after a repressive era, sex is, in a way, "new" and exciting. However, because of the prior taboo of discussing sex, a sense of responsibility, self-respect, and self-care was likely not passed down to Brett. Because of this, she, as a "new woman," binges on sex. This is not necessarily because she is an emasculating man-eater. Rather, this is a reflection on her being almost child-like in her behavior, being given power without being made aware of the responsibility of it. As Martin expresses, for Brett, the need to rebel against the traditional idea of the feminine outweighs the practice of responsible sex (67-8, 71).

However, her existence during such a cultural transition takes a toll on Brett's psychological well-being. In trying to cope with Robert Cohn's infatuation with her, for example, she turns to alcohol: As Jake returns a bottle of Fundador to the bartender, she stops him. "'Let's have one more drink of that,' Brett said. 'My nerves are rotten'" (Hemingway 186). As stated by Martin, "In spite of the fact that Brett tries to break free of patriarchal control, she often vacillates between the extremes of self-abnegation and self-indulgence, and her relationships... are filled with ambivalence, anxiety, and frequently alienation" (69). Among one of her many discussions with Jake where she admits her dissatisfaction and misery, Brett confides in him that "When I think of all the hell I put chaps through. I'm paying for it all now" (34). Thus, Brett is not without a sense of guilt. Despite this, she continues with one affair after another, knowing how it has affected the men she has been and will be with. There must then be other driving factors in her behavior beyond a desire for sexual pleasure.

Like many people of her generation, in testing out a life free of restrictive and seemingly worn-out Victorian ideologies, Brett feels disillusionment and a loss of agency after World War I, leaving her with a "moral and emotional vacuum" (Spilka 36). She cannot even take solace in religion. When she attempts to pray for her young lover Romero before his bull fight, she becomes uncomfortable in the atmosphere of the chapel: "'Come on,' she whispered throatily. 'Let's get out of here. Makes me damned nervous'" (Hemingway 212). She attempts to fill this void using intimate encounters with men, seeking a momentary feeling of human connection, but remains unwilling to submit herself to anyone long term. This is particularly seen in her relationship with Jake, as she constantly uses him as a financial source and emotional support, all the while knowing that he is tormented by all her lovers (Spilka 42-3). Onderdonk points out that, at times, Brett appears to want a true relationship, such as with Romero, before he attempts to "tame" her (81). Yet, as Djos notes, she generally manipulates men, asserts her dominance over them, and avoids commitment to them

(143, 148). This behavior might be interpreted as a sign that the sexual freedom Brett is trying out inevitably leads to an ethical dead end.

Unlike an imperialistic government, however, Brett is a human being with a conscience, giving rise to the aforementioned guilt. This guilt, coupled with the internal void common to the Lost Generation, is what drives her and her colleagues to seek comfort in a bottle. Often taken for a sign of immorality, alcoholism here signifies quite the opposite. It is Brett's conscience and her discomfort with the lack of moral direction that drive her to drink. Djos presents the following theory, based on real-life alcoholics: "There is a great deal of fear here, fear of self-understanding, fear of emotional and physical inadequacy, and ... fear of each other" (141-2). Because Brett and her friends are travelling an unmapped road, with no signs pointing to ethical landmarks or spiritual meaning, they must deal with the uncertainty of their situation. The characters throughout the novel do seem to have shallow interactions and relationships with each other, yet the fact that so much is left unsaid between them is evidence of Hemingway's "tip of the iceberg" style. For them alcohol is a social lubricant, and even a means to survive day by day, minute by minute, suggesting that these characters are navigating great psychological challenges (Djos 141) and must suffer in isolation as they do so. Brett is no exception to this experience. Early on in the novel, Brett alludes to this despair when she bemoans to Jake, "Oh, darling, I've been so miserable" (Hemingway 32).

Brett is far from being a role model or the picture of perfection. Yet, she is not a cold-hearted succubus, either. She is a woman attempting to find her place in the wake of a war and a gender revolution, surrounded by changing ideas, gender roles, and cultural standards. Hiding behind a wall of alcohol abuse, she struggles, as did many women of her time, between her libido and desire for freedom from patriarchy and male ownership, and her sense of guilt and discomfort with herself and others. Brett is nothing more, or less, than a human being experiencing the tumultuous waves produced by life.

Works Cited

Djos, Matts. "Alcoholism in Ernest Hemingway's The Sun Also Rises: A Wine and Roses Perspective on the Lost Generation." 1995. *Ernest Hemingway's The Sun Also Rises*, edited by Linda Wagner-Martin, Oxford UP, 2002, pp. 139-53.

Hemingway, Ernest. *The Sun Also Rises*. Scribner, 1926.

Martin, Wendy. "Brett Ashley as New Woman in The Sun Also Rises." *New Essays on The Sun Also Rises*, edited by Linda Wagner-Martin, Cambridge UP, 1987, pp. 65-81.

Onderdonk, Todd. "'Bitched': Feminization, Identity, and the Hemingwayesque in The Sun Also Rises." Twentieth Century Literature, vol. 52, no 1, 1 Mar. 2006, pp. 61-91. Academic Search Complete. doi:10.1215/0041462X-2006-2007. Accessed 16 Sept. 2013.

Spilka, Mark. "The Death of Love in The Sun Also Rises." 1958. *Ernest Hemingway's The Sun Also Rises*, edited by Linda Wagner-Martin, Oxford UP, 2002, pp. 33-45.

In chapters 8 and 9, we will elaborate on ways of incorporating literary analysis and secondary sources into your essays, and we will explore ways to structure this kind of argument. Bill's and Katherine's essays above will provide helpful examples as we move forward in our study of writing about literature. For more novels available free and online, visit the Gutenberg Project at gutenberg.org, where you can find such works as Charles A. Chesnutt's *The House Behind the Cedars*, Kate Chopin's *The Awakening*, E.M. Forster's *A Room with a View*, Nathaniel Hawthorne's *The Scarlet Letter*, Jack London's *The Sea-Wolf*, and Mary Shelley's *Frankenstein*.

All the World's a Stage

6.1 Drama as a Genre

Like fiction, **drama** features characters caught up in a plot. In fact, some plays have been based on novels, and novels on plays. Yet, whereas the narrator of a novel can spend pages painting a picture of the story's circumstances for the reader, a play is restricted to the space of the stage and the time frame of a couple of hours. What strategies are available to the playwright to ensure that the play successfully conveys its intended effects and themes?

To provide the story's setting, a play requires sets. If you've ever been involved with a play, you know that the **set** can be made up of detailed backdrops, specifically designed props, strategic lighting, and sometimes even background noise. A set, along with the characters' subtle indications of the scene, can generate a full setting in the audience's imagination.

Another difference between fiction and drama is that usually a play's **plot** is primarily forwarded through dialogue and action. Although a novel's narrator can describe in detail the thoughts and impressions of its characters, a play's effects depend much more heavily on what the characters say and do. A play is a performance, a spectacle, rather than words on paper. Some plays do include a narrator or a chorus, to introduce the scene or set the tone of the play, but the bulk of the production's effect is generated through the dialogue and its visual devices, and since the play's **script** dictates what the characters will say and often, through **stage direction**, its production strategies as well, the script is crucial to a successful performance.

6.2 A One-Act Play

Although the following script is only that, a script, it does give us a place to start as we investigate drama as a genre. *Trifles* is a **one-act play**, which is a drama that can usually be performed in an hour or less and in which the entire story is performed in one *act* as opposed to several. Although a one-act play can contain scene changes, this one only employs one scene.

Trifles
By Susan Glaspell

First performed by the Provincetown Players at the Wharf Theatre, Provincetown, Mass., August 8, 1916.

GEORGE HENDERSON (County Attorney)
HENRY PETERS (Sheriff)
LEWIS HALE, A neighboring farmer
MRS. PETERS
MRS. HALE

SCENE: *The kitchen is the now abandoned farmhouse of* JOHN WRIGHT, *a gloomy kitchen, and left without having been put in order—unwashed pans under the sink, a loaf of bread outside the bread-box, a dish-towel on the table—other signs of incompleted work. At the rear the outer door opens and the* SHERIFF *comes in followed by the* COUNTY ATTORNEY *and* HALE. *The* SHERIFF *and* HALE *are men in middle life, the* COUNTY ATTORNEY *is a young man; all are much bundled up and go at once to the stove. They are followed by the two women—the* SHERIFF's *wife first; she is a slight wiry woman, a thin nervous face.* MRS. HALE *is larger and would ordinarily be called more comfortable looking, but she is disturbed now and looks fearfully about as she enters. The women have come in slowly, and stand close together near the door.*

COUNTY ATTORNEY
(*rubbing his hands*)
This feels good. Come up to the fire, ladies.

MRS. PETERS
(*after taking a step forward*)
I'm not—cold.

SHERIFF

(*unbuttoning his overcoat and stepping away from the
stove as if to mark the beginning of official business*)
Now, Mr. Hale, before we move things about, you
explain to Mr. Henderson just what you saw when you
came here yesterday morning.

COUNTY ATTORNEY

By the way, has anything been moved? Are things just as
you left them yesterday?

SHERIFF

(*looking about*)
It's just the same. When it dropped below zero last
night I thought I'd better send Frank out this morning to
make a fire for us—no use getting pneumonia with a big
case on, but I told him not to touch anything except the
stove—and you know Frank.

COUNTY ATTORNEY

Somebody should have been left here yesterday.

SHERIFF

Oh—yesterday. When I had to send Frank to Morris
Center for that man who went crazy—I want you to
know I had my hands full yesterday. I knew you could
get back from Omaha by today and as long as I went
over everything here myself—

COUNTY ATTORNEY

Well, Mr. Hale, tell just what happened when you came
here yesterday morning.

HALE

Harry and I had started to town with a load of potatoes.
We came along the road from my place and as I got here
I said, I'm going to see if I can't get John Wright to go in
with me on a party telephone.' I spoke to Wright about
it once before and he put me off, saying folks talked too
much anyway, and all he asked was peace and quiet—I

guess you know about how much he talked himself; but I
thought maybe if I went to the house and talked about it
before his wife, though I said to Harry that I didn't know
as what his wife wanted made much difference to John—

COUNTY ATTORNEY
Let's talk about that later, Mr. Hale. I do want to talk
about that, but tell now just what happened when you got
to the house.

HALE
I didn't hear or see anything; I knocked at the door, and
still it was all quiet inside. I knew they must be up, it
was past eight o'clock. So I knocked again, and I thought
I heard somebody say, 'Come in.' I wasn't sure, I'm not
sure yet, but I opened the door—this door
(*indicating the door by which the two women are still
standing*)
and there in that rocker—
(*pointing to it*)
sat Mrs. Wright.
(*They all look at the rocker.*)

COUNTY ATTORNEY
What—was she doing?

HALE
She was rockin' back and forth. She had her apron in her
hand and was kind of—pleating it.

COUNTY ATTORNEY
And how did she—look?

HALE
Well, she looked queer.

COUNTY ATTORNEY
How do you mean—queer?

HALE
Well, as if she didn't know what she was going to do
next. And kind of done up.

116

COUNTY ATTORNEY
How did she seem to feel about your coming?

HALE
Why, I don't think she minded—one way or other. She
didn't pay much attention. I said, 'How do, Mrs. Wright
it's cold, ain't it?' And she said, 'Is it?'—and went on
kind of pleating at her apron. Well, I was surprised; she
didn't ask me to come up to the stove, or to set down,
but just sat there, not even looking at me, so I said, 'I
want to see John.' And then she—laughed. I guess you
would call it a laugh. I thought of Harry and the team
outside, so I said a little sharp: 'Can't I see John?' 'No',
she says, kind o' dull like. 'Ain't he home?' says I. 'Yes',
says she, 'he's home'. 'Then why can't I see him?' I
asked her, out of patience. ''Cause he's dead', says she.
'Dead?' says I. She just nodded her head, not getting a
bit excited, but rockin' back and forth. 'Why—where is
he?' says I, not knowing what to say. She just pointed
upstairs—like that
(*himself pointing to the room above.*)
I got up, with the idea of going up there. I walked from
there to here—then I says, 'Why, what did he die of?'
'He died of a rope round his neck', says she, and just
went on pleatin' at her apron. Well, I went out and called
Harry. I thought I might—need help. We went upstairs
and there he was lyin'—

COUNTY ATTORNEY
I think I'd rather have you go into that upstairs, where
you can point it all out. Just go on now with the rest of
the story.

HALE
Well, my first thought was to get that rope off. It
looked...
(*stops, his face twitches*)
... but Harry, he went up to him, and he said, 'No, he's
dead all right, and we'd better not touch anything.' So
we went back down stairs. She was still sitting that same
way. 'Has anybody been notified?' I asked. 'No', says

she unconcerned. 'Who did this, Mrs. Wright?' said
Harry. He said it business-like—and she stopped pleatin'
of her apron. 'I don't know', she says. 'You don't *know*?'
says Harry. 'No', says she. 'Weren't you sleepin' in the
bed with him?' says Harry. 'Yes', says she, 'but I was
on the inside'. 'Somebody slipped a rope round his neck
and strangled him and you didn't wake up?' says Harry.
'I didn't wake up', she said after him. We must 'a looked
as if we didn't see how that could be, for after a minute
she said, 'I sleep sound'. Harry was going to ask her more
questions but I said maybe we ought to let her tell her
story first to the coroner, or the sheriff, so Harry went fast
as he could to Rivers' place, where there's a telephone.

COUNTY ATTORNEY
And what did Mrs. Wright do when she knew that you
had gone for the coroner?

HALE
She moved from that chair to this one over here
(*pointing to a small chair in the corner*)
and just sat there with her hands held together and
looking down. I got a feeling that I ought to make some
conversation, so I said I had come in to see if John
wanted to put in a telephone, and at that she started to
laugh, and then she stopped and looked at me—scared,
(*the* COUNTY ATTORNEY, *who has had his notebook
out, makes a note.*)
I dunno, maybe it wasn't scared. I wouldn't like to say it
was. Soon Harry got back, and then Dr. Lloyd came, and
you, Mr. Peters, and so I guess that's all I know that you
don't.

COUNTY ATTORNEY
(*looking around.*)
I guess we'll go upstairs first—and then out to the barn
and around there,
(*to the* SHERIFF.)
You're convinced that there was nothing important
here—nothing that would point to any motive.

SHERIFF

Nothing here but kitchen things.

(*The* COUNTY ATTORNEY, *after again looking around the kitchen, opens the door of a cupboard closet. He gets up on a chair and looks on a shelf. Pulls his hand away, sticky.*)

COUNTY ATTORNEY

Here's a nice mess.

(*The women draw nearer.*)

MRS. PETERS

(*to the other woman*)

Oh, her fruit; it did freeze,

(*to the* LAWYER)

She worried about that when it turned so cold. She said the fire'd go out and her jars would break.

SHERIFF

Well, can you beat the women! Held for murder and worryin' about her preserves.

COUNTY ATTORNEY

I guess before we're through she may have something more serious than preserves to worry about.

HALE

Well, women are used to worrying over trifles.

(*The two women move a little closer together.*)

COUNTY ATTORNEY

(*with the gallantry of a young politician*)

And yet, for all their worries, what would we do without the ladies?

(*the women do not unbend. He goes to the sink, takes a dipperful of water from the pail and pouring it into a basin, washes his hands. Starts to wipe them on the roller-towel, turns it for a cleaner place*)

Dirty towels!

(*kicks his foot against the pans under the sink*)

Not much of a housekeeper, would you say, ladies?

MRS. HALE

(*stiffly*)

There's a great deal of work to be done on a farm.

COUNTY ATTORNEY

To be sure. And yet

(*with a little bow to her*)

I know there are some Dickson county farmhouses
which do not have such roller towels.

(*He gives it a pull to expose its length again.*)

MRS. HALE

Those towels get dirty awful quick. Men's hands aren't
always as clean as they might be.

COUNTY ATTORNEY

Ah, loyal to your sex, I see. But you and Mrs. Wright
were neighbors. I suppose you were friends, too.

MRS. HALE

(*shaking her head*)

I've not seen much of her of late years. I've not been in
this house—it's more than a year.

COUNTY ATTORNEY

And why was that? You didn't like her?

MRS. HALE

I liked her all well enough. Farmers' wives have their
hands full, Mr. Henderson. And then—

COUNTY ATTORNEY

Yes—?

MRS. HALE

(*looking about.*)

It never seemed a very cheerful place.

COUNTY ATTORNEY

No—it's not cheerful. I shouldn't say she had the home-
making instinct.

MRS. HALE

Well, I don't know as Wright had, either.

COUNTY ATTORNEY

You mean that they didn't get on very well?

MRS. HALE

No, I don't mean anything. But I don't think a place'd be any cheerfuller for John Wright's being in it.

COUNTY ATTORNEY

I'd like to talk more of that a little later. I want to get the lay of things upstairs now.
(*He goes to the left, where three steps lead to a stair door.*)

SHERIFF

I suppose anything Mrs. Peters does'll be all right. She was to take in some clothes for her, you know, and a few little things. We left in such a hurry yesterday.

COUNTY ATTORNEY

Yes, but I would like to see what you take, Mrs. Peters, and keep an eye out for anything that might be of use to us.

MRS. PETERS

Yes, Mr. Henderson.
(*The women listen to the men's steps on the stairs, then look about the kitchen.*)

MRS. HALE

I'd hate to have men coming into my kitchen, snooping around and criticizing.
(*She arranges the pans under sink which the* LAWYER *had shoved out of place.*)

MRS. PETERS

Of course it's no more than their duty.

MRS. HALE

Duty's all right, but I guess that deputy sheriff that came out to make the fire might have got a little of this on.
(*gives the roller towel a pull.*)

Wish I'd thought of that sooner. Seems mean to talk about her for not having things slicked up when she had to come away in such a hurry.

MRS. PETERS
(*who has gone to a small table in the left rear corner of the room, and lifted one end of a towel that covers a pan*) She had bread set.
(*Stands still.*)

MRS. HALE
(*eyes fixed on a loaf of bread beside the bread-box, which is on a low shelf at the other side of the room. Moves slowly toward it.*)
She was going to put this in there,
(*picks up loaf, then abruptly drops it. In a manner of returning to familiar things.*)
 It's a shame about her fruit. I wonder if it's all gone.
(*gets up on the chair and looks.*)
I think there's some here that's all right, Mrs. Peters.
Yes—here;
(*holding it toward the window.*)
 this is cherries, too.
(*looking again.*)
 I declare I believe that's the only one.
(*gets down, bottle in her hand. Goes to the sink and wipes it off on the outside.*)
She'll feel awful bad after all her hard work in the hot weather. I remember the afternoon I put up my cherries last summer.
(*She puts the bottle on the big kitchen table, center of the room. With a sigh, is about to sit down in the rocking-chair. Before she is seated realizes what chair it is; with a slow look at it, steps back. The chair which she has touched rocks back and forth.*)

MRS. PETERS
Well, I must get those things from the front room closet,
(*she goes to the door at the right, but after looking into the other room, steps back.*)

You coming with me, Mrs. Hale? You could help me
carry them.
(*They go in the other room; reappear,* MRS. PETERS
carrying a dress and skirt, MRS. HALE *following with a
pair of shoes.*)

MRS. PETERS

My, it's cold in there.
(*She puts the clothes on the big table, and hurries to the
stove.*)

MRS. HALE

(*examining the skirt.*)
Wright was close. I think maybe that's why she kept so
much to herself. She didn't even belong to the Ladies Aid.
I suppose she felt she couldn't do her part, and then you
don't enjoy things when you feel shabby. She used to wear
pretty clothes and be lively, when she was Minnie Foster,
one of the town girls singing in the choir. But that—oh,
that was thirty years ago. This all you was to take in?

MRS. PETERS

She said she wanted an apron. Funny thing to want, for
there isn't much to get you dirty in jail, goodness knows.
But I suppose just to make her feel more natural. She
said they was in the top drawer in this cupboard. Yes,
here. And then her little shawl that always hung behind
the door.
(*opens stair door and looks.*)
Yes, here it is.
(*Quickly shuts door leading upstairs.*)

MRS. HALE

(*abruptly moving toward her*)
Mrs. Peters?

MRS. PETERS

Yes, Mrs. Hale?

MRS. HALE

Do you think she did it?

MRS. PETERS

(*in a frightened voice*)
Oh, I don't know.

MRS. HALE

Well, I don't think she did. Asking for an apron and her little shawl. Worrying about her fruit.

MRS. PETERS

(*starts to speak, glances up, where footsteps are heard in the room above. In a low voice*)
Mr. Peters says it looks bad for her. Mr. Henderson is awful sarcastic in a speech and he'll make fun of her sayin' she didn't wake up.

MRS. HALE

Well, I guess John Wright didn't wake when they was slipping that rope under his neck.

MRS. PETERS

No, it's strange. It must have been done awful crafty and still. They say it was such a—funny way to kill a man, rigging it all up like that.

MRS. HALE

That's just what Mr. Hale said. There was a gun in the house. He says that's what he can't understand.

MRS. PETERS

Mr. Henderson said coming out that what was needed for the case was a motive; something to show anger, or— sudden feeling.

MRS. HALE

(*who is standing by the table.*)
Well, I don't see any signs of anger around here,
(*she puts her hand on the dish towel which lies on the table, stands looking down at table, one half of which is clean, the other half messy.*)
It's wiped to here,
(*makes a move as if to finish work, then turns and looks at loaf of bread outside the breadbox. Drops towel. In that voice of coming back to familiar things.*)

Wonder how they are finding things upstairs. I hope she had it a little more red-up up there. You know, it seems kind of sneaking. Locking her up in town and then coming out here and trying to get her own house to turn against her!

MRS. PETERS
But Mrs. Hale, the law is the law.

MRS. HALE
I s'pose 'tis,
(*unbuttoning her coat.*)
Better loosen up your things, Mrs. Peters. You won't feel them when you go out.
(MRS. PETERS *takes off her fur tippet, goes to hang it on hook at back of room, stands looking at the under part of the small corner table.*)

MRS. PETERS
She was piecing a quilt.
(*She brings the large sewing basket and they look at the bright pieces.*)

MRS. HALE
It's log cabin pattern. Pretty, isn't it? I wonder if she was goin' to quilt it or just knot it?
(*Footsteps have been heard coming down the stairs.* The SHERIFF enters followed by HALE and the COUNTY ATTORNEY.)

SHERIFF
They wonder if she was going to quilt it or just knot it!
(*The men laugh, the women look abashed.*)

COUNTY ATTORNEY
(*rubbing his hands over the stove*)
Frank's fire didn't do much up there, did it? Well, let's go out to the barn and get that cleared up.
(*The men go outside.*)

MRS. HALE
(*resentfully*)
I don't know as there's anything so strange, our takin' up

our time with little things while we're waiting for them to get the evidence.
(*she sits down at the big table smoothing out a block with decision*)
I don't see as it's anything to laugh about.

MRS. PETERS

(*apologetically*)
Of course they've got awful important things on their minds.
(*Pulls up a chair and joins MRS HALE at the table.*)

MRS. HALE

(*examining another block*)
Mrs. Peters, look at this one. Here, this is the one she was working on, and look at the sewing! All the rest of it has been so nice and even. And look at this! It's all over the place! Why, it looks as if she didn't know what she was about!
(*After she has said this they look at each other, then start to glance back at the door. After an instant* MRS. HALE *has pulled at a knot and ripped the sewing.*)

MRS. PETERS

Oh, what are you doing, Mrs. Hale?

MRS. HALE

(*mildly*)
Just pulling out a stitch or two that's not sewed very good.
(*threading a needle*)
Bad sewing always made me fidgety.

MRS. PETERS

(nervously)
I don't think we ought to touch things.

MRS. HALE

I'll just finish up this end.
(*suddenly stopping and leaning forward*)
Mrs. Peters?

MRS. PETERS

Yes, Mrs. Hale?

MRS. HALE

What do you suppose she was so nervous about?

MRS. PETERS

Oh—I don't know. I don't know as she was nervous. I
sometimes sew awful queer when I'm just tired.
(MRS. HALE *starts to say something, looks at* MRS.
PETERS, *then goes on sewing*)
Well I must get these things wrapped up. They may be
through sooner than we think,
(*putting apron and other things together*)
I wonder where I can find a piece of paper, and string.

MRS. HALE

In that cupboard, maybe.

MRS. PETERS

(*looking in cupboard*)
Why, here's a bird-cage,
(*holds it up.*)
Did she have a bird, Mrs. Hale?

MRS. HALE

Why, I don't know whether she did or not—I've not
been here for so long. There was a man around last year
selling canaries cheap, but I don't know as she took one;
maybe she did. She used to sing real pretty herself.

MRS. PETERS

(*glancing around.*)
Seems funny to think of a bird here. But she must have
had one, or why would she have a cage? I wonder what
happened to it.

MRS. HALE

I s'pose maybe the cat got it.

MRS. PETERS

No, she didn't have a cat. She's got that feeling some

people have about cats—being afraid of them. My cat got in her room and she was real upset and asked me to take it out.

MRS. HALE

My sister Bessie was like that. Queer, ain't it?

MRS. PETERS

(*examining the cage.*)
Why, look at this door. It's broke. One hinge is pulled apart.

MRS. HALE

(*looking too.*)
Looks as if someone must have been rough with it.

MRS. PETERS

Why, yes.
(*She brings the cage forward and puts it on the table.*)

MRS. HALE

I wish if they're going to find any evidence they'd be about it. I don't like this place.

MRS. PETERS

But I'm awful glad you came with me, Mrs. Hale. It would be lonesome for me sitting here alone.

MRS. HALE

It would, wouldn't it?
(*dropping her sewing*)
But I tell you what I do wish, Mrs. Peters. I wish I had come over sometimes when *she* was here. I—
(*looking around the room*)
—wish I had.

MRS. PETERS

But of course you were awful busy, Mrs. Hale—your house and your children.

MRS. HALE

I could've come. I stayed away because it weren't cheerful—and that's why I ought to have come. I—I've

never liked this place. Maybe because it's down in a
hollow and you don't see the road. I dunno what it is, but
it's a lonesome place and always was. I wish I had come
over to see Minnie Foster sometimes. I can see now—
(*shakes her head*)

MRS. PETERS

Well, you mustn't reproach yourself, Mrs. Hale. Somehow we just don't see how it is with other folks until—
something comes up.

MRS. HALE

Not having children makes less work—but it makes
a quiet house, and Wright out to work all day, and no
company when he did come in. Did you know John
Wright, Mrs. Peters?

MRS. PETERS

Not to know him; I've seen him in town. They say he
was a good man.

MRS. HALE

Yes—good; he didn't drink, and kept his word as well as
most, I guess, and paid his debts. But he was a hard man,
Mrs. Peters. Just to pass the time of day with him—
(*shivers.*)
Like a raw wind that gets to the bone,
(*pauses, her eye falling on the cage.*)
I should think she would 'a wanted a bird. But what do
you suppose went with it?

MRS. PETERS

I don't know, unless it got sick and died.
(*She reaches over and swings the broken door, swings it
again, both women watch it.*)

MRS. HALE

You weren't raised round here, were you?
(*MRS. PETERS shakes her head.*)
You didn't know—her?

129

MRS. PETERS

Not till they brought her yesterday.

MRS. HALE

She—come to think of it, she was kind of like a bird
herself—real sweet and pretty, but kind of timid and—
fluttery. How—she—did—change.
(*silence; then as if struck by a happy thought and
relieved to get back to everyday things.*)
Tell you what, Mrs. Peters, why don't you take the quilt
in with you? It might take up her mind.

MRS. PETERS

Why, I think that's a real nice idea, Mrs. Hale. There
couldn't possibly be any objection to it, could there?
Now, just what would I take? I wonder if her patches are
in here—and her things.
(*They look in the sewing basket.*)

MRS. HALE

Here's some red. I expect this has got sewing things in it.
(*brings out a fancy box*)
What a pretty box. Looks like something somebody
would give you. Maybe her scissors are in here.
(*Opens box. Suddenly puts her hand to her nose*)
Why—
(MRS. PETERS *bends nearer, then turns her face away*)
There's something wrapped up in this piece of silk.

MRS. PETERS

Why, this isn't her scissors.

MRS. HALE

(*lifting the silk*)
Oh, Mrs. Peters—it's—
(MRS. PETERS *bends closer.*)
MRS. PETERS
It's the bird.

MRS. HALE

(*jumping up*)
But, Mrs. Peters—look at it! It's neck! Look at its neck!
It's all—other side *to.*

MRS. PETERS

Somebody—wrung—its—neck.
(*Their eyes meet. A look of growing comprehension,
of horror. Steps are heard outside.* MRS. HALE *slips
box under quilt pieces, and sinks into her chair. Enter*
SHERIFF *and* COUNTY ATTORNEY. MRS. PETERS
rises.)

COUNTY ATTORNEY

(*as one turning from serious things to little pleasantries*)
Well ladies, have you decided whether she was going to
quilt it or knot it?

MRS. PETERS

We think she was going to—knot it.

COUNTY ATTORNEY

Well, that's interesting, I'm sure.
(*seeing the birdcage*)
Has the bird flown?

MRS. HALE

(*putting more quilt pieces over the box*)
We think the—cat got it.

COUNTY ATTORNEY

(*preoccupied*)
Is there a cat?
(MRS. HALE *glances in a quick covert way at* MRS.
PETERS.)

MRS. PETERS

Well, not now. They're superstitious, you know. They
leave.

COUNTY ATTORNEY
(*to* SHERIFF PETERS, *continuing an interrupted con-*
versation)
No sign at all of anyone having come from the outside.
Their own rope. Now let's go up again and go over it
piece by piece.
(*they start upstairs*)
It would have to have been someone who knew just the—
(MRS. PETERS *sits down. The two women sit there not*
looking at one another, but as if peering into something
and at the same time holding back. When they talk now
it is in the manner of feeling their way over strange
ground, as if afraid of what they are saying, but as if they
can not help saying it.)

MRS. HALE
She liked the bird. She was going to bury it in that pretty
box.

MRS. PETERS
(*in a whisper*)
When I was a girl—my kitten—there was a boy took
a hatchet, and before my eyes—and before I could get
there—
(*covers her face an instant*)
If they hadn't held me back I would have—
(*catches herself, looks upstairs where steps are heard,*
falters weakly)
—hurt him.

MRS. HALE
(*with a slow look around her*)
I wonder how it would seem never to have had any
children around,
(*pause*)
No, Wright wouldn't like the bird—a thing that sang.
She used to sing. He killed that, too.

MRS. PETERS
(*moving uneasily*)
We don't know who killed the bird.

MRS. HALE
I knew John Wright.

MRS. PETERS
It was an awful thing was done in this house that night,
Mrs. Hale. Killing a man while he slept, slipping a rope
around his neck that choked the life out of him.

MRS. HALE
His neck. Choked the life out of him.
(*Her hand goes out and rests on the bird-cage.*)

MRS. PETERS
(*with rising voice*)
We don't know who killed him. We don't *know*.

MRS. HALE
(*her own feeling not interrupted*)
If there'd been years and years of nothing, then a bird to
sing to you, it would be awful—still, after the bird was still.

MRS. PETERS
(*something within her speaking.*)
I know what stillness is. When we homesteaded in
Dakota, and my first baby died—after he was two years
old, and me with no other then—

MRS. HALE
(*moving.*)
How soon do you suppose they'll be through, looking
for the evidence?

MRS. PETERS
I know what stillness is.
(*pulling herself back.*)
The law has got to punish crime, Mrs. Hale.

MRS. HALE
(*not as if answering that.*)
I wish you'd seen Minnie Foster when she wore a white
dress with blue ribbons and stood up there in the choir
and sang.

(*a look around the room.*)
Oh, I *wish* I'd come over here once in a while! That was a crime! That was a crime! Who's going to punish that?

MRS. PETERS

(*looking upstairs.*)
We mustn't—take on.

MRS. HALE

I might have known she needed help! I know how things can be—for women. I tell you, it's queer, Mrs. Peters. We live close together and we live far apart. We all go through the same things—it's all just a different kind of the same thing,
(*brushes her eyes, noticing the bottle of fruit, reaches out for it.*)
If I was you, I wouldn't tell her her fruit was gone. Tell her it *ain't*. Tell her it's all right. Take this in to prove it to her. She—she may never know whether it was broke or not.

MRS. PETERS

(*takes the bottle, looks about for something to wrap it in; takes petticoat from the clothes brought from the other room, very nervously begins winding this around the bottle. In a false voice.*)
My, it's a good thing the men couldn't hear us. Wouldn't they just laugh! Getting all stirred up over a little thing like a—dead canary. As if that could have anything to do with—with—wouldn't they *laugh*!
(*The men are heard coming down stairs.*)

MRS. HALE

(*under her breath.*)
Maybe they would—maybe they wouldn't.

COUNTY ATTORNEY

No, Peters, it's all perfectly clear except a reason for doing it. But you know juries when it comes to women. If there was some definite thing. Something to show— something to make a story about—a thing that would connect up with this strange way of doing it—

(The women's eyes meet for an instant. Enter HALE from outer door.)

HALE
Well, I've got the team around. Pretty cold out there.

COUNTY ATTORNEY
I'm going to stay here a while by myself,
(to the SHERIFF.)
You can send Frank out for me, can't you? I want to go over everything. I'm not satisfied that we can't do better.

SHERIFF
Do you want to see what Mrs. Peters is going to take in?
(The LAWYER goes to the table, picks up the apron, laughs.)

COUNTY ATTORNEY
Oh, I guess they're not very dangerous things the ladies have picked out.
(Moves a few things about, disturbing the quilt pieces which cover the box. Steps back)
No, Mrs. Peters doesn't need supervising. For that matter, a sheriff's wife is married to the law. Ever think of it that way, Mrs. Peters?

MRS. PETERS
Not—just that way.

SHERIFF
(chuckling)
Married to the law.
(moves toward the other room)
I just want you to come in here a minute, George. We ought to take a look at these windows.

COUNTY ATTORNEY
(scoffingly)
Oh, windows!

SHERIFF

We'll be right out, Mr. Hale.

(HALE *goes outside. The* SHERIFF *follows the* COUNTY ATTORNEY *into the other room. Then* MRS. HALE *rises, hands tight together, looking intensely at* MRS. PETERS, *whose eyes make a slow turn, finally meeting* MRS. HALE*'s. A moment* MRS. HALE *holds her, then her own eyes point the way to where the box is concealed. Suddenly* MRS. PETERS *throws back quilt pieces and tries to put the box in the bag she is wearing. It is too big. She opens box, starts to take bird out, cannot touch it, goes to pieces, stands there helpless. Sound of a knob turning in the other room.* MRS. HALE *snatches the box and puts it in the pocket of her big coat. Enter* COUNTY ATTORNEY *and* SHERIFF.)

COUNTY ATTORNEY

(*facetiously*)

Well, Henry, at least we found out that she was not going to quilt it. She was going to—what is it you call it, ladies?

MRS. HALE

(*her hand against her pocket*)

We call it—knot it, Mr. Henderson.

(CURTAIN)

(1916)

Questions for Consideration:

1. Discuss what sort of backdrop, props, and costumes would be required to perform this play. How much of this detail is dictated by the stage directions and how much of it is left for the director to create?

2. How are the characters revealed? Which lines of dialogue are especially tell-tale regarding certain characters' values and personalities?

3. How does the play develop the audience's impression of Mrs. Wright, though she never appears in the play?

4. In light of the play's themes, what does the bird cage symbolize? How does that symbol develop our impression of Mr. and Mrs. Wright?

5. How does the metaphor of the quilt serve to develop the theme of women's undervalued work?

6. Consider the order and pace whereby clues are revealed to the audience. How does the plot unfold to generate suspense and interest for the audience?

In *Trifles*, Glaspell employs some round characters and some flat, or stock, characters. Round, complex characters, like Mrs. Wright, Mrs. Hale, and Mrs. Peters, reflect the complicated personalities and experiences that most of us can identify with. When Mrs. Peters seems torn between following the wishes of her husband, who represents the law, and showing sympathy with Mrs. Wright, we understand her conflict. Most of us have encountered similar conflicts in our daily lives. However, we tend to dislike Mr. Henderson, partly because he insults Mrs. Wright, but also, notably, because he is a flat character. He does not reveal the capacity or the habit of complex thought, but rather reacts to his surroundings based on his stereotype-based assumptions. Since the male characters represent dominant male society, including familiar patriarchs (Mr. Wright is the authority in his house), a society in which women have not yet been granted the right to vote, and a legal system that does not recognize women as full citizens, they are sustained as flat. While it may seem that the use of flat characters would yield a weak play, it is important to consider why writers use flat characters at all. Since these characters carry with them a ready-made impression, less dialogue has to be devoted to developing them, thereby creating more dialogue-space for other important characters or ideas. In this short play, most of the script focuses on the dialogue and actions of Mrs. Hale and Mrs. Peters, allowing Glaspell to develop the theme successfully.

6.3 Shakespeare's *The Tempest*

In a longer play, of several acts, a playwright has more room for development. Like the novel relative to the short story, a longer play can elaborate on the central theme and can even develop several plot and theme threads. Consider William Shakespeare's *The Tempest* and the various storylines he develops in this play.

CHARACTERS:

PROSPERO, former Duke of Milan; father of Miranda

MIRANDA: Prospero's young daughter

IRIS, JUNO, CERES, Nymphs, Reapers: Spirits

TRINCULO, a jester

SEBASTIAN, Alonso's brother

STEPHANO, a drunken butler

GONZALO, an old and honest lord

ANTONIO, Prospero's brother

ARIEL, an airy spirit, servant to Prospero

ADRIAN and FRANCISCO, noblemen; companions of Alonzo

ALONSO, king of Naples; father of Ferdinand

FERDINAND, son and heir of Alonso

CALIBAN, Prospero's servant, savage and deformed; son of Sycorax

Master of a Ship, Boatswains, Mariners

SETTING: A ship at sea during a terrible storm; later, a Mediterranean island to which Prospero has been banished with Miranda since she was a young child and where the ship's travelers come ashore

ACT I

SCENE I. On a ship at sea: a tempestuous noise of thunder and lightning heard.
Enter a Master and a Boatswain

Master

Boatswain!

Boatswain

Here, master: what cheer?

Master

Good, speak to the mariners: fall to't, yarely, or we run ourselves aground: bestir, bestir.
Exit
Enter Mariners

Boatswain

Heigh, my hearts! cheerly, cheerly, my hearts!
yare, yare! Take in the topsail. Tend to the
master's whistle. Blow, till thou burst thy wind,
if room enough!
Enter ALONSO, SEBASTIAN, ANTONIO, FERDINAND,
GONZALO, and others

ALONSO

Good boatswain, have care. Where's the master?
Play the men.   10

Boatswain

I pray now, keep below.

ANTONIO

Where is the master, boatswain?

Boatswain

Do you not hear him? You mar our labour: keep your
cabins: you do assist the storm.

GONZALO

Nay, good, be patient.

Boatswain

When the sea is. Hence! What cares these roarersfor the
name of king? To cabin: silence! trouble us not.

GONZALO

Good, yet remember whom thou hast aboard.

Boatswain

None that I more love than myself. You are a
counsellor; if you can command these elements to   20
silence, and work the peace of the present, we will
not hand a rope more; use your authority: if you
cannot, give thanks you have lived so long, and make
yourself ready in your cabin for the mischance of
the hour, if it so hap. Cheerly, good hearts! Out
of our way, I say.
Exit

GONZALO

I have great comfort from this fellow: methinks he
hath no drowning mark upon him; his complexion is
perfect gallows. Stand fast, good Fate, to his
hanging: make the rope of his destiny our cable,   30
for our own doth little advantage. If he be not
born to be hanged, our case is miserable.
Exeunt
Re-enter Boatswain

Boatswain

Down with the topmast! yare! lower, lower! Bring
her to try with main-course.
A cry within
A plague upon this howling! they are louder than
the weather or our office.
Re-enter SEBASTIAN, ANTONIO, and GONZALO
Yet again! what do you here? Shall we give o'er
and drown? Have you a mind to sink?

SEBASTIAN

A pox o' your throat, you bawling, blasphemous,   40
incharitable dog!

Boatswain

Work you then.

ANTONIO

Hang, cur! hang, you whoreson, insolent noisemaker!
We are less afraid to be drowned than thou art.

GONZALO

I'll warrant him for drowning; though the ship were
no stronger than a nutshell and as leaky as an
unstanched wench.

Boatswain

Lay her a-hold, a-hold! set her two courses off to
sea again; lay her off.
Enter Mariners wet   50

Mariners

All lost! to prayers, to prayers! all lost!

Boatswain

What, must our mouths be cold?

GONZALO

The king and prince at prayers! let's assist them,
For our case is as theirs.

SEBASTIAN

I'm out of patience.

ANTONIO

We are merely cheated of our lives by drunkards:
This wide-chapp'd rascal—would thou mightst lie drown-
ing
The washing of ten tides!

GONZALO

He'll be hang'd yet,
Though every drop of water swear against it
And gape at widest to glut him.
A confused noise within: 'Mercy on us!'—   60
'We split, we split!'—'Farewell, my wife and children!'—
'Farewell, brother!'—'We split, we split, we split!'

ANTONIO

Let's all sink with the king.

SEBASTIAN

Let's take leave of him.
Exeunt ANTONIO and SEBASTIAN

GONZALO

Now would I give a thousand furlongs of sea for an
acre of barren ground, long heath, brown furze, any
thing. The wills above be done! but I would fain
die a dry death.
Exeunt

SCENE II. The island. Before PROSPERO'S cell.
Enter PROSPERO and MIRANDA

MIRANDA

If by your art, my dearest father, you have   70
Put the wild waters in this roar, allay them.
The sky, it seems, would pour down stinking pitch,
But that the sea, mounting to the welkin's cheek,
Dashes the fire out. O, I have suffered
With those that I saw suffer: a brave vessel,
Who had, no doubt, some noble creature in her,
Dash'd all to pieces. O, the cry did knock
Against my very heart. Poor souls, they perish'd.
Had I been any god of power, I would
Have sunk the sea within the earth or ere   80
It should the good ship so have swallow'd and
The fraughting souls within her.

PROSPERO

Be collected:
No more amazement: tell your piteous heart
There's no harm done.

MIRANDA

O, woe the day!

PROSPERO

No harm.
I have done nothing but in care of thee,
Of thee, my dear one, thee, my daughter, who
Art ignorant of what thou art, nought knowing   90
Of whence I am, nor that I am more better
Than Prospero, master of a full poor cell,
And thy no greater father.

MIRANDA

More to know
Did never meddle with my thoughts.

PROSPERO

'Tis time
I should inform thee farther. Lend thy hand,
And pluck my magic garment from me. So:
Lays down his mantle
Lie there, my art. Wipe thou thine eyes; have comfort.   100
The direful spectacle of the wreck, which touch'd
The very virtue of compassion in thee,
I have with such provision in mine art
So safely ordered that there is no soul—
No, not so much perdition as an hair
Betid to any creature in the vessel
Which thou heard'st cry, which thou saw'st sink. Sit down;
For thou must now know farther.

MIRANDA

You have often
Begun to tell me what I am, but stopp'd   110
And left me to a bootless inquisition,
Concluding 'Stay: not yet.'

PROSPERO

The hour's now come;
The very minute bids thee ope thine ear;
Obey and be attentive. Canst thou remember
A time before we came unto this cell?
I do not think thou canst, for then thou wast not
Out three years old.

MIRANDA

Certainly, sir, I can.

PROSPERO

By what? by any other house or person?   120
Of any thing the image tell me that
Hath kept with thy remembrance.

MIRANDA

'Tis far off
And rather like a dream than an assurance

143

That my remembrance warrants. Had I not
Four or five women once that tended me?

PROSPERO

Thou hadst, and more, Miranda. But how is it
That this lives in thy mind? What seest thou else
In the dark backward and abysm of time?
If thou remember'st aught ere thou camest here,   130
How thou camest here thou mayst.

MIRANDA

But that I do not.

PROSPERO

Twelve year since, Miranda, twelve year since,
Thy father was the Duke of Milan and
A prince of power.

MIRANDA

Sir, are not you my father?

PROSPERO

Thy mother was a piece of virtue, and
She said thou wast my daughter; and thy father
Was Duke of Milan; and thou his only heir
And princess no worse issued.   140

MIRANDA

O the heavens!
What foul play had we, that we came from thence?
Or blessed was't we did?

PROSPERO

Both, both, my girl:
By foul play, as thou say'st, were we heaved thence,
But blessedly holp hither.

MIRANDA

O, my heart bleeds
To think o' the teen that I have turn'd you to,
Which is from my remembrance! Please you, farther.

PROSPERO

My brother and thy uncle, call'd Antonio—   150
I pray thee, mark me—that a brother should
Be so perfidious!—he whom next thyself
Of all the world I loved and to him put
The manage of my state; as at that time
Through all the signories it was the first
And Prospero the prime duke, being so reputed
In dignity, and for the liberal arts
Without a parallel; those being all my study,
The government I cast upon my brother
And to my state grew stranger, being transported   160
And rapt in secret studies. Thy false uncle—
Dost thou attend me?

MIRANDA

Sir, most heedfully.

PROSPERO

Being once perfected how to grant suits,
How to deny them, who to advance and who
To trash for over-topping, new created
The creatures that were mine, I say, or changed 'em,
Or else new form'd 'em; having both the key
Of officer and office, set all hearts i' the state
To what tune pleased his ear; that now he was   170
The ivy which had hid my princely trunk,
And suck'd my verdure out on't. Thou attend'st not.

MIRANDA

O, good sir, I do.

PROSPERO

I pray thee, mark me.
I, thus neglecting worldly ends, all dedicated
To closeness and the bettering of my mind
With that which, but by being so retired,
O'er-prized all popular rate, in my false brother
Awaked an evil nature; and my trust,
Like a good parent, did beget of him   180
A falsehood in its contrary as great

145

As my trust was; which had indeed no limit,
A confidence sans bound. He being thus lorded,
Not only with what my revenue yielded,
But what my power might else exact, like one
Who having into truth, by telling of it,
Made such a sinner of his memory,
To credit his own lie, he did believe
He was indeed the duke; out o' the substitution
And executing the outward face of royalty,   190
With all prerogative: hence his ambition growing—
Dost thou hear?

MIRANDA
Your tale, sir, would cure deafness.

PROSPERO
To have no screen between this part he play'd
And him he play'd it for, he needs will be
Absolute Milan. Me, poor man, my library
Was dukedom large enough: of temporal royalties
He thinks me now incapable; confederates—
So dry he was for sway—wi' the King of Naples
To give him annual tribute, do him homage,   200
Subject his coronet to his crown and bend
The dukedom yet unbow'd—alas, poor Milan!—
To most ignoble stooping.

MIRANDA
O the heavens!

PROSPERO
Mark his condition and the event; then tell me
If this might be a brother.

MIRANDA
I should sin
To think but nobly of my grandmother:
Good wombs have borne bad sons.

PROSPERO
Now the condition.   210

The King of Naples, being an enemy
To me inveterate, hearkens my brother's suit;
Which was, that he, in lieu o' the premises
Of homage and I know not how much tribute,
Should presently extirpate me and mine
Out of the dukedom and confer fair Milan
With all the honours on my brother: whereon,
A treacherous army levied, one midnight
Fated to the purpose did Antonio open
The gates of Milan, and, i' the dead of darkness,   220
The ministers for the purpose hurried thence
Me and thy crying self.

MIRANDA

Alack, for pity!
I, not remembering how I cried out then,
Will cry it o'er again: it is a hint
That wrings mine eyes to't.

PROSPERO

Hear a little further
And then I'll bring thee to the present business
Which now's upon's; without the which this story
Were most impertinent.   230

MIRANDA

Wherefore did they not
That hour destroy us?

PROSPERO

Well demanded, wench:
My tale provokes that question. Dear, they durst not,
So dear the love my people bore me, nor set
A mark so bloody on the business, but
With colours fairer painted their foul ends.
In few, they hurried us aboard a bark,
Bore us some leagues to sea; where they prepared
A rotten carcass of a boat, not rigg'd,   240
Nor tackle, sail, nor mast; the very rats
Instinctively had quit it: there they hoist us,
To cry to the sea that roar'd to us, to sigh

To the winds whose pity, sighing back again,
Did us but loving wrong.

MIRANDA

Alack, what trouble
Was I then to you!

PROSPERO

O, a cherubim
Thou wast that did preserve me. Thou didst smile.
Infused with a fortitude from heaven,   250
When I have deck'd the sea with drops full salt,
Under my burthen groan'd; which raised in me
An undergoing stomach, to bear up
Against what should ensue.

MIRANDA

How came we ashore?

PROSPERO

By Providence divine.
Some food we had and some fresh water that
A noble Neapolitan, Gonzalo,
Out of his charity, being then appointed
Master of this design, did give us, with   260
Rich garments, linens, stuffs and necessaries,
Which since have steaded much; so, of his gentleness,
Knowing I loved my books, he furnish'd me
From mine own library with volumes that
I prize above my dukedom.

MIRANDA

Would I might
But ever see that man!

PROSPERO

Now I arise:
Resumes his mantle
Sit still, and hear the last of our sea-sorrow.   270
Here in this island we arrived; and here

Have I, thy schoolmaster, made thee more profit
Than other princesses can that have more time
For vainer hours and tutors not so careful.

MIRANDA

Heavens thank you for't! And now, I pray you, sir,
For still 'tis beating in my mind, your reason
For raising this sea-storm?

PROSPERO

Know thus far forth.
By accident most strange, bountiful Fortune,
Now my dear lady, hath mine enemies   280
Brought to this shore; and by my prescience
I find my zenith doth depend upon
A most auspicious star, whose influence
If now I court not but omit, my fortunes
Will ever after droop. Here cease more questions:
Thou art inclined to sleep; 'tis a good dulness,
And give it way: I know thou canst not choose.
MIRANDA sleeps
Come away, servant, come. I am ready now.
Approach, my Ariel, come.
Enter ARIEL

ARIEL

All hail, great master! grave sir, hail! I come   290
To answer thy best pleasure; be't to fly,
To swim, to dive into the fire, to ride
On the curl'd clouds, to thy strong bidding task
Ariel and all his quality.

PROSPERO

Hast thou, spirit,
Perform'd to point the tempest that I bade thee?

ARIEL

To every article.
I boarded the king's ship; now on the beak,
Now in the waist, the deck, in every cabin,

I flamed amazement: sometime I'ld divide,   300
And burn in many places; on the topmast,
The yards and bowsprit, would I flame distinctly,
Then meet and join. Jove's lightnings, the precursors
O' the dreadful thunder-claps, more momentary
And sight-outrunning were not; the fire and cracks
Of sulphurous roaring the most mighty Neptune
Seem to besiege and make his bold waves tremble,
Yea, his dread trident shake.

PROSPERO

My brave spirit!
Who was so firm, so constant, that this coil   310
Would not infect his reason?

ARIEL

Not a soul
But felt a fever of the mad and play'd
Some tricks of desperation. All but mariners
Plunged in the foaming brine and quit the vessel,
Then all afire with me: the king's son, Ferdinand,
With hair up-staring,—then like reeds, not hair,—
Was the first man that leap'd; cried, 'Hell is empty
And all the devils are here.'

PROSPERO

Why that's my spirit!   320
But was not this nigh shore?

ARIEL

Close by, my master.

PROSPERO

But are they, Ariel, safe?

ARIEL

Not a hair perish'd;
On their sustaining garments not a blemish,
But fresher than before: and, as thou badest me,
In troops I have dispersed them 'bout the isle.
The king's son have I landed by himself;
Whom I left cooling of the air with sighs

In an odd angle of the isle and sitting,   330
His arms in this sad knot.

PROSPERO

Of the king's ship
The mariners say how thou hast disposed
And all the rest o' the fleet.

ARIEL

Safely in harbour
Is the king's ship; in the deep nook, where once
Thou call'dst me up at midnight to fetch dew
From the still-vex'd Bermoothes, there she's hid:
The mariners all under hatches stow'd;
Who, with a charm join'd to their suffer'd labour,   340
I have left asleep; and for the rest o' the fleet
Which I dispersed, they all have met again
And are upon the Mediterranean flote,
Bound sadly home for Naples,
Supposing that they saw the king's ship wreck'd
And his great person perish.

PROSPERO

Ariel, thy charge
Exactly is perform'd: but there's more work.
What is the time o' the day?

ARIEL

Past the mid season.   350

PROSPERO

At least two glasses. The time 'twixt six and now
Must by us both be spent most preciously.

ARIEL

Is there more toil? Since thou dost give me pains,
Let me remember thee what thou hast promised,
Which is not yet perform'd me.

PROSPERO

How now? moody?
What is't thou canst demand?

ARIEL

My liberty.

PROSPERO

Before the time be out? no more!

ARIEL

I prithee,   360
Remember I have done thee worthy service;
Told thee no lies, made thee no mistakings, served
Without or grudge or grumblings: thou didst promise
To bate me a full year.

PROSPERO

Dost thou forget
From what a torment I did free thee?

ARIEL

No.

PROSPERO

Thou dost, and think'st it much to tread the ooze
Of the salt deep,
To run upon the sharp wind of the north,   370
To do me business in the veins o' the earth
When it is baked with frost.

ARIEL

I do not, sir.

PROSPERO

Thou liest, malignant thing! Hast thou forgot
The foul witch Sycorax, who with age and envy
Was grown into a hoop? hast thou forgot her?

ARIEL

No, sir.

PROSPERO

Thou hast. Where was she born? speak; tell me.

ARIEL

Sir, in Argier.

PROSPERO

O, was she so? I must   380
Once in a month recount what thou hast been,
Which thou forget'st. This damn'd witch Sycorax,
For mischiefs manifold and sorceries terrible
To enter human hearing, from Argier,
Thou know'st, was banish'd: for one thing she did
They would not take her life. Is not this true?

ARIEL

Ay, sir.

PROSPERO

This blue-eyed hag was hither brought with child
And here was left by the sailors. Thou, my slave,
As thou report'st thyself, wast then her servant;   390
And, for thou wast a spirit too delicate
To act her earthy and abhorr'd commands,
Refusing her grand hests, she did confine thee,
By help of her more potent ministers
And in her most unmitigable rage,
Into a cloven pine; within which rift
Imprison'd thou didst painfully remain
A dozen years; within which space she died
And left thee there; where thou didst vent thy groans
As fast as mill-wheels strike. Then was this island—   400
Save for the son that she did litter here,
A freckled whelp hag-born—not honour'd with
A human shape.

ARIEL

Yes, Caliban her son.

PROSPERO

Dull thing, I say so; he, that Caliban
Whom now I keep in service. Thou best know'st
What torment I did find thee in; thy groans
Did make wolves howl and penetrate the breasts
Of ever angry bears: it was a torment
To lay upon the damn'd, which Sycorax   410

Could not again undo: it was mine art,
When I arrived and heard thee, that made gape
The pine and let thee out.

ARIEL

I thank thee, master.

PROSPERO

If thou more murmur'st, I will rend an oak
And peg thee in his knotty entrails till
Thou hast howl'd away twelve winters.

ARIEL

Pardon, master; I will be correspondent to command
And do my spiriting gently.

PROSPERO

Do so, and after two days   420
I will discharge thee.

ARIEL

That's my noble master!
What shall I do? say what; what shall I do?

PROSPERO

Go make thyself like a nymph o' the sea: be subject
To no sight but thine and mine, invisible
To every eyeball else. Go take this shape
And hither come in't: go, hence with diligence!
Exit ARIEL
Awake, dear heart, awake! thou hast slept well; Awake!

MIRANDA

The strangeness of your story put
Heaviness in me.   430

PROSPERO

Shake it off. Come on;
We'll visit Caliban my slave, who never
Yields us kind answer.

MIRANDA

'Tis a villain, sir,
I do not love to look on.

PROSPERO

But, as 'tis,
We cannot miss him: he does make our fire,
Fetch in our wood and serves in offices
That profit us. What, ho! slave! Caliban!
Thou earth, thou! speak.   440

CALIBAN

[Within] There's wood enough within.

PROSPERO

Come forth, I say! there's other business for thee:
Come, thou tortoise! when?
Re-enter ARIEL like a water-nymph
Fine apparition! My quaint Ariel,
Hark in thine ear.

ARIEL

My lord it shall be done.
Exit

PROSPERO

Thou poisonous slave, got by the devil himself
Upon thy wicked dam, come forth!
Enter CALIBAN

CALIBAN

As wicked dew as e'er my mother brush'd
With raven's feather from unwholesome fen   450
Drop on you both! a south-west blow on ye
And blister you all o'er!

PROSPERO

For this, be sure, to-night thou shalt have cramps,
Side-stitches that shall pen thy breath up; urchins
Shall, for that vast of night that they may work,
All exercise on thee; thou shalt be pinch'd

As thick as honeycomb, each pinch more stinging
Than bees that made 'em.

CALIBAN

I must eat my dinner.
This island's mine, by Sycorax my mother,   460
Which thou takest from me. When thou camest first,
Thou strokedst me and madest much of me, wouldst give me
Water with berries in't, and teach me how
To name the bigger light, and how the less,
That burn by day and night: and then I loved thee
And show'd thee all the qualities o' the isle,
The fresh springs, brine-pits, barren place and fertile:
Cursed be I that did so! All the charms
Of Sycorax, toads, beetles, bats, light on you!
For I am all the subjects that you have,   470
Which first was mine own king: and here you sty me
In this hard rock, whiles you do keep from me
The rest o' the island.

PROSPERO

Thou most lying slave,
Whom stripes may move, not kindness! I have used thee,
Filth as thou art, with human care, and lodged thee
In mine own cell, till thou didst seek to violate
The honour of my child.

CALIBAN

O ho, O ho! would't had been done!
Thou didst prevent me; I had peopled else   480
This isle with Calibans.

PROSPERO

Abhorred slave,
Which any print of goodness wilt not take,
Being capable of all ill! I pitied thee,
Took pains to make thee speak, taught thee each hour
One thing or other: when thou didst not, savage,
Know thine own meaning, but wouldst gabble like
A thing most brutish, I endow'd thy purposes
With words that made them known. But thy vile race,

Though thou didst learn, had that in't which 490
good natures
Could not abide to be with; therefore wast thou
Deservedly confined into this rock,
Who hadst deserved more than a prison.

CALIBAN

You taught me language; and my profit on't
Is, I know how to curse. The red plague rid you
For learning me your language!

PROSPERO

Hag-seed, hence!
Fetch us in fuel; and be quick, thou'rt best,
To answer other business. Shrug'st thou, malice? 500
If thou neglect'st or dost unwillingly
What I command, I'll rack thee with old cramps,
Fill all thy bones with aches, make thee roar
That beasts shall tremble at thy din.

CALIBAN

No, pray thee.
[*Aside*] I must obey: his art is of such power,
It would control my dam's god, Setebos,
and make a vassal of him.

PROSPERO

So, slave; hence! 510
Exit CALIBAN
Re-enter ARIEL, invisible, playing and singing;
FERDINAND following

ARIEL'S song.
Come unto these yellow sands,
And then take hands:
Courtsied when you have and kiss'd
The wild waves whist,
Foot it featly here and there;
And, sweet sprites, the burthen bear.
Hark, hark!
Burthen dispersedly, within

The watch-dogs bark!
Burthen Bow-wow   520
Hark, hark! I hear
The strain of strutting chanticleer
Cry, Cock-a-diddle-dow.

FERDINAND

Where should this music be? i' the air or the earth?
It sounds no more: and sure, it waits upon
Some god o' the island. Sitting on a bank,
Weeping again the king my father's wreck,
This music crept by me upon the waters,
Allaying both their fury and my passion
With its sweet air: thence I have follow'd it,   530
Or it hath drawn me rather. But 'tis gone.
No, it begins again.

ARIEL sings
Full fathom five thy father lies;
Of his bones are coral made;
Those are pearls that were his eyes:
Nothing of him that doth fade
But doth suffer a sea-change
Into something rich and strange.
Sea-nymphs hourly ring his knell   540
Burthen Ding-dong
Hark! now I hear them,—Ding-dong, bell.

FERDINAND

The ditty does remember my drown'd father.
This is no mortal business, nor no sound
That the earth owes. I hear it now above me.

PROSPERO

The fringed curtains of thine eye advance
And say what thou seest yond.

MIRANDA

What is't? a spirit?
Lord, how it looks about! Believe me, sir,
It carries a brave form. But 'tis a spirit.   550

PROSPERO

No, wench; it eats and sleeps and hath such senses
As we have, such. This gallant which thou seest
Was in the wreck; and, but he's something stain'd
With grief that's beauty's canker, thou mightst call him
A goodly person: he hath lost his fellows
And strays about to find 'em.

MIRANDA

I might call him
A thing divine, for nothing natural
I ever saw so noble.

PROSPERO

[*Aside*] It goes on, I see,   560
As my soul prompts it. Spirit, fine spirit! I'll free thee
Within two days for this.

FERDINAND

Most sure, the goddess
On whom these airs attend! Vouchsafe my prayer
May know if you remain upon this island;
And that you will some good instruction give
How I may bear me here: my prime request,
Which I do last pronounce, is, O you wonder!
If you be maid or no?

MIRANDA

No wonder, sir;   570
But certainly a maid.

FERDINAND

My language! heavens!
I am the best of them that speak this speech,
Were I but where 'tis spoken.

PROSPERO

How? the best?
What wert thou, if the King of Naples heard thee?

FERDINAND

A single thing, as I am now, that wonders
To hear thee speak of Naples. He does hear me;
And that he does I weep: myself am Naples,
Who with mine eyes, never since at ebb, beheld   580
The king my father wreck'd.

MIRANDA

Alack, for mercy!

FERDINAND

Yes, faith, and all his lords; the Duke of Milan
And his brave son being twain.

PROSPERO

[*Aside*] The Duke of Milan
And his more braver daughter could control thee,
If now 'twere fit to do't. At the first sight
They have changed eyes. Delicate Ariel,
I'll set thee free for this.
To FERDINAND
A word, good sir;   590
I fear you have done yourself some wrong: a word.

MIRANDA

Why speaks my father so ungently? This
Is the third man that e'er I saw, the first   That e'er I
sigh'd for: pity move my father
To be inclined my way!

FERDINAND

O, if a virgin,
And your affection not gone forth, I'll make you
The queen of Naples.

PROSPERO

Soft, sir! one word more.
[*Aside*]
They are both in either's powers; but this swift business   600
I must uneasy make, lest too light winning
Make the prize light.

To FERDINAND
One word more; I charge thee
That thou attend me: thou dost here usurp
The name thou owest not; and hast put thyself
Upon this island as a spy, to win it
From me, the lord on't.

FERDINAND

No, as I am a man.

MIRANDA

There's nothing ill can dwell in such a temple:
If the ill spirit have so fair a house,   610
Good things will strive to dwell with't.

PROSPERO

Follow me.
Speak not you for him; he's a traitor. Come;
I'll manacle thy neck and feet together:
Sea-water shalt thou drink; thy food shall be
The fresh-brook muscles, wither'd roots and husks
Wherein the acorn cradled. Follow.

FERDINAND

No;
I will resist such entertainment till
Mine enemy has more power.   620
Draws, and is charmed from moving

MIRANDA

O dear father,
Make not too rash a trial of him, for
He's gentle and not fearful.

PROSPERO

What? I say,
My foot my tutor? Put thy sword up, traitor;
Who makest a show but darest not strike, thy conscience
Is so possess'd with guilt: come from thy ward,
For I can here disarm thee with this stick
And make thy weapon drop.   630

MIRANDA

Beseech you, father.

PROSPERO

Hence! hang not on my garments.

MIRANDA

Sir, have pity;
I'll be his surety.

PROSPERO

Silence! one word more
Shall make me chide thee, if not hate thee. What!
An advocate for an imposter! hush!
Thou think'st there is no more such shapes as he,
Having seen but him and Caliban: foolish wench!
To the most of men this is a Caliban   640
And they to him are angels.

MIRANDA

My affections
Are then most humble; I have no ambition
To see a goodlier man.

PROSPERO

Come on; obey:
Thy nerves are in their infancy again
And have no vigour in them.

FERDINAND

So they are;
My spirits, as in a dream, are all bound up.
My father's loss, the weakness which I feel,   650
The wreck of all my friends, nor this man's threats,
To whom I am subdued, are but light to me,
Might I but through my prison once a day
Behold this maid: all corners else o' the earth
Let liberty make use of; space enough
Have I in such a prison.

PROSPERO

[*Aside*] It works.

To FERDINAND
Come on.
Thou hast done well, fine Ariel!
To FERDINAND
Follow me.   660
To ARIEL
Hark what thou else shalt do me.

MIRANDA

Be of comfort;
My father's of a better nature, sir,
Than he appears by speech: this is unwonted
Which now came from him.

PROSPERO

Thou shalt be free
As mountain winds: but then exactly do
All points of my command.

ARIEL

To the syllable.

PROSPERO

Come, follow. Speak not for him.   670
Exeunt

ACT II

SCENE I. Another part of the island.
Enter ALONSO, SEBASTIAN, ANTONIO, GONZALO,
ADRIAN, FRANCISCO, and others

GONZALO

Beseech you, sir, be merry; you have cause,
So have we all, of joy; for our escape
Is much beyond our loss. Our hint of woe
Is common; every day some sailor's wife,
The masters of some merchant and the merchant
Have just our theme of woe; but for the miracle,
I mean our preservation, few in millions
Can speak like us: then wisely, good sir, weigh
Our sorrow with our comfort.

ALONSO

Prithee, peace.   680

SEBASTIAN

He receives comfort like cold porridge.

ANTONIO

The visitor will not give him o'er so.

SEBASTIAN

Look he's winding up the watch of his wit;
by and by it will strike.

GONZALO

Sir,—

SEBASTIAN

One: tell.

GONZALO

When every grief is entertain'd that's offer'd,
Comes to the entertainer—

SEBASTIAN

A dollar.

GONZALO

Dolour comes to him, indeed: you   690
have spoken truer than you purposed.

SEBASTIAN

You have taken it wiselier than I meant you should.

GONZALO

Therefore, my lord,—

ANTONIO

Fie, what a spendthrift is he of his tongue!

ALONSO

I prithee, spare.

GONZALO

Well, I have done: but yet,—

SEBASTIAN

He will be talking.

ANTONIO

Which, of he or Adrian, for a good
wager, first begins to crow?

SEBASTIAN

The old cock.   700

ANTONIO

The cockerel.

SEBASTIAN

Done. The wager?

ANTONIO

A laughter.

SEBASTIAN

A match!

ADRIAN

Though this island seem to be desert,—

SEBASTIAN

Ha, ha, ha! So, you're paid.

ADRIAN

Uninhabitable and almost inaccessible,—

SEBASTIAN

Yet,—

ADRIAN

Yet,—

ANTONIO

He could not miss't.   710

ADRIAN

It must needs be of subtle, tender and delicate temperance.

ANTONIO

Temperance was a delicate wench.

SEBASTIAN

Ay, and a subtle; as he most learnedly delivered.

ADRIAN

The air breathes upon us here most sweetly.

SEBASTIAN

As if it had lungs and rotten ones.

ANTONIO

Or as 'twere perfumed by a fen.

GONZALO

Here is everything advantageous to life.

ANTONIO

True; save means to live.

SEBASTIAN

Of that there's none, or little.

GONZALO

How lush and lusty the grass looks! how green!   720

ANTONIO

The ground indeed is tawny.

SEBASTIAN
With an eye of green in't.

ANTONIO
He misses not much.

SEBASTIAN
No; he doth but mistake the truth totally.

GONZALO
But the rarity of it is,—which is indeed almost beyond credit,—

SEBASTIAN
As many vouched rarities are.

GONZALO
That our garments, being, as they were, drenched in the sea, hold notwithstanding their freshness and glosses, being rather new-dyed than stained with salt water. 730

ANTONIO
If but one of his pockets could speak, would it not say he lies?
SEBASTIAN
Ay, or very falsely pocket up his report

GONZALO
Methinks our garments are now as fresh as when we put them on first in Afric, at the marriage of the king's fair daughter Claribel to the King of Tunis.

SEBASTIAN
'Twas a sweet marriage, and we prosper well in our return.

ADRIAN
Tunis was never graced before with such a paragon to their queen. 740

GONZALO

Not since widow Dido's time.

ANTONIO

Widow! a pox o' that! How came that widow in? Widow
Dido!

SEBASTIAN

What if he had said 'widower Aeneas' too? Good Lord,
how you take it!

ADRIAN

'Widow Dido' said you? you make me study of that:
she was of Carthage, not of Tunis.

GONZALO

This Tunis, sir, was Carthage.

ADRIAN

Carthage?

GONZALO

I assure you, Carthage.   750

SEBASTIAN

His word is more than the miraculous harp; he hath
raised the wall and houses too.

ANTONIO

What impossible matter will he make easy next?

SEBASTIAN

I think he will carry this island home in his pocket
and give it his son for an apple.

ANTONIO

And, sowing the kernels of it in the sea, bring
forth more islands.

GONZALO

Ay.

ANTONIO

Why, in good time.

GONZALO

Sir, we were talking that our garments seem now   760
as fresh as when we were at Tunis at the marriage
of your daughter, who is now queen.

ANTONIO

And the rarest that e'er came there.

SEBASTIAN

Bate, I beseech you, widow Dido.

ANTONIO

O, widow Dido! ay, widow Dido.

GONZALO

Is not, sir, my doublet as fresh as the first day I
wore it? I mean, in a sort.

ANTONIO

That sort was well fished for.

GONZALO

When I wore it at your daughter's marriage?

ALONSO

You cram these words into mine ears against   770
The stomach of my sense. Would I had never
Married my daughter there! for, coming thence,
My son is lost and, in my rate, she too,
Who is so far from Italy removed
I ne'er again shall see her. O thou mine heir
Of Naples and of Milan, what strange fish
Hath made his meal on thee?

FRANCISCO

Sir, he may live:
I saw him beat the surges under him,
And ride upon their backs; he trod the water, 780
Whose enmity he flung aside, and breasted
The surge most swoln that met him; his bold head
'Bove the contentious waves he kept, and oar'd
Himself with his good arms in lusty stroke
To the shore, that o'er his wave-worn basis bow'd,
As stooping to relieve him: I not doubt
He came alive to land.

ALONSO

No, no, he's gone.

SEBASTIAN

Sir, you may thank yourself for this great loss,
That would not bless our Europe with your daughter, 790
But rather lose her to an African;
Where she at least is banish'd from your eye,
Who hath cause to wet the grief on't.

ALONSO

Prithee, peace.

SEBASTIAN

You were kneel'd to and importuned otherwise
By all of us, and the fair soul herself
Weigh'd between loathness and obedience, at
Which end o' the beam should bow. We have lost your
son,
I fear, for ever: Milan and Naples have 800
More widows in them of this business' making
Than we bring men to comfort them:
The fault's your own.

ALONSO

So is the dear'st o' the loss.

GONZALO

My lord Sebastian,
The truth you speak doth lack some gentleness

And time to speak it in: you rub the sore,
When you should bring the plaster.

SEBASTIAN

Very well.

ANTONIO

And most chirurgeonly.   810

GONZALO

It is foul weather in us all, good sir,
When you are cloudy.

SEBASTIAN

Foul weather?

ANTONIO

Very foul.

GONZALO

Had I plantation of this isle, my lord,—

ANTONIO

He'ld sow't with nettle-seed.

SEBASTIAN

Or docks, or mallows.

GONZALO

And were the king on't, what would I do?

SEBASTIAN

'Scape being drunk for want of wine.

GONZALO

I' the commonwealth I would by contraries   820
Execute all things; for no kind of traffic
Would I admit; no name of magistrate;
Letters should not be known; riches, poverty,
And use of service, none; contract, succession,
Bourn, bound of land, tilth, vineyard, none;
No use of metal, corn, or wine, or oil;
No occupation; all men idle, all;

And women too, but innocent and pure;
No sovereignty;—

SEBASTIAN

Yet he would be king on't.   830

ANTONIO

The latter end of his commonwealth forgets the beginning.

GONZALO

All things in common nature should produce
Without sweat or endeavour: treason, felony,
Sword, pike, knife, gun, or need of any engine,
Would I not have; but nature should bring forth,
Of its own kind, all foison, all abundance,
To feed my innocent people.

SEBASTIAN

No marrying 'mong his subjects?

ANTONIO

None, man; all idle: whores and knaves.

GONZALO

I would with such perfection govern, sir,   840
To excel the golden age.

SEBASTIAN

God save his majesty!

ANTONIO

Long live Gonzalo!

GONZALO

And,—do you mark me, sir?

ALONSO

Prithee, no more: thou dost talk nothing to me.

GONZALO

I do well believe your highness; and
did it to minister occasion to these gentlemen,

who are of such sensible and nimble lungs that
they always use to laugh at nothing.

ANTONIO

'Twas you we laughed at.   850

GONZALO

Who in this kind of merry fooling am nothing
to you: so you may continue and laugh at
nothing still.

ANTONIO

What a blow was there given!

SEBASTIAN

An it had not fallen flat-long.

GONZALO

You are gentlemen of brave metal; you would lift
the moon out of her sphere, if she would continue
in it five weeks without changing.
Enter ARIEL, invisible, playing solemn music

SEBASTIAN

We would so, and then go a bat-fowling.

ANTONIO

Nay, good my lord, be not angry.   860

GONZALO

No, I warrant you; I will not adventure
my discretion so weakly. Will you laugh
me asleep, for I am very heavy?

ANTONIO

Go sleep, and hear us.
All sleep except ALONSO, SEBASTIAN, and ANTONIO

ALONSO

What, all so soon asleep! I wish mine eyes
Would, with themselves, shut up my thoughts: I find
They are inclined to do so.

SEBASTIAN

Please you, sir,
Do not omit the heavy offer of it:
It seldom visits sorrow; when it doth,   870
It is a comforter.

ANTONIO

We two, my lord,
Will guard your person while you take your rest,
And watch your safety.

ALONSO

Thank you. Wondrous heavy.
ALONSO sleeps. Exit ARIEL

SEBASTIAN

What a strange drowsiness possesses them!

ANTONIO

It is the quality o' the climate.

SEBASTIAN

Why
Doth it not then our eyelids sink? I find not
Myself disposed to sleep.   880

ANTONIO

Nor I; my spirits are nimble.
They fell together all, as by consent;
They dropp'd, as by a thunder-stroke. What might,
Worthy Sebastian? O, what might?—No more:—
And yet me thinks I see it in thy face,
What thou shouldst be: the occasion speaks thee, and
My strong imagination sees a crown
Dropping upon thy head.

SEBASTIAN

What, art thou waking?

ANTONIO

Do you not hear me speak?   890

SEBASTIAN

I do; and surely
It is a sleepy language and thou speak'st
Out of thy sleep. What is it thou didst say?
This is a strange repose, to be asleep
With eyes wide open; standing, speaking, moving,
And yet so fast asleep.

ANTONIO

Noble Sebastian,
Thou let'st thy fortune sleep—die, rather; wink'st
Whiles thou art waking.

SEBASTIAN

Thou dost snore distinctly;   900
There's meaning in thy snores.

ANTONIO

I am more serious than my custom: you
Must be so too, if heed me; which to do
Trebles thee o'er.

SEBASTIAN

Well, I am standing water.

ANTONIO

I'll teach you how to flow.

SEBASTIAN

Do so: to ebb
Hereditary sloth instructs me.

ANTONIO

O,
If you but knew how you the purpose cherish   910
Whiles thus you mock it! how, in stripping it,
You more invest it! Ebbing men, indeed,
Most often do so near the bottom run
By their own fear or sloth.

SEBASTIAN

Prithee, say on:
The setting of thine eye and cheek proclaim
A matter from thee, and a birth indeed
Which throes thee much to yield.

ANTONIO

Thus, sir:
Although this lord of weak remembrance, this,   920
Who shall be of as little memory
When he is earth'd, hath here almost persuade,—
For he's a spirit of persuasion, only
Professes to persuade,—the king his son's alive,
'Tis as impossible that he's undrown'd
And he that sleeps here swims.

SEBASTIAN

I have no hope
That he's undrown'd.

ANTONIO

O, out of that 'no hope'
What great hope have you! no hope that way is   930
Another way so high a hope that even
Ambition cannot pierce a wink beyond,
But doubt discovery there. Will you grant with me
That Ferdinand is drown'd?

SEBASTIAN

He's gone.

ANTONIO

Then, tell me,
Who's the next heir of Naples?

SEBASTIAN

Claribel.

ANTONIO

She that is queen of Tunis; she that dwells
Ten leagues beyond man's life; she that from Naples   940
Can have no note, unless the sun were post—

176

The man i' the moon's too slow—till new-born chins
Be rough and razorable; she that—from whom?
We all were sea-swallow'd, though some cast again,
And by that destiny to perform an act
Whereof what's past is prologue, what to come
In yours and my discharge.

SEBASTIAN

What stuff is this! how say you?
'Tis true, my brother's daughter's queen of Tunis;
So is she heir of Naples; 'twixt which regions   950
There is some space.

ANTONIO

A space whose every cubit
Seems to cry out, 'How shall that Claribel
Measure us back to Naples? Keep in Tunis,
And let Sebastian wake.' Say, this were death
That now hath seized them; why, they were no worse
Than now they are. There be that can rule Naples
As well as he that sleeps; lords that can prate
As amply and unnecessarily
As this Gonzalo; I myself could make   960
A chough of as deep chat. O, that you bore
The mind that I do! what a sleep were this
For your advancement! Do you understand me?

SEBASTIAN

Methinks I do.

ANTONIO

And how does your content
Tender your own good fortune?

SEBASTIAN

I remember
You did supplant your brother Prospero.

ANTONIO

True:
And look how well my garments sit upon me;   970

177

Much feater than before: my brother's servants
Were then my fellows; now they are my men.

SEBASTIAN

But, for your conscience?

ANTONIO

Ay, sir; where lies that? if 'twere a kibe,
'Twould put me to my slipper: but I feel not
This deity in my bosom: twenty consciences,
That stand 'twixt me and Milan, candied be they
And melt ere they molest! Here lies your brother,
No better than the earth he lies upon,
If he were that which now he's like, that's dead;   980
Whom I, with this obedient steel, three inches of it,
Can lay to bed for ever; whiles you, doing thus,
To the perpetual wink for aye might put
This ancient morsel, this Sir Prudence, who
Should not upbraid our course. For all the rest,
They'll take suggestion as a cat laps milk;
They'll tell the clock to any business that
We say befits the hour.

SEBASTIAN

Thy case, dear friend,
Shall be my precedent; as thou got'st Milan,   990
I'll come by Naples. Draw thy sword: one stroke
Shall free thee from the tribute which thou payest;
And I the king shall love thee.

ANTONIO

Draw together;
And when I rear my hand, do you the like,
To fall it on Gonzalo.

SEBASTIAN

O, but one word.
They talk apart
Re-enter ARIEL, invisible

ARIEL

My master through his art foresees the danger

That you, his friend, are in; and sends me forth—   1000
For else his project dies—to keep them living.
Sings in GONZALO's ear
While you here do snoring lie,
Open-eyed conspiracy
His time doth take.
If of life you keep a care,
Shake off slumber, and beware:
Awake, awake!

ANTONIO

Then let us both be sudden.

GONZALO

Now, good angels
Preserve the king.   1010
They wake

ALONSO

Why, how now? ho, awake! Why are you drawn?
Wherefore this ghastly looking?

GONZALO

What's the matter?

SEBASTIAN

Whiles we stood here securing your repose,
Even now, we heard a hollow burst of bellowing
Like bulls, or rather lions: did't not wake you?
It struck mine ear most terribly.

ALONSO

I heard nothing.

ANTONIO

O, 'twas a din to fright a monster's ear,   1020
To make an earthquake! sure, it was the roar
Of a whole herd of lions.

ALONSO

Heard you this, Gonzalo?

GONZALO

Upon mine honour, sir, I heard a humming,
And that a strange one too, which did awake me:
I shaked you, sir, and cried: as mine eyes open'd,
I saw their weapons drawn: there was a noise,
That's verily. 'Tis best we stand upon our guard,
Or that we quit this place; let's draw our weapons.

ALONSO

Lead off this ground; and let's make further search   1030
For my poor son.

GONZALO

Heavens keep him from these beasts!
For he is, sure, i' the island.

ALONSO

Lead away.

ARIEL

Prospero my lord shall know what I have done:
So, king, go safely on to seek thy son.
Exeunt

SCENE II. Another part of the island.
*Enter CALIBAN with a burden of wood. A noise of
thunder heard*

CALIBAN

All the infections that the sun sucks up
From bogs, fens, flats, on Prosper fall and make him
By inch-meal a disease! His spirits hear me
And yet I needs must curse. But they'll nor pinch,   1040
Fright me with urchin—shows, pitch me i' the mire,
Nor lead me, like a firebrand, in the dark
Out of my way, unless he bid 'em; but
For every trifle are they set upon me;
Sometime like apes that mow and chatter at me
And after bite me, then like hedgehogs which
Lie tumbling in my barefoot way and mount
Their pricks at my footfall; sometime am I

All wound with adders who with cloven tongues
Do hiss me into madness.   1050
Enter TRINCULO
Lo, now, lo!
Here comes a spirit of his, and to torment me
For bringing wood in slowly. I'll fall flat;
Perchance he will not mind me.

TRINCULO

Here's neither bush nor shrub, to bear off
any weather at all, and another storm brewing;
I hear it sing i' the wind: yond same black
cloud, yond huge one, looks like a foul
bombard that would shed his liquor. If it should thunder
as it did before, I know not   1060
where to hide my head: yond same cloud cannot
choose but fall by pailfuls. What have we
here? a man or a fish? dead or alive? A fish:
he smells like a fish; a very ancient and fish-
like smell; a kind of not of the newest Poor-
John. A strange fish! Were I in England now,
as once I was, and had but this fish painted,
not a holiday fool there but would give a piece
of silver: there would this monster make a man; any
strange beast there makes a man: 1070
when they will not give a doit to relieve a lame
beggar, they will lazy out ten to see a dead
Indian. Legged like a man and his fins like
arms! Warm o' my troth! I do now let loose
my opinion; hold it no longer: this is no fish,
but an islander, that hath lately suffered by a
thunderbolt.
Thunder
Alas, the storm is come again! my best way is to
creep under his gaberdine; there is no other
shelter hereabouts: misery acquaints a man with   1080
strange bed-fellows. I will here shroud till the
dregs of the storm be past.
Enter STEPHANO, singing: a bottle in his hand

STEPHANO

I shall no more to sea, to sea,
Here shall I die ashore—
This is a very scurvy tune to sing at a man's
funeral: well, here's my comfort.
Drinks
Sings
The master, the swabber, the boatswain and I,
The gunner and his mate
Loved Mall, Meg and Marian and Margery,
But none of us cared for Kate;   1090
For she had a tongue with a tang,
Would cry to a sailor, Go hang!
She loved not the savour of tar nor of pitch,
Yet a tailor might scratch her where'er she did itch:
Then to sea, boys, and let her go hang!
This is a scurvy tune too: but here's my comfort.
Drinks

CALIBAN

Do not torment me: Oh!

STEPHANO

What's the matter? Have we devils here? Do you put
tricks upon's with savages and men of Ind, ha?
I have not scaped drowning to be afeard now of your   1100
four legs; for it hath been said, As proper a man as
ever went on four legs cannot make him give ground;
and it shall be said so again while Stephano
breathes at's nostrils.

CALIBAN

The spirit torments me; Oh!

STEPHANO

This is some monster of the isle with four legs, who
hath got, as I take it, an ague. Where the devil
should he learn our language? I will give him some
relief, if it be but for that. if I can recover him

and keep him tame and get to Naples with him, he's a   1110
present for any emperor that ever trod on neat's leather.

CALIBAN

Do not torment me, prithee; I'll bring my wood home
faster.

STEPHANO

He's in his fit now and does not talk after the
wisest. He shall taste of my bottle: if he have
never drunk wine afore will go near to remove his
fit. If I can recover him and keep him tame, I will
not take too much for him; he shall pay for him that
hath him, and that soundly.

CALIBAN

Thou dost me yet but little hurt; thou wilt anon,   1120
I know it by thy trembling: now Prosper works upon thee.

STEPHANO

Come on your ways; open your mouth; here is that
which will give language to you, cat: open your
mouth; this will shake your shaking, I can tell you,
and that soundly: you cannot tell who's your friend:
open your chaps again.

TRINCULO

I should know that voice: it should be—but he is
drowned; and these are devils: O defend me!

STEPHANO

Four legs and two voices: a most delicate monster!
His forward voice now is to speak well of his
friend; his backward voice is to utter foul speeches   1130
and to detract. If all the wine in my bottle will
recover him, I will help his ague. Come. Amen! I
will pour some in thy other mouth.

TRINCULO

Stephano!

STEPHANO

Doth thy other mouth call me? Mercy, mercy! This is
a devil, and no monster: I will leave him; I have no
long spoon.

TRINCULO

Stephano! If thou beest Stephano, touch me and
speak to me: for I am Trinculo—be not afeard—thy
good friend Trinculo.   1140

STEPHANO

If thou beest Trinculo, come forth: I'll pull thee
by the lesser legs: if any be Trinculo's legs,
these are they. Thou art very Trinculo indeed! How
camest thou to be the siege of this moon-calf? can
he vent Trinculos?

TRINCULO

I took him to be killed with a thunder-stroke. But
art thou not drowned, Stephano? I hope now thou art
not drowned. Is the storm overblown? I hid me
under the dead moon-calf's gaberdine for fear of
the storm. And art thou living, Stephano? O   1150
Stephano, two Neapolitans 'scaped!

STEPHANO

Prithee, do not turn me about; my stomach is not constant.

CALIBAN

[*Aside*] These be fine things, an if they be not sprites.
That's a brave god and bears celestial liquor.
I will kneel to him.

STEPHANO

How didst thou 'scape? How camest thou hither?
swear by this bottle how thou camest hither. I
escaped upon a butt of sack which the sailors
heaved o'erboard, by this bottle; which I made of
the bark of a tree with mine own hands since I was   1160
cast ashore.

CALIBAN

I'll swear upon that bottle to be thy true subject;
for the liquor is not earthly.

STEPHANO

Here; swear then how thou escapedst.

TRINCULO

Swum ashore, man, like a duck: I can swim like a
duck, I'll be sworn.

STEPHANO

Here, kiss the book. Though thou canst swim like a
duck, thou art made like a goose.

TRINCULO

O Stephano, hast any more of this?

STEPHANO

The whole butt, man: my cellar is in a rock by the   1170
sea-side where my wine is hid. How now, moon-calf!
how does thine ague?

CALIBAN

Hast thou not dropp'd from heaven?

STEPHANO

Out o' the moon, I do assure thee: I was the man i'
the moon when time was.

CALIBAN

I have seen thee in her and I do adore thee:
My mistress show'd me thee and thy dog and thy bush.

STEPHANO

Come, swear to that; kiss the book: I will furnish
it anon with new contents swear.

TRINCULO

By this good light, this is a very shallow monster!   1180
I afeard of him! A very weak monster! The man i'

185

the moon! A most poor credulous monster! Well
drawn, monster, in good sooth!

CALIBAN

I'll show thee every fertile inch o' th' island;
And I will kiss thy foot: I prithee, be my god.

TRINCULO

By this light, a most perfidious and drunken
monster! when 's god's asleep, he'll rob his bottle.

CALIBAN

I'll kiss thy foot; I'll swear myself thy subject.

STEPHANO

Come on then; down, and swear.

TRINCULO

I shall laugh myself to death at this puppy-headed   1190
monster. A most scurvy monster! I could find in my
heart to beat him,—

STEPHANO

Come, kiss.

TRINCULO

But that the poor monster's in drink: an abominable monster!

CALIBAN

I'll show thee the best springs; I'll pluck thee berries;
I'll fish for thee and get thee wood enough.
A plague upon the tyrant that I serve!
I'll bear him no more sticks, but follow thee,
Thou wondrous man.

TRINCULO

A most ridiculous monster, to make a wonder of a   1200
Poor drunkard!

CALIBAN

I prithee, let me bring thee where crabs grow;
And I with my long nails will dig thee pignuts;

Show thee a jay's nest and instruct thee how
To snare the nimble marmoset; I'll bring thee
To clustering filberts and sometimes I'll get thee
Young scamels from the rock. Wilt thou go with me?

STEPHANO

I prithee now, lead the way without any more
talking. Trinculo, the king and all our company
else being drowned, we will inherit here: here;   1210
bear my bottle: fellow Trinculo, we'll fill him by and by again.

CALIBAN

Sings drunkenly
Farewell master; farewell, farewell!

TRINCULO

A howling monster: a drunken monster!

CALIBAN

No more dams I'll make for fish
Nor fetch in firing
At requiring;
Nor scrape trencher, nor wash dish
'Ban, 'Ban, Cacaliban
Has a new master: get a new man.   1220
Freedom, hey-day! hey-day, freedom! freedom,
hey-day, freedom!

STEPHANO

O brave monster! Lead the way.
Exeunt

ACT III

SCENE I. Before PROSPERO'S Cell.
Enter FERDINAND, bearing a log

FERDINAND

There be some sports are painful, and their labour
Delight in them sets off: some kinds of baseness
Are nobly undergone and most poor matters
Point to rich ends. This my mean task

Would be as heavy to me as odious, but
The mistress which I serve quickens what's dead
And makes my labours pleasures: O, she is   1230
Ten times more gentle than her father's crabbed,
And he's composed of harshness. I must remove
Some thousands of these logs and pile them up,
Upon a sore injunction: my sweet mistress
Weeps when she sees me work, and says, such baseness
Had never like executor. I forget:
But these sweet thoughts do even refresh my labours,
Most busy lest, when I do it.
Enter MIRANDA; and PROSPERO at a distance, unseen

MIRANDA

Alas, now, pray you,
Work not so hard: I would the lightning had   1240
Burnt up those logs that you are enjoin'd to pile!
Pray, set it down and rest you: when this burns,
'Twill weep for having wearied you. My father
Is hard at study; pray now, rest yourself;
He's safe for these three hours.

FERDINAND

O most dear mistress,
The sun will set before I shall discharge
What I must strive to do.

MIRANDA

If you'll sit down,
I'll bear your logs the while: pray, give me that;   1250
I'll carry it to the pile.

FERDINAND

No, precious creature;
I had rather crack my sinews, break my back,
Than you should such dishonour undergo,
While I sit lazy by.

MIRANDA

It would become me
As well as it does you: and I should do it

With much more ease; for my good will is to it,
And yours it is against.

PROSPERO

Poor worm, thou art infected!   1260
This visitation shows it.

MIRANDA

You look wearily.

FERDINAND

No, noble mistress;'tis fresh morning with me
When you are by at night. I do beseech you—
Chiefly that I might set it in my prayers—
What is your name?

MIRANDA

Miranda.—O my father,
I have broke your hest to say so!

FERDINAND

Admired Miranda!
Indeed the top of admiration! worth   1270
What's dearest to the world! Full many a lady
I have eyed with best regard and many a time
The harmony of their tongues hath into bondage
Brought my too diligent ear: for several virtues
Have I liked several women; never any
With so fun soul, but some defect in her
Did quarrel with the noblest grace she owed
And put it to the foil: but you, O you,
So perfect and so peerless, are created
Of every creature's best!   1280

MIRANDA

I do not know
One of my sex; no woman's face remember,
Save, from my glass, mine own; nor have I seen
More that I may call men than you, good friend,
And my dear father: how features are abroad,
I am skilless of; but, by my modesty,

The jewel in my dower, I would not wish
Any companion in the world but you,
Nor can imagination form a shape,
Besides yourself, to like of. But I prattle   1290
Something too wildly and my father's precepts
I therein do forget.

FERDINAND

I am in my condition
A prince, Miranda; I do think, a king;
I would, not so!—and would no more endure
This wooden slavery than to suffer
The flesh-fly blow my mouth. Hear my soul speak:
The very instant that I saw you, did
My heart fly to your service; there resides,
To make me slave to it; and for your sake   1300
Am I this patient log—man.

MIRANDA

Do you love me?

FERDINAND

O heaven, O earth, bear witness to this sound
And crown what I profess with kind event
If I speak true! if hollowly, invert
What best is boded me to mischief! I
Beyond all limit of what else i' the world
Do love, prize, honour you.

MIRANDA

I am a fool
To weep at what I am glad of.   1310

PROSPERO

Fair encounter
Of two most rare affections! Heavens rain grace
On that which breeds between 'em!

FERDINAND

Wherefore weep you?

MIRANDA

At mine unworthiness that dare not offer
What I desire to give, and much less take
What I shall die to want. But this is trifling;
And all the more it seeks to hide itself,
The bigger bulk it shows. Hence, bashful cunning!
And prompt me, plain and holy innocence!   1320
I am your wife, if you will marry me;
If not, I'll die your maid: to be your fellow
You may deny me; but I'll be your servant,
Whether you will or no.

FERDINAND

My mistress, dearest;
And I thus humble ever.

MIRANDA

My husband, then?

FERDINAND

Ay, with a heart as willing
As bondage e'er of freedom: here's my hand.

MIRANDA

And mine, with my heart in't; and now farewell   1330
Till half an hour hence.

FERDINAND

A thousand thousand!
Exeunt FERDINAND and MIRANDA severally

PROSPERO

So glad of this as they I cannot be,
Who are surprised withal; but my rejoicing
At nothing can be more. I'll to my book,
For yet ere supper-time must I perform
Much business appertaining.
Exit

SCENE II. Another part of the island.
Enter CALIBAN, STEPHANO, and TRINCULO

STEPHANO

Tell not me; when the butt is out, we will drink
water; not a drop before: therefore bear up, and
board 'em. Servant-monster, drink to me. 1340

TRINCULO

Servant-monster! the folly of this island! They
say there's but five upon this isle: we are three
of them; if th' other two be brained like us, the
state totters.

STEPHANO

Drink, servant-monster, when I bid thee: thy eyes
are almost set in thy head.

TRINCULO

Where should they be set else? he were a brave
monster indeed, if they were set in his tail.

STEPHANO

My man-monster hath drown'd his tongue in sack:
for my part, the sea cannot drown me; I swam, ere 1350
I could recover the shore, five and thirty leagues off
and on. By this light, thou shalt be my lieutenant,
monster, or my standard.

TRINCULO

Your lieutenant, if you list; he's no standard.

STEPHANO

We'll not run, Monsieur Monster.

TRINCULO

Nor go neither; but you'll lie like dogs and yet say
nothing neither.

STEPHANO

Moon-calf, speak once in thy life, if thou beest a
good moon-calf.

CALIBAN

How does thy honour? Let me lick thy shoe.   1360
I'll not serve him; he's not valiant.

TRINCULO

Thou liest, most ignorant monster: I am in case to
justle a constable. Why, thou deboshed fish thou,
was there ever man a coward that hath drunk so much
sack as I to-day? Wilt thou tell a monstrous lie,
being but half a fish and half a monster?

CALIBAN

Lo, how he mocks me! wilt thou let him, my lord?

TRINCULO

'Lord' quoth he! That a monster should be such a natural!

CALIBAN

Lo, lo, again! bite him to death, I prithee.

STEPHANO

Trinculo, keep a good tongue in your head: if you   1370
prove a mutineer,—the next tree! The poor monster's
my subject and he shall not suffer indignity.

CALIBAN

I thank my noble lord. Wilt thou be pleased to
hearken once again to the suit I made to thee?

STEPHANO

Marry, will I kneel and repeat it; I will stand,
and so shall Trinculo.
Enter ARIEL, invisible

CALIBAN

As I told thee before, I am subject to a tyrant, a sorcerer,
that by his cunning hath cheated me of the island.

ARIEL

Thou liest.

CALIBAN

Thou liest, thou jesting monkey, thou: I would my   1380
valiant master would destroy thee! I do not lie.

STEPHANO

Trinculo, if you trouble him any more in's tale, by
this hand, I will supplant some of your teeth.

TRINCULO

Why, I said nothing.

STEPHANO

Mum, then, and no more. Proceed.

CALIBAN

I say, by sorcery he got this isle;
From me he got it. if thy greatness will
Revenge it on him,—for I know thou darest,
But this thing dare not,—

STEPHANO

That's most certain.   1390

CALIBAN

Thou shalt be lord of it and I'll serve thee.

STEPHANO

How now shall this be compassed?
Canst thou bring me to the party?

CALIBAN

Yea, yea, my lord: I'll yield him thee asleep,
Where thou mayst knock a nail into his bead.

ARIEL

Thou liest; thou canst not.

CALIBAN

What a pied ninny's this! Thou scurvy patch!
I do beseech thy greatness, give him blows

And take his bottle from him: when that's gone
He shall drink nought but brine; for I'll not show him   1400
Where the quick freshes are.

STEPHANO

Trinculo, run into no further danger:
interrupt the monster one word further, and,
by this hand, I'll turn my mercy out o' doors
and make a stock-fish of thee.

TRINCULO

Why, what did I? I did nothing. I'll go farther off.

STEPHANO

Didst thou not say he lied?

ARIEL

Thou liest.

STEPHANO

Do I so? take thou that.
Beats TRINCULO
As you like this, give me the lie another time.   1410

TRINCULO

I did not give the lie. Out o' your
wits and bearing too? A pox o' your bottle!
this can sack and drinking do. A murrain on
your monster, and the devil take your fingers!

CALIBAN

Ha, ha, ha!

STEPHANO

Now, forward with your tale. Prithee, stand farther off.

CALIBAN

Beat him enough: after a little time
I'll beat him too.

STEPHANO
Stand farther. Come, proceed.

CALIBAN
Why, as I told thee, 'tis a custom with him,   1420
I' th' afternoon to sleep: there thou mayst brain him,
Having first seized his books, or with a log
Batter his skull, or paunch him with a stake,
Or cut his wezand with thy knife. Remember
First to possess his books; for without them
He's but a sot, as I am, nor hath not
One spirit to command: they all do hate him
As rootedly as I. Burn but his books.
He has brave utensils,—for so he calls them—
Which when he has a house, he'll deck withal   1430
And that most deeply to consider is
The beauty of his daughter; he himself
Calls her a nonpareil: I never saw a woman,
But only Sycorax my dam and she;
But she as far surpasseth Sycorax
As great'st does least.

STEPHANO
Is it so brave a lass?

CALIBAN
Ay, lord; she will become thy bed, I warrant.
And bring thee forth brave brood.

STEPHANO
Monster, I will kill this man: his daughter and I   1440
will be king and queen—save our graces!—and
Trinculo and thyself shall be viceroys. Dost thou
like the plot, Trinculo?

TRINCULO
Excellent.

STEPHANO
Give me thy hand: I am sorry I beat thee; but,
while thou livest, keep a good tongue in thy head.

CALIBAN

Within this half hour will he be asleep:
Wilt thou destroy him then?

STEPHANO

Ay, on mine honour.

ARIEL

This will I tell my master.   1450

CALIBAN

Thou makest me merry; I am full of pleasure:
Let us be jocund: will you troll the catch
You taught me but while-ere?

STEPHANO

At thy request, monster, I will do reason, any
reason. Come on, Trinculo, let us sing.
Sings
Flout 'em and scout 'em
And scout 'em and flout 'em
Thought is free.

CALIBAN

That's not the tune.
ARIEL plays the tune on a tabour and pipe   1460

STEPHANO

What is this same?

TRINCULO

This is the tune of our catch, played by the picture
of Nobody.

STEPHANO

If thou beest a man, show thyself in thy likeness:
if thou beest a devil, take't as thou list.

TRINCULO

O, forgive me my sins!

STEPHANO

He that dies pays all debts: I defy thee. Mercy upon us!

CALIBAN

Art thou afeard?

STEPHANO

No, monster, not I.

CALIBAN

Be not afeard; the isle is full of noises,   1470
Sounds and sweet airs, that give delight and hurt not.
Sometimes a thousand twangling instruments
Will hum about mine ears, and sometime voices
That, if I then had waked after long sleep,
Will make me sleep again: and then, in dreaming,
The clouds methought would open and show riches
Ready to drop upon me that, when I waked,
I cried to dream again.

STEPHANO

This will prove a brave kingdom to me, where I shall
have my music for nothing.   1480

CALIBAN

When Prospero is destroyed.

STEPHANO

That shall be by and by: I remember the story.

TRINCULO

The sound is going away; let's follow it, and
after do our work.

STEPHANO

Lead, monster; we'll follow. I would I could see
this tabourer; he lays it on.

TRINCULO

Wilt come? I'll follow, Stephano.
Exeunt

SCENE III. Another part of the island.

Enter ALONSO, SEBASTIAN, ANTONIO, GONZALO, ADRIAN, FRANCISCO, and others

GONZALO

By'r lakin, I can go no further, sir;
My old bones ache: here's a maze trod indeed
Through forth-rights and meanders! By your patience,   1490
I needs must rest me.

ALONSO

Old lord, I cannot blame thee,
Who am myself attach'd with weariness,
To the dulling of my spirits: sit down, and rest.
Even here I will put off my hope and keep it
No longer for my flatterer: he is drown'd
Whom thus we stray to find, and the sea mocks
Our frustrate search on land. Well, let him go.

ANTONIO

[*Aside to SEBASTIAN*]
I am right glad that he's so out of hope.
Do not, for one repulse, forego the purpose   1500
That you resolved to effect.

SEBASTIAN

[*Aside to ANTONIO*] The next advantage
Will we take throughly.

ANTONIO

[*Aside to SEBASTIAN*] Let it be to-night;
For, now they are oppress'd with travel, they
Will not, nor cannot, use such vigilance
As when they are fresh.

SEBASTIAN

[*Aside to ANTONIO*] I say, to-night: no more.
Solemn and strange music

ALONSO

What harmony is this? My good friends, hark!   1510

GONZALO

Marvellous sweet music!
*Enter PROSPERO above, invisible. Enter several
strange Shapes, bringing in a banquet; they dance about
it with gentle actions of salutation; and, inviting the
King, &c. to eat, they depart*

ALONSO

Give us kind keepers, heavens! What were these?

SEBASTIAN

A living drollery. Now I will believe
That there are unicorns, that in Arabia
There is one tree, the phoenix' throne, one phoenix
At this hour reigning there.

ANTONIO

I'll believe both;
And what does else want credit, come to me,
And I'll be sworn 'tis true: travellers ne'er did lie,
Though fools at home condemn 'em.   1520

GONZALO

If in Naples
I should report this now, would they believe me?
If I should say, I saw such islanders—
For, certes, these are people of the island—
Who, though they are of monstrous shape, yet, note,
Their manners are more gentle-kind than of
Our human generation you shall find
Many, nay, almost any.

PROSPERO

[*Aside*] Honest lord,
Thou hast said well; for some of you there present   1530
Are worse than devils.

ALONSO

I cannot too much muse
Such shapes, such gesture and such sound, expressing,
Although they want the use of tongue, a kind
Of excellent dumb discourse.

PROSPERO

[*Aside*] Praise in departing.

FRANCISCO

They vanish'd strangely.

SEBASTIAN

No matter, since
They have left their viands behind; for we have stomachs.
Will't please you taste of what is here?   1540

ALONSO

Not I.

GONZALO

Faith, sir, you need not fear. When we were boys,
Who would believe that there were mountaineers
Dew-lapp'd like bulls, whose throats had hanging at 'em
Wallets of flesh? or that there were such men
Whose heads stood in their breasts? which now we find
Each putter-out of five for one will bring us
Good warrant of.

ALONSO

I will stand to and feed,
Although my last: no matter, since I feel   1550
The best is past. Brother, my lord the duke,
Stand to and do as we.
*Thunder and lightning. Enter ARIEL, like a harpy; claps
his wings upon the table; and, with a quaint device, the
banquet vanishes*

ARIEL

You are three men of sin, whom Destiny,
That hath to instrument this lower world
And what is in't, the never-surfeited sea
Hath caused to belch up you; and on this island
Where man doth not inhabit; you 'mongst men
Being most unfit to live. I have made you mad;
And even with such-like valour men hang and drown
Their proper selves.   1560
ALONSO, SEBASTIAN &c. draw their swords

201

You fools! I and my fellows
Are ministers of Fate: the elements,
Of whom your swords are temper'd, may as well
Wound the loud winds, or with bemock'd-at stabs
Kill the still-closing waters, as diminish
One dowle that's in my plume: my fellow-ministers
Are like invulnerable. If you could hurt,
Your swords are now too massy for your strengths
And will not be uplifted. But remember—
For that's my business to you—that you three   1570
From Milan did supplant good Prospero;
Exposed unto the sea, which hath requit it,
Him and his innocent child: for which foul deed
The powers, delaying, not forgetting, have
Incensed the seas and shores, yea, all the creatures,
Against your peace. Thee of thy son, Alonso,
They have bereft; and do pronounce by me:
Lingering perdition, worse than any death
Can be at once, shall step by step attend
You and your ways; whose wraths to guard you from—   1580
Which here, in this most desolate isle, else falls
Upon your heads—is nothing but heart-sorrow
And a clear life ensuing.
He vanishes in thunder; then, to soft music enter the
Shapes again, and dance, with mocks and mows, and
carrying out the table

PROSPERO

Bravely the figure of this harpy hast thou
Perform'd, my Ariel; a grace it had, devouring:
Of my instruction hast thou nothing bated
In what thou hadst to say: so, with good life
And observation strange, my meaner ministers
Their several kinds have done. My high charms work
And these mine enemies are all knit up   1590
In their distractions; they now are in my power;
And in these fits I leave them, while I visit
Young Ferdinand, whom they suppose is drown'd,
And his and mine loved darling.
Exit above

GONZALO
I' the name of something holy, sir, why stand you
In this strange stare?

ALONSO
O, it is monstrous, monstrous:
Methought the billows spoke and told me of it;
The winds did sing it to me, and the thunder,
That deep and dreadful organ-pipe, pronounced   1600
The name of Prosper: it did bass my trespass.
Therefore my son i' the ooze is bedded, and
I'll seek him deeper than e'er plummet sounded
And with him there lie mudded.
Exit

SEBASTIAN
But one fiend at a time,
I'll fight their legions o'er.

ANTONIO
I'll be thy second.
Exeunt SEBASTIAN, and ANTONIO

GONZALO
All three of them are desperate: their great guilt,
Like poison given to work a great time after,
Now 'gins to bite the spirits. I do beseech you   1610
That are of suppler joints, follow them swiftly
And hinder them from what this ecstasy
May now provoke them to.

ADRIAN
Follow, I pray you.
Exeunt

ACT IV

SCENE I. Before PROSPERO'S cell.
Enter PROSPERO, FERDINAND, and MIRANDA

PROSPERO

If I have too austerely punish'd you,
Your compensation makes amends, for I
Have given you here a third of mine own life,
Or that for which I live; who once again
I tender to thy hand: all thy vexations
Were but my trials of thy love and thou   1620
Hast strangely stood the test here, afore Heaven,
I ratify this my rich gift. O Ferdinand,
Do not smile at me that I boast her off,
For thou shalt find she will outstrip all praise
And make it halt behind her.

FERDINAND

I do believe it
Against an oracle.

PROSPERO

Then, as my gift and thine own acquisition
Worthily purchased take my daughter: but
If thou dost break her virgin-knot before   1630
All sanctimonious ceremonies may
With full and holy rite be minister'd,
No sweet aspersion shall the heavens let fall
To make this contract grow: but barren hate,
Sour-eyed disdain and discord shall bestrew
The union of your bed with weeds so loathly
That you shall hate it both: therefore take heed,
As Hymen's lamps shall light you.

FERDINAND

As I hope
For quiet days, fair issue and long life,   1640
With such love as 'tis now, the murkiest den,
The most opportune place, the strong'st suggestion.
Our worser genius can, shall never melt
Mine honour into lust, to take away
The edge of that day's celebration
When I shall think: or Phoebus' steeds are founder'd,
Or Night kept chain'd below.

PROSPERO

Fairly spoke.
Sit then and talk with her; she is thine own.
What, Ariel! my industrious servant, Ariel!   1650
Enter ARIEL

ARIEL

What would my potent master? here I am.

PROSPERO

Thou and thy meaner fellows your last service
Did worthily perform; and I must use you
In such another trick. Go bring the rabble,
O'er whom I give thee power, here to this place:
Incite them to quick motion; for I must
Bestow upon the eyes of this young couple
Some vanity of mine art: it is my promise,
And they expect it from me.

ARIEL

Presently?   1660

PROSPERO

Ay, with a twink.

ARIEL

Before you can say 'come' and 'go,'
And breathe twice and cry 'so, so,'
Each one, tripping on his toe,
Will be here with mop and mow.
Do you love me, master? no?

PROSPERO

Dearly my delicate Ariel. Do not approach
Till thou dost hear me call.

ARIEL

Well, I conceive.
Exit

PROSPERO

Look thou be true; do not give dalliance   1670
Too much the rein: the strongest oaths are straw
To the fire i' the blood: be more abstemious,
Or else, good night your vow!

FERDINAND

I warrant you sir;
The white cold virgin snow upon my heart
Abates the ardour of my liver.

PROSPERO

Well.
Now come, my Ariel! bring a corollary,
Rather than want a spirit: appear and pertly!
No tongue! all eyes! be silent.   1680
Soft music
Enter IRIS

IRIS

Ceres, most bounteous lady, thy rich leas
Of wheat, rye, barley, vetches, oats and pease;
Thy turfy mountains, where live nibbling sheep,
And flat meads thatch'd with stover, them to keep;
Thy banks with pioned and twilled brims,
Which spongy April at thy hest betrims,
To make cold nymphs chaste crowns; and thy broom-groves,
Whose shadow the dismissed bachelor loves,
Being lass-lorn: thy pole-clipt vineyard;
And thy sea-marge, sterile and rocky-hard,   1690
Where thou thyself dost air;—the queen o' the sky,
Whose watery arch and messenger am I,
Bids thee leave these, and with her sovereign grace,
Here on this grass-plot, in this very place,
To come and sport: her peacocks fly amain:
Approach, rich Ceres, her to entertain.
Enter CERES

CERES

Hail, many-colour'd messenger, that ne'er
Dost disobey the wife of Jupiter;
Who with thy saffron wings upon my flowers

Diffusest honey-drops, refreshing showers, 1700
And with each end of thy blue bow dost crown
My bosky acres and my unshrubb'd down,
Rich scarf to my proud earth; why hath thy queen
Summon'd me hither, to this short-grass'd green?

IRIS

A contract of true love to celebrate;
And some donation freely to estate
On the blest lovers.

CERES

Tell me, heavenly bow,
If Venus or her son, as thou dost know,
Do now attend the queen? Since they did plot 1710
The means that dusky Dis my daughter got,
Her and her blind boy's scandal'd company
I have forsworn.

IRIS

Of her society
Be not afraid: I met her deity
Cutting the clouds towards Paphos and her son
Dove-drawn with her. Here thought they to have done
Some wanton charm upon this man and maid,
Whose vows are, that no bed-right shall be paid
Till Hymen's torch be lighted: but vain; 1720
Mars's hot minion is returned again;
Her waspish-headed son has broke his arrows,
Swears he will shoot no more but play with sparrows
And be a boy right out.

CERES

High'st queen of state,
Great Juno, comes; I know her by her gait.
Enter JUNO

JUNO

How does my bounteous sister? Go with me
To bless this twain, that they may prosperous be
And honour'd in their issue.
They sing:

JUNO

Honour, riches, marriage-blessing,   1730
Long continuance, and increasing,
Hourly joys be still upon you!
Juno sings her blessings upon you.

CERES

Earth's increase, foison plenty,
Barns and garners never empty,
Vines and clustering bunches growing,
Plants with goodly burthen bowing;
Spring come to you at the farthest
In the very end of harvest!
Scarcity and want shall shun you;   1740
Ceres' blessing so is on you.

FERDINAND

This is a most majestic vision, and
Harmoniously charmingly. May I be bold
To think these spirits?

PROSPERO

Spirits, which by mine art
I have from their confines call'd to enact
My present fancies.

FERDINAND

Let me live here ever;
So rare a wonder'd father and a wife
Makes this place Paradise.   1750
*JUNO and CERES whisper, and send IRIS on
employment*

PROSPERO

Sweet, now, silence!
JUNO and CERES whisper seriously;
There's something else to do: hush, and be mute,
Or else our spell is marr'd.

IRIS

You nymphs, call'd Naiads, of the windring brooks,
With your sedged crowns and ever-harmless looks,

Leave your crisp channels and on this green land
Answer your summons; Juno does command:
Come, temperate nymphs, and help to celebrate   1760
A contract of true love; be not too late.
Enter certain Nymphs
You sunburnt sicklemen, of August weary,
Come hither from the furrow and be merry:
Make holiday; your rye-straw hats put on
And these fresh nymphs encounter every one
In country footing.
*Enter certain Reapers, properly habited: they join with
the Nymphs in a graceful dance; towards the end whereof
PROSPERO starts suddenly, and speaks; after which, to a
strange, hollow, and confused noise, they heavily vanish*

PROSPERO

[*Aside*] I had forgot that foul conspiracy
Of the beast Caliban and his confederates
Against my life: the minute of their plot
Is almost come.   1770
To the Spirits
Well done! avoid; no more!

FERDINAND

This is strange: your father's in some passion
That works him strongly.

MIRANDA

Never till this day
Saw I him touch'd with anger so distemper'd.

PROSPERO

You do look, my son, in a moved sort,
As if you were dismay'd: be cheerful, sir.
Our revels now are ended. These our actors,
As I foretold you, were all spirits and
Are melted into air, into thin air: 1780
And, like the baseless fabric of this vision,
The cloud-capp'd towers, the gorgeous palaces,
The solemn temples, the great globe itself,
Ye all which it inherit, shall dissolve

And, like this insubstantial pageant faded,
Leave not a rack behind. We are such stuff
As dreams are made on, and our little life
Is rounded with a sleep. Sir, I am vex'd;
Bear with my weakness; my, brain is troubled:
Be not disturb'd with my infirmity: 1790
If you be pleased, retire into my cell
And there repose: a turn or two I'll walk,
To still my beating mind.

FERDINAND AND MIRANDA

We wish your peace.
Exeunt

PROSPERO

Come with a thought I thank thee, Ariel: come.
Enter ARIEL

ARIEL

Thy thoughts I cleave to. What's thy pleasure?

PROSPERO

Spirit,
We must prepare to meet with Caliban.

ARIEL

Ay, my commander: when I presented Ceres,
I thought to have told thee of it, but I fear'd
Lest I might anger thee.   1800

PROSPERO

Say again, where didst thou leave these varlets?

ARIEL

I told you, sir, they were red-hot with drinking;
So fun of valour that they smote the air
For breathing in their faces; beat the ground
For kissing of their feet; yet always bending
Towards their project. Then I beat my tabour;
At which, like unback'd colts, they prick'd their ears,

Advanced their eyelids, lifted up their noses
As they smelt music: so I charm'd their ears
That calf-like they my lowing follow'd through   1810
Tooth'd briers, sharp furzes, pricking goss and thorns,
Which entered their frail shins: at last I left them
I' the filthy-mantled pool beyond your cell,
There dancing up to the chins, that the foul lake
O'erstunk their feet.

PROSPERO

This was well done, my bird.
Thy shape invisible retain thou still:
The trumpery in my house, go bring it hither,
For stale to catch these thieves.

ARIEL

I go, I go.   1820
Exit

PROSPERO

A devil, a born devil, on whose nature
Nurture can never stick; on whom my pains,
Humanely taken, all, all lost, quite lost;
And as with age his body uglier grows,
So his mind cankers. I will plague them all,
Even to roaring.
Re-enter ARIEL, loaden with glistering apparel, &c.
Come, hang them on this line.
PROSPERO and ARIEL remain invisible.
Enter CALIBAN, STEPHANO, and TRINCULO, all wet

CALIBAN

Pray you, tread softly, that the blind mole may not
Hear a foot fall: we now are near his cell.

STEPHANO

Monster, your fairy, which you say is   1830
a harmless fairy, has done little better than
played the Jack with us.

TRINCULO

Monster, I do smell all horse-piss; at
which my nose is in great indignation.

STEPHANO

So is mine. Do you hear, monster? If I should take
a displeasure against you, look you,—

TRINCULO

Thou wert but a lost monster.

CALIBAN

Good my lord, give me thy favour still.
Be patient, for the prize I'll bring thee to
Shall hoodwink this mischance: therefore speak softly.   1840
All's hush'd as midnight yet.

TRINCULO

Ay, but to lose our bottles in the pool,—

STEPHANO

There is not only disgrace and dishonour in that,
monster, but an infinite loss.

TRINCULO

That's more to me than my wetting: yet this is your
harmless fairy, monster.

STEPHANO

I will fetch off my bottle, though I be o'er ears
for my labour.

CALIBAN

Prithee, my king, be quiet. Seest thou here,
This is the mouth o' the cell: no noise, and enter.   1850
Do that good mischief which may make this island
Thine own for ever, and I, thy Caliban,
For aye thy foot-licker.

STEPHANO

Give me thy hand. I do begin to have bloody thoughts.

TRINCULO

O king Stephano! O peer! O worthy Stephano! look
what a wardrobe here is for thee!

CALIBAN

Let it alone, thou fool; it is but trash.

TRINCULO

O, ho, monster! we know what belongs to a frippery.
O king Stephano!

STEPHANO

Put off that gown, Trinculo; by this hand, I'll have   1860
that gown.

TRINCULO

Thy grace shall have it.

CALIBAN

The dropsy drown this fool I what do you mean
To dote thus on such luggage? Let's alone
And do the murder first: if he awake,
From toe to crown he'll fill our skins with pinches,
Make us strange stuff.

STEPHANO

Be you quiet, monster. Mistress line,
is not this my jerkin? Now is the jerkin under
the line: now, jerkin, you are like to lose your   1870
hair and prove a bald jerkin.

TRINCULO

Do, do: we steal by line and level, an't like your grace.

STEPHANO

I thank thee for that jest; here's a garment for't:
wit shall not go unrewarded while I am king of this
country. 'Steal by line and level' is an excellent
pass of pate; there's another garment for't.

TRINCULO

Monster, come, put some lime upon your fingers, and
away with the rest.

CALIBAN

I will have none on't: we shall lose our time,
And all be turn'd to barnacles, or to apes   1880
With foreheads villanous low.

STEPHANO

Monster, lay-to your fingers: help to bear this
away where my hogshead of wine is, or I'll turn you
out of my kingdom: go to, carry this.

TRINCULO

And this.

STEPHANO

Ay, and this.
*A noise of hunters heard. Enter divers Spirits, in shape
of dogs and hounds, and hunt them about, PROSPERO
and ARIEL setting them on*

PROSPERO

Hey, Mountain, hey!

ARIEL

Silver I there it goes, Silver!

PROSPERO

Fury, Fury! there, Tyrant, there! hark! hark!
CALIBAN, STEPHANO, and TRINCULO, are driven out
Go charge my goblins that they grind their joints   1890
With dry convulsions, shorten up their sinews
With aged cramps, and more pinch-spotted make them
Than pard or cat o' mountain.

ARIEL

Hark, they roar!

PROSPERO

Let them be hunted soundly. At this hour

Lie at my mercy all mine enemies:
Shortly shall all my labours end, and thou
Shalt have the air at freedom: for a little
Follow, and do me service.
Exeunt

ACT V

SCENE I. Before PROSPERO'S cell.
Enter PROSPERO in his magic robes, and ARIEL

PROSPERO
Now does my project gather to a head: 1900
My charms crack not; my spirits obey; and time
Goes upright with his carriage. How's the day?

ARIEL
On the sixth hour; at which time, my lord,
You said our work should cease.

PROSPERO
I did say so,
When first I raised the tempest. Say, my spirit,
How fares the king and's followers?

ARIEL
Confined together
In the same fashion as you gave in charge,
Just as you left them; all prisoners, sir,   1910
In the line-grove which weather-fends your cell;
They cannot budge till your release. The king,
His brother and yours, abide all three distracted
And the remainder mourning over them,
Brimful of sorrow and dismay; but chiefly
Him that you term'd, sir, 'The good old lord Gonzalo;'
His tears run down his beard, like winter's drops
From eaves of reeds. Your charm so strongly works 'em
That if you now beheld them, your affections
Would become tender.   1920

PROSPERO

Dost thou think so, spirit?

ARIEL

Mine would, sir, were I human.

PROSPERO

And mine shall.
Hast thou, which art but air, a touch, a feeling
Of their afflictions, and shall not myself,
One of their kind, that relish all as sharply,
Passion as they, be kindlier moved than thou art?
Though with their high wrongs I am struck to the quick,
Yet with my nobler reason 'gaitist my fury
Do I take part: the rarer action is   1930
In virtue than in vengeance: they being penitent,
The sole drift of my purpose doth extend
Not a frown further. Go release them, Ariel:
My charms I'll break, their senses I'll restore,
And they shall be themselves.

ARIEL

I'll fetch them, sir.
Exit

PROSPERO

Ye elves of hills, brooks, standing lakes and groves,
And ye that on the sands with printless foot
Do chase the ebbing Neptune and do fly him
When he comes back; you demi-puppets that   1940
By moonshine do the green sour ringlets make,
Whereof the ewe not bites, and you whose pastime
Is to make midnight mushrooms, that rejoice
To hear the solemn curfew; by whose aid,
Weak masters though ye be, I have bedimm'd
The noontide sun, call'd forth the mutinous winds,
And 'twixt the green sea and the azured vault
Set roaring war: to the dread rattling thunder
Have I given fire and rifted Jove's stout oak
With his own bolt; the strong-based promontory   1950

Have I made shake and by the spurs pluck'd up
The pine and cedar: graves at my command
Have waked their sleepers, oped, and let 'em forth
By my so potent art. But this rough magic
I here abjure, and, when I have required
Some heavenly music, which even now I do,
To work mine end upon their senses that
This airy charm is for, I'll break my staff,
Bury it certain fathoms in the earth,
And deeper than did ever plummet sound   1960
I'll drown my book.
Solemn music
Re-enter ARIEL before: then ALONSO, with a frantic
gesture, attended by GONZALO; SEBASTIAN and
ANTONIO in like manner, attended by ADRIAN and
FRANCISCO they all enter the circle which PROSPERO
had made, and there stand charmed; which PROSPERO
observing, speaks:
A solemn air and the best comforter
To an unsettled fancy cure thy brains,
Now useless, boil'd within thy skull! There stand,
For you are spell-stopp'd.
Holy Gonzalo, honourable man,
Mine eyes, even sociable to the show of thine,
Fall fellowly drops. The charm dissolves apace,
And as the morning steals upon the night,   1970
Melting the darkness, so their rising senses
Begin to chase the ignorant fumes that mantle
Their clearer reason. O good Gonzalo,
My true preserver, and a loyal sir
To him you follow'st! I will pay thy graces
Home both in word and deed. Most cruelly
Didst thou, Alonso, use me and my daughter:
Thy brother was a furtherer in the act.
Thou art pinch'd fort now, Sebastian. Flesh and blood,
You, brother mine, that entertain'd ambition,   1980
Expell'd remorse and nature; who, with Sebastian,
Whose inward pinches therefore are most strong,
Would here have kill'd your king; I do forgive thee,
Unnatural though thou art. Their understanding

Begins to swell, and the approaching tide
Will shortly fill the reasonable shore
That now lies foul and muddy. Not one of them
That yet looks on me, or would know me Ariel,
Fetch me the hat and rapier in my cell:
I will discase me, and myself present   1990
As I was sometime Milan: quickly, spirit;
Thou shalt ere long be free.
ARIEL sings and helps to attire him
Where the bee sucks, there suck I:
In a cowslip's bell I lie;
There I couch when owls do cry.
On the bat's back I do fly
After summer merrily.
Merrily, merrily shall I live now
Under the blossom that hangs on the bough.

PROSPERO

Why, that's my dainty Ariel! I shall miss thee: 2000
But yet thou shalt have freedom: so, so, so.
To the king's ship, invisible as thou art:
There shalt thou find the mariners asleep
Under the hatches; the master and the boatswain
Being awake, enforce them to this place,
And presently, I prithee.

ARIEL

I drink the air before me, and return
Or ere your pulse twice beat.
Exit

GONZALO

All torment, trouble, wonder and amazement
Inhabits here: some heavenly power guide us   2010
Out of this fearful country!

PROSPERO

Behold, sir king,
The wronged Duke of Milan, Prospero:
For more assurance that a living prince

Does now speak to thee, I embrace thy body;
And to thee and thy company I bid
A hearty welcome.

ALONSO

Whether thou best he or no,
Or some enchanted trifle to abuse me,
As late I have been, I not know: thy pulse   2020
Beats as of flesh and blood; and, since I saw thee,
The affliction of my mind amends, with which,
I fear, a madness held me: this must crave,
An if this be at all, a most strange story.
Thy dukedom I resign and do entreat
Thou pardon me my wrongs. But how should Prospero
Be living and be here?

PROSPERO

First, noble friend,
Let me embrace thine age, whose honour cannot
Be measured or confined.   2030

GONZALO

Whether this be
Or be not, I'll not swear.

PROSPERO

You do yet taste
Some subtilties o' the isle, that will not let you
Believe things certain. Welcome, my friends all!
Aside to SEBASTIAN and ANTONIO
But you, my brace of lords, were I so minded,
I here could pluck his highness' frown upon you
And justify you traitors: at this time
I will tell no tales.

SEBASTIAN

[*Aside*]
The devil speaks in him.   2040

219

PROSPERO

No.
For you, most wicked sir, whom to call brother
Would even infect my mouth, I do forgive
Thy rankest fault; all of them; and require
My dukedom of thee, which perforce, I know,
Thou must restore.

ALONSO

If thou be'st Prospero,
Give us particulars of thy preservation;
How thou hast met us here, who three hours since
Were wreck'd upon this shore; where I have lost—   2050
How sharp the point of this remembrance is!—
My dear son Ferdinand.

PROSPERO

I am woe for't, sir.

ALONSO

Irreparable is the loss, and patience
Says it is past her cure.

PROSPERO

I rather think
You have not sought her help, of whose soft grace
For the like loss I have her sovereign aid
And rest myself content.

ALONSO

You the like loss!   2060

PROSPERO

As great to me as late; and, supportable
To make the dear loss, have I means much weaker
Than you may call to comfort you, for I
Have lost my daughter.

ALONSO

A daughter?
O heavens, that they were living both in Naples,

The king and queen there! that they were, I wish
Myself were mudded in that oozy bed
Where my son lies. When did you lose your daughter?

PROSPERO

In this last tempest. I perceive these lords   2070
At this encounter do so much admire
That they devour their reason and scarce think
Their eyes do offices of truth, their words
Are natural breath: but, howsoe'er you have
Been justled from your senses, know for certain
That I am Prospero and that very duke
Which was thrust forth of Milan, who most strangely
Upon this shore, where you were wreck'd, was landed,
To be the lord on't. No more yet of this;
For 'tis a chronicle of day by day,   2080
Not a relation for a breakfast nor
Befitting this first meeting. Welcome, sir;
This cell's my court: here have I few attendants
And subjects none abroad: pray you, look in.
My dukedom since you have given me again,
I will requite you with as good a thing;
At least bring forth a wonder, to content ye
As much as me my dukedom.
Here PROSPERO discovers FERDINAND and
MIRANDA playing at chess

MIRANDA

Sweet lord, you play me false.

FERDINAND

No, my dear'st love,   2090
I would not for the world.

MIRANDA

Yes, for a score of kingdoms you should wrangle,
And I would call it, fair play.

ALONSO

If this prove
A vision of the Island, one dear son
Shall I twice lose.

221

SEBASTIAN

A most high miracle!

FERDINAND

Though the seas threaten, they are merciful;
I have cursed them without cause.
Kneels

ALONSO

Now all the blessings   2100
Of a glad father compass thee about!
Arise, and say how thou camest here.

MIRANDA

O, wonder!
How many goodly creatures are there here!
How beauteous mankind is! O brave new world,
That has such people in't!

PROSPERO

'Tis new to thee.

ALONSO

What is this maid with whom thou wast at play?
Your eld'st acquaintance cannot be three hours:
Is she the goddess that hath sever'd us,   2110
And brought us thus together?

FERDINAND

Sir, she is mortal;
But by immortal Providence she's mine:
I chose her when I could not ask my father
For his advice, nor thought I had one. She
Is daughter to this famous Duke of Milan,
Of whom so often I have heard renown,
But never saw before; of whom I have
Received a second life; and second father
This lady makes him to me.   2120

ALONSO

I am hers:
But, O, how oddly will it sound that I
Must ask my child forgiveness!

PROSPERO

There, sir, stop:
Let us not burthen our remembrance with
A heaviness that's gone.

GONZALO

I have inly wept,
Or should have spoke ere this. Look down, you god,
And on this couple drop a blessed crown!
For it is you that have chalk'd forth the way   2130
Which brought us hither.

ALONSO

I say, Amen, Gonzalo!

GONZALO

Was Milan thrust from Milan, that his issue
Should become kings of Naples? O, rejoice
Beyond a common joy, and set it down
With gold on lasting pillars: In one voyage
Did Claribel her husband find at Tunis,
And Ferdinand, her brother, found a wife
Where he himself was lost, Prospero his dukedom
In a poor isle and all of us ourselves   2140
When no man was his own.

ALONSO

To FERDINAND and MIRANDA
Give me your hands:
Let grief and sorrow still embrace his heart
That doth not wish you joy!

GONZALO

Be it so! Amen!
*Re-enter ARIEL, with the Master and Boatswain
amazedly following*
O, look, sir, look, sir! here is more of us:
I prophesied, if a gallows were on land,
This fellow could not drown. Now, blasphemy,
That swear'st grace o'erboard, not an oath on shore?
Hast thou no mouth by land? What is the news?   2150

223

Boatswain

The best news is, that we have safely found
Our king and company; the next, our ship—
Which, but three glasses since, we gave out split—
Is tight and yare and bravely rigg'd as when
We first put out to sea.

ARIEL

[*Aside to PROSPERO*]
Sir, all this service
Have I done since I went.

PROSPERO

[*Aside to ARIEL*]
My tricksy spirit!

ALONSO

These are not natural events; they strengthen
From strange to stranger. Say, how came you hither?   2160

Boatswain

If I did think, sir, I were well awake,
I'ld strive to tell you. We were dead of sleep,
And—how we know not—all clapp'd under hatches;
Where but even now with strange and several noises
Of roaring, shrieking, howling, jingling chains,
And more diversity of sounds, all horrible,
We were awaked; straightway, at liberty;
Where we, in all her trim, freshly beheld
Our royal, good and gallant ship, our master
Capering to eye her: on a trice, so please you,   2170
Even in a dream, were we divided from them
And were brought moping hither.

ARIEL

[*Aside to PROSPERO*]
Was't well done?

PROSPERO

[*Aside to ARIEL*]
Bravely, my diligence. Thou shalt be free.

ALONSO

This is as strange a maze as e'er men trod
And there is in this business more than nature
Was ever conduct of: some oracle
Must rectify our knowledge.

PROSPERO

Sir, my liege,
Do not infest your mind with beating on   2180
The strangeness of this business; at pick'd leisure
Which shall be shortly, single I'll resolve you,
Which to you shall seem probable, of every
These happen'd accidents; till when, be cheerful
And think of each thing well.
[*Aside to ARIEL*]
Come hither, spirit:
Set Caliban and his companions free;
Untie the spell.
Exit ARIEL
How fares my gracious sir?
There are yet missing of your company   2190
Some few odd lads that you remember not.
Re-enter ARIEL, driving in CALIBAN, STEPHANO and
TRINCULO, in their stolen apparel

STEPHANO

Every man shift for all the rest, and
let no man take care for himself; for all is
but fortune. Coragio, bully-monster, coragio!

TRINCULO

If these be true spies which I wear in my head,
here's a goodly sight.

CALIBAN

O Setebos, these be brave spirits indeed!
How fine my master is! I am afraid
He will chastise me.

SEBASTIAN

Ha, ha!

What things are these, my lord Antonio?
Will money buy 'em?   2200

ANTONIO

Very like; one of them
Is a plain fish, and, no doubt, marketable.

PROSPERO

Mark but the badges of these men, my lords,
Then say if they be true. This mis-shapen knave,
His mother was a witch, and one so strong
That could control the moon, make flows and ebbs,
And deal in her command without her power.
These three have robb'd me; and this demi-devil—
For he's a bastard one—had plotted with them
To take my life. Two of these fellows you   2210
Must know and own; this thing of darkness!
Acknowledge mine.

CALIBAN

I shall be pinch'd to death.

ALONSO

Is not this Stephano, my drunken butler?

SEBASTIAN

He is drunk now: where had he wine?

ALONSO

And Trinculo is reeling ripe: where should they
Find this grand liquor that hath gilded 'em?
How camest thou in this pickle?

TRINCULO

I have been in such a pickle since I
saw you last that, I fear me, will never out of   2220
my bones: I shall not fear fly-blowing.

SEBASTIAN

Why, how now, Stephano!

STEPHANO

O, touch me not; I am not Stephano, but a cramp.

PROSPERO

You'ld be king o' the isle, sirrah?

STEPHANO

I should have been a sore one then.

ALONSO

This is a strange thing as e'er I look'd on.
Pointing to Caliban

PROSPERO

He is as disproportion'd in his manners
As in his shape. Go, sirrah, to my cell;
Take with you your companions; as you look   2230
To have my pardon, trim it handsomely.

CALIBAN

Ay, that I will; and I'll be wise hereafter
And seek for grace. What a thrice-double ass
Was I, to take this drunkard for a god
And worship this dull fool!

PROSPERO

Go to; away!

ALONSO

Hence, and bestow your luggage where you found it.   2240

SEBASTIAN

Or stole it, rather.
Exeunt CALIBAN, STEPHANO, and TRINCULO

PROSPERO

Sir, I invite your highness and your train
To my poor cell, where you shall take your rest   2250
For this one night; which, part of it, I'll waste
With such discourse as, I not doubt, shall make it
Go quick away; the story of my life
And the particular accidents gone by

Since I came to this isle: and in the morn
I'll bring you to your ship and so to Naples,
Where I have hope to see the nuptial
Of these our dear-beloved solemnized;
And thence retire me to my Milan, where
Every third thought shall be my grave.   2260

ALONSO

I long
To hear the story of your life, which must
Take the ear strangely.

PROSPERO

I'll deliver all;
And promise you calm seas, auspicious gales
And sail so expeditious that shall catch
Your royal fleet far off.
[*Aside to ARIEL*]
My Ariel, chick,
That is thy charge: then to the elements
Be free, and fare thou well! Please you, draw near.   2270
Exeunt

EPILOGUE
SPOKEN BY PROSPERO

Now my charms are all o'erthrown,
And what strength I have's mine own,
Which is most faint: now, 'tis true,
I must be here confined by you,
Or sent to Naples. Let me not,
Since I have my dukedom got
And pardon'd the deceiver, dwell
In this bare island by your spell;
But release me from my bands
With the help of your good hands: 2280
Gentle breath of yours my sails
Must fill, or else my project fails,
Which was to please. Now I want
Spirits to enforce, art to enchant,
And my ending is despair,

Unless I be relieved by prayer,
Which pierces so that it assaults
Mercy itself and frees all faults.
As you from crimes would pardon'd be,
Let your indulgence set me free.   2290

(1611)

Questions for Consideration:

1. Unlike *Trifles*, this play is written in verse. Most lines tend to contain 10-11 syllables and some can be read as blank verse, unrhymed iambic pentameter. Why would Shakespeare have written it this way in his day? What is the effect of this use of verse in the characters' lines?

2. Gonzalo comments that he believes the boatswain's fate is to be hanged rather than drowned. What point is he making? What larger notion of fate in the play is introduced in this passage? How does Prospero's magic affect our notion of fate?

3. What do we learn of Miranda's character in her first speech?

4. What does Prospero reveal to Miranda in their first exchange?

5. In *The Tempest*, how does Shakespeare develop the theme of ambition and its power to corrupt?

6. What evidence does the play present of Prospero's magical powers?

7. Why is Ariel loyal to Prospero?

8. How does Prospero describe Caliban, son of Sycorax?

9. How does Miranda feel about Caliban? Why?

10. How does Caliban feel about Prospero? Why?

11. Is Prospero good?

12. How does Shakespeare use "asides" to convey to the audience character attitudes and information that some characters are not privy to?

13. Why does Prospero treat Ferdinand so roughly in the beginning?

14. What is the effect of metaphors and similes in the play?

15. How does Gonzalo describe the perfect commonwealth?

16. Find a passage in the dialogue of Act I, Scene 2 that reveals Antonio's character.

17. What is the effect of the play-within-a-play, the masque put on by Juno, Ceres, and Iris for Miranda and Ferdinand?

18. How does Prospero's epilogue further develop the audience's acknowledgement of the play's being a play? In what way has the audience's power kept Prospero "confined" to the island?

19. How is the script a kind of fate for the characters?

20. As traditional to Greek drama, tragedies end in death, comedies in marriage. As a comedy, how does this play resolve its conflicts in the final events, including the impending marriage of Miranda and Ferdinand?

Shakespeare's influence on Western culture is undeniable. Not only is his work a touchstone for Western literature in general, but many of his characters have both drawn from and shaped important literary **archetypes** (figures that appear over and over again in literature for their familiar roles in general human dynamics). *The Tempest* has certainly made its mark in this regard, establishing Prospero and Caliban as two important widely-recognized archetypes. Prospero is the magician: a powerful figure able to orchestrate events and control outcomes, but held accountable on some level for his decisions in doing so. Caliban is the savage: tragic, malformed, and yet sensitive to the injustice of his circumstances. Further, this play's archetypal influence is evidenced by the many versions of it that have been produced—in theatre, film, and fiction—since Shakespeare's time. For example, Paul Mazursky's 1982 film *Tempest*, set in the twentieth century yet based on Shakespeare's play, stars John Cassavetes as the self-exiled architect Philip Dimitrius (Prospero) and Molly Ringwald as his teenaged daughter Miranda. In two other interesting retellings of the story, Julie Taymor's 2010 film *The Tempest* stars Helen Mirren as Prospera, and Gloria Naylor's 1988 novel *Mama Day* employs the storm as plot-vehicle as well as featuring Mama Day herself as a black female Prospero-type figure.

The themes of *The Tempest*, then, are considered by many to be "universal" in their connection to common human experiences such as feeling relegated to an unjustly-restricted and inferior status (as Caliban is) and deciding whether use of one's power to alter others' lives is justified or not (like Prospero). Dramatic productions have great potential to move an audience, and both *Trifles* and *The Tempest* offer examples of how a play might do so. Through effective use of dramatic strategies and powerfully written lines, a play can tap into the most basic and profound aspects of human experience.

Creative Nonfiction, the Fourth Genre

7

7.1 Creative Nonfiction as a Genre

Creative nonfiction seems to have existed for as long as poetry, fiction, and drama have, but only in the last forty years or so has the term become common as a label for *creative, factual prose*. The length is not a factor in characterizing this genre: Such prose can take the form of an essay or a book. For this chapter's discussion, we will focus on the *essay*, since not only will this shorter version of the form allow us to examine multiple examples for a better understanding of the genre, but also, you may have written creative nonfiction essays yourself. Looking carefully at the strategies exhibited by some successful essay writers will give us new ideas for achieving goals in our own writing.

First, let's do what we can to more clearly define the creative nonfiction **essay**. What is the difference between this kind of essay and a...well, what shall we call essays outside this category? *Non*-creative nonfiction essays? This title does not work very well for our purposes; the distinction is a muddy one, since even a researched academic essay can exhibit creativity. However, we can make some general observations about the differences between creative nonfiction and works that do not fit neatly into this genre: Although written in prose form (**prose** is writing *not* visually broken into distinct lines as poetry is), the creative nonfiction essay often strives for a poetic *effect*, employing a kind of compressed, distilled language so that most words carry more meaning than their simple denotation (or literal meaning). Generally, this kind of essay is not heavy with researched information or formal argument; its priority, instead, is to generate a powerful emotional and **aesthetic** effect (*aesthetic* referring to *artistic* and/or *beautiful* qualities).

Virginia Woolf's 1942 "The Death of the Moth" is an illuminating example of such a work. While the essay does not present a stated argument and proceed to offer evidence in the same way conventional academic argument would, it does strive to *persuade*. Consider this piece carefully at http://gutenberg.net.au/ebooks12/1203811h.html#ch-02 and see if you can detect the theme that Woolf is developing.

The title of Woolf's essay, "The Death of the Moth," offers us, from the start, the knowledge of the work's theme of death. Woolf's choice of tone for an essay on this topic is, perhaps, what distinguishes it from the many other literary works on the subject. The attitude is not one of tragedy, horror, or indignation, as we might expect. Rather, through imagery and diction, Woolf generates a tone of *wistfulness*. By carefully crafting the reader's experience of the moth's death, through the author's own first person point of view, she reminds us of our own human struggle against death, which is both heroic and inevitable.

While this piece is not a poem, what aspects of it are *poetic*? Consider the imagery employed to suggest the season of death, for all of nature. The writer describes her experience sitting at her desk next to the window, observing the signs of autumn: the plow "scoring the field" where the crop (or "share") has already been harvested. Although the scene begins in morning—characterized by energetic exertions of nature, including the rooks, rising and settling into the trees again and again with a great deal of noise, "as though to be thrown into the air and settle slowly down upon the tree tops were a tremendously exciting experience"—the day shifts, as the essay progresses, to afternoon, the birds having left the trees of this field for some other place. Like the moth, the day and the year are waning. The energy that each began with is now diminishing, as is the case for all living things.

The writer is impressed with the moth's valiant struggle against its impending death because she is also aware of its inevitable doom: "[T]here was something marvellous as well as pathetic about him." As is common in poetry, Woolf's diction not only suggests her attitude toward the subject, but also exhibits a lyrical quality that enhances the work's effect: She introduces words whose meanings are associated with youth and energy, as well as *sounding* strong with the "vigorous" consonants of "g," "c," "z," and "t"—words such as "vigour," "clamour," and "zest." Yet, the author counters this positive tone with other words that suggest, both in meaning and in their softer sounds, the vulnerability of living things: "thin," "frail," "diminutive," and "futile." In a third category of diction, with words of compliment—"extraordinary" and "uncomplainingly"—

Woolf acknowledges the moth's admirable fight. In addition to indicating the moth's heroism, the very length of these words seems to model the moth's attempts to drag out its last moments of life.

What impression does the essay, as a whole, convey? The writer acknowledges that watching even such a small creature as the moth struggle against death, she sympathizes with the moth and not with the "power of such magnitude" that carries on outside the window—that of time and inevitable change, for this power is ultimately her own "enemy" as well. In her last line, "O yes, he seemed to say, death is stronger than I am," what lesson has she internalized regarding *herself,* a human being who at first observed the autumn day with no immediate sense of her own mortality?

7.2 Models of Creative Nonfiction

Now that we have analyzed a creative nonfiction essay together, try your own hand at this process. With each of the following essays, I have included Questions for Consideration to help guide you to some of the key elements that generate particular effects and meanings. Once you have observed *how* these works make meaning, you might choose one on which to formulate a perspective and then compose a written argument making a case for that perspective.

Let's begin with "Goodbye to All That," by Joan Didion, 1967, at http://juliaallison.com/goodbye-to-all-that-by-joan-didion/.

Questions for Consideration:

1. How does Didion employ sensory detail to draw us into her experience of New York City?

2. Of her images of New York, which are the most striking to you? What gives these images their impact?

3. What general impression of New York is created by the essay?

4. How does Didion use **catalogs** (or lists) to help generate a panoramic impression of the city in her early years there?

5. How does the writer experience her memories of New York City now? How does she use the notion of "film dissolve" to convey this perspective?

6. Why did her experience of the city change when she was twenty-eight?

7. What do you think is the general message of this essay?

While Didion's "Goodbye to All That" is a *personal essay*, offering a glimpse into Didion's own life as a vehicle for more general insight into human experience, Richard P. Feynman's work "The Value of Science" focuses on the subject of science in a context more *social* than personal. In fact, it was originally offered as a *lecture* in 1955 for the National Academy of Sciences. As you read the work in its written form at http://calteches.library.caltech.edu/40/2/Science.htm, consider how it might have been shaped by its original intent for lecture delivery to an audience composed primarily of scientists.

Questions for Consideration:

1. In the beginning of the lecture, Feynman says that in talking not about scientific subjects but rather about *values*, he is "as dumb as the next guy." How does this notion fit into his later argument that one important value of science is that it teaches us to live with uncertainty?

2. How does Feynman differentiate between scientific knowledge and moral choice? How does he make his case for the value of the *key* to heaven *and* hell?

3. The second value of science, according to Feynman, is that it stimulates a unique imaginative process, one that causes those who get turned onto the scientific perspective to "turn over each new stone." How does his poem exemplify this unique kind of imagining? What is the meaning of line 17, "A mite makes the sea roar"?

4. How does Feynman use the metaphor of playing music to explain why perhaps more people are not "inspired by our present picture of the universe"?

5. What is your personal response to his reminder that our brain, which we equate with our *mind* (on which we base our notion of our individuality) is not made of the same atoms it was made of two weeks ago? Does this point affect you the way Feynman desired it to? Why or why not?

6. What, according to Feynman, is the importance of our learning to live in a state of uncertainty? How does science help foster this world view?

George Orwell, author of the novels *Animal Farm* and *Nineteen Eighty-Four*, among many other works, brings us back to the personal essay in his 1946 "Why I Write." This essay not only offers a useful example of effective creative nonfiction, but it also gives us a glimpse into the subject of writing itself, raising questions about our own reasons for writing. You can read it at http://gutenberg.net.au/ebooks03/0300011h.html#part47.

Questions for Consideration:

1. What does Orwell mean when he says that in his early resistance to becoming a writer, he was "outraging my true nature"? Can you identify with this sentiment in light of your own "natural" tendencies?

2. What kind of "literary activities" did Orwell engage in even when he was not purposefully developing his aspirations of becoming a writer? How then does his attitude contrast his perspective on that period as he looks back now, writing this essay?

3. What is the "joy of mere words" he describes? Can you give examples of words that affect you this way?

4. Consider the "four great motives for writing" listed by Orwell. According to him, how might these motives work against one another?

5. How does Orwell use his poem to explain why he eventually became political even though it was not in his "nature" to do so?

6. What is the role of aestheticism for Orwell even in writing a book with a political theme?

7. What does he mean when he says that "every book is a failure"?

8. If you were to write a similar essay tracing your development into a _____ major, what details of your life would you focus on? If this major, and the profession it leads to, does not always fit well with your character and habits, where do the discrepancies lie?

9. If you were to write an essay about your development as a writer, how would your story be similar to Orwell's? How would it be different?

The essays presented in this chapter reveal the potential power of creative nonfiction. Exhibiting strong differences from one another, these pieces illuminate the ways that various literary strategies can be used to generate particular effects. You may end up writing your own essay that provides a literary analysis of one of these works, giving you a chance to practice composing argument based on textual evidence. Whether you write *about* these essays or not, these works *model* strategies available to you as a writer.

Since the length of this chapter is limited by the constraints of space, I have included a brief list, below, of additional essays that might be of interest to you. These should be accessible, free of charge, on the internet. Like the other essays whose links are included in this chapter, these works provide both fascinating subjects for analysis and useful models for your own writing.

Anzaldua, Gloria. "How to Tame a Wild Tongue." *Borderlands / La Frontera*, 2nd ed., Aunt Lute Books, 1987. https://www.sfu.ca/iirp/documents/Anzaldua%201999.pdf. Accessed 21 Dec. 2014.

Postman, Neil. "Of Luddites, Learning, and Life." *Technos Quarterly*, vol. 2, no. 4, Winter 1993. http://www.faculty.rsu.edu/users/f/felwell/www/Theorists/Postman/Articles/TECHNOS_NET.htm. Accessed 3 June 2014.

Sedaris, David. "Old Lady Down the Hall." *Esquire*, http://www.esquire.com/news-politics/a498/old-lady-hall-sedaris-1000/. Accessed 5 Feb. 2014.

Wimsatt, William Upski. "How I Got My D.I.Y Degree." *Unte Reader*, May/June 1998. Self Education Foundation. https://selfeducationfoundation.wordpress.com/sef-history/diy-degree/. Accessed 7 Feb. 2014.

The Literary Analysis Essay

Now that we have discussed the basic conventions and terminology associated with poetry, fiction, drama, and creative nonfiction, let's explore how one progresses from reading a piece of literature to producing a literary analysis paper on that work. It is important to note that the process of writing discussed in this chapter can be used in writing for any discipline. As stated in this book's Introduction, literature provides a fruitful context for development of writing skills, but the skills themselves are transferable into a multitude of communication situations.

8.1 Literary Analysis Arguments

Analysis means to break something down in order to better understand how it works. To analyze a literary work is to pull it apart and look at its discrete components to see how those components contribute to the meaning and/or effect of the whole. Thus, a literary analysis argument considers what has been learned in analyzing a work (What do the parts look like and how do they function?) and forwards a particular *perspective* on their contribution to the whole (In light of the author's use of diction, for example, what meaning does the novel, as a whole, yield?).

Consider, once again, the literary analysis arguments presented in this book so far:

> Marion Velis (Chapter 2): "At first glance, Theodore Roethke's poem 'My Papa's Waltz' may seem like a poem about a boy's fear of his controlling, abusive, alcoholic father. But the poem goes much deeper than that. Roethke uses specific rhythm, word choice, and

a controlling metaphor to give the poem a reminiscent tone that looks back on the father in love."

Bill Day (Chapter 5): "Through the metaphors of Jake's wound and the tainted Pamplona fiesta, the novel [*The Sun Also Rises*] conveys the possibility that we can dangerously disrupt the cycle of renewal."

Katherine Jones (Chapter 5): "Brett, as she is developed in the novel [*The Sun Also Rises*], has been painted in different lights, depending on the interpreter, ranging from a sympathetic view to one of condemnation. The portrait of her that I will attempt to show is one of a human being, caught between the ideologies of two eras."

Each of these essays engages in analysis of the text in question, pointing to and considering plot events, images, character traits, dialogue, and other *components* of the work to understand the meaning of the text as a *whole*. Although in her thesis, Katherine does not list the "parts" that her paper investigates, she goes on to focus on Brett's specific *behaviors* and *expressions* that support the essay's interpretation of *The Sun Also Rises*.

8.2 Writing as a Process: Breaking It Down

For many students, approaching a writing assignment can be overwhelming. They know that there are many tasks that must be completed, such as gathering information about the topic, forming a perspective on it, brainstorming ideas to be included in the paper, organizing those ideas, integrating the evidence, and articulating the argument with clarity and eloquence, not to mention accommodating the assigned format guidelines. This job is not unlike building a house. You look at the empty lot and imagine the beautiful house you want to build, but you know that the tasks necessary to get from nothing to the final product are many and varied. The prospect can certainly be overwhelming. Yet, any builder understands that the best approach to a big job like this one is breaking it down into a methodical and carefully scheduled process. In response to a challenging writing assignment, you are encouraged to do the same.

Let's consider the writing assignment Bill originally received from his English 1102 instructor:

> *For this essay, write a literary analysis of Ernest Hemingway's* The Sun Also Rises *using a formalist*

*approach. The essay should forward a specific perspective
on the novel (articulated in your thesis), and the evidence
for your argument should come from the novel itself. The
essay should be three-four pages in length.
Due date: February 3.*

Bill remembers that in his high school senior English class, he once procrastinated on a major paper assignment and ended up writing the whole essay in one night. The result was a "D" on the paper and a tendency to experience writer's block, which still plagued him all during his first semester of college. But he has one tool this second semester that he has not had before: his instructor's handout on "Writing as a Process." The literary analysis essay for this class is not due for three weeks, but he decides to review the handout *now* as a first step to avoiding writer's block and another low grade. Here is the advice recommended in his instructor's handout:

1. Investigate the general topic; in this case, read the novel and make notes and annotations as you go.

2. Brainstorm points of interest regarding what you've learned so far. As you brainstorm, do not try to write in full sentences or to organize your thoughts. Instead, simply write down everything that comes to mind.

3. Read back over your notes and decide on a focus. Considering this focus, decide *what you think* about this topic, based on your observations so far. Form a *perspective* on the topic.

4. Again considering your brainstorming notes, determine a very general organization for the *major points* on this topic. Once you have completed this basic outline, categorize all the leftover *"smaller" items* under the most relevant *major points*. If some items on your brainstorming page don't seem relevant, mark through them. Keep only the items that fit your paper's focus.

5. With the paper topic and its major supporting points in mind, write a *working thesis*. This thesis is not set in stone yet, but it will help you stay on track as you move forward.

6. Go back to your materials on the general topic now—in this case, comb through your notes on the novel, annotations, and highlighted passages. Would any of these words, ideas, and/ or passages make effective *evidence* to develop one or more of your major points? As you find fruitful items, jot down a quote, summary, or paraphrase of each item, along with the page number of the novel where you found it. Make a note to yourself indicating which *major point* each item supports.

7. Revise your paper outline now to include not only the working thesis and the major points, but also the pieces of evidence that will go under each major point.

8. Begin drafting the paper. If the introduction does not come quickly, skip it. Keep your working thesis in mind and write out the major sections of your paper which support that thesis.

9. Now go back to the introduction. Consider your audience. How are you trying to alter your audience's perspective on the novel with this paper? How can you use the introduction to (a) draw your reader's interest to your new way of looking at the novel and (b) lay the groundwork for your argument? The introduction should accomplish these goals. Write your conclusion with similar goals in mind. This is your last chance to persuade your reader that your perspective is convincing and important. How can you leave your reader with a strong and lasting impression?

10. Once you have drafted the entire essay, start at the beginning and revise. Pay particular attention to coherence during this phase. In a coherent paper, everything in the essay promotes its central purpose. During this phase, you may want to *clarify and strengthen the relationships among ideas* with transition words and explanations. A coherent paper exhibits a certain *tightness* that produces the desired impact on the reader. Imagine that you are reading the paper aloud to an actual audience of fellow students who have their own values and opinions. How can you shape the prose to (1) keep their attention, (2) clearly and persuasively convey your case, and (3) convince these readers that your perspective is a valuable one?

11. Final revision phase: Read through the essay as many times as you need to, checking grammar and spelling and giving the language its final polish. Read it aloud again, this time slowly, to be sure that the essay sounds as eloquent as you intended for it to.

12. Be sure that the essay follows the format guidelines and is ready for submission.

In class, after handing out this sheet, Bill's instructor told the students to take out their datebooks. She told the students to consult their schedules and assign "dummy" dates for each item on the task list. Here is how Bill divided up his time for addressing the tasks necessary for completing the paper:

January 12	13	14	15	16	17	18
	Attend math, English, and history class **Read and annotate novel (2 hrs.)** Math homework Read chapter in history	Attend biology **Read and annotate novel (2 hrs.)** Read biology chapter Fraternity meeting	Attend math, English, and history class **Read and annotate novel (2 hrs.)** Math homework	Attend biology and lab **Read and annotate novel (2 hrs.)** Review biology notes	Attend math, English, and history class **Brainstorm for essay 1 (1 hr.); Decide on and write down paper's focus (30 min.)**	Fraternity workday
19	**20**	**21**	**22**	**23**	**24**	**25**
Make a tentative outline of major and supporting points for essay 1 (1 hr.) Review history notes	Attend math, English, and history class Math homework **Compose a working thesis for essay 1 (30 min.)**	Attend biology **Review notes and novel itself for best evidence/examples (2 hrs.)** Read biology chapter Fraternity meeting	Attend math, English, and history class **Continue finding evidence for essay 1 (2 hrs.)** Math homework	Attend biology and lab **Revise essay 1 outline to include specific evidence items (1 hr.)** Review biology notes	Attend math, English, and history class Go home for Granny's birthday	Granny's birthday party

26	27	28	29	30	31	February 1
Draft essay 1 (3 hrs.)	Attend math, English, and history class	Attend biology	Attend math, English, and history class	Attend biology and lab	Attend math, English, and history class	Work on math group project
Review history notes	Math homework	Study for history exam	History exam	Submit lab report	Math exam	
Study for math test	Community service	Write biology lab report	**Write introduction and conclusion for essay 1 (1 hr.)**	Study for math test	**Revise essay 1 (2 hrs.)**	
		Fraternity meeting	Math homework	Review biology notes		
				Revise essay 1 (2 hrs.)		

2	3	4	5	6	7	8
Format, proofread, and polish and print essay 1 (2 hrs.)	Attend math, English, and history class	Attend biology	Attend math, English, and history class	Attend biology and lab	Attend math, English, and history class	Work on math group project
Review history notes	**Submit essay 1**	**Begin working on Essay 2**	Math homework	Review biology notes		
	Math homework	Read biology chapter				
		Fraternity meeting				

To some students, the idea of working for an entire three weeks on a three to four page essay might seem extreme. Yet, anyone who writes for a living will attest that all of these tasks are necessary for a high quality product. Professional writers may allocate their time a bit differently, perhaps working for eight or nine hours in one day on a single project, and undoubtedly they gain speed over time at completing each stage of the process. Even so, they understand that for a product with the desired impact, one must spend time planning and crafting the piece. Since students are usually taking other classes in addition to English, and must often hold down jobs and fulfill personal obligations, Bill's Essay 1 plan is much more likely to work out than a twenty-hour writing marathon beginning two days before the paper's due-date. Notice that Bill did not schedule any Essay 1 tasks for January 18, 24-25, 27-28, and February 1. Looking ahead in his date book, he realized that he has fraternity events on January 18 and 27, and he wants to save time on the other dates to join his family for his grandmother's birthday celebration, as well as to study intensively for a history test and work with a group on a math project.

As Bill discovers in carrying out his plans, he experiences much less stress than before as he tackles the "small" daily writing tasks he has assigned himself. On the day he does his brainstorming for Essay 1, he does not feel pressured by the fact that he still needs to write and revise the essay—he knows the time-slots for those tasks are already carved out in his calendar and he will be able to address those items on the designated dates. Let's look at the products of two of Bill's writing process tasks:

Brainstorming Sheet:

1. The Sun Also Rises—Why this title?
2. Jake seems tough but does cry and feel bad often.
3. Brett shaky—an alcoholic?
4. Jake's wound—mysterious, his groin
5. Bullfights—gory but exciting; but gets ruined for Jake
6. World War I
7. Party-time all the time
8. But the characters don't always like each other—Jake and Robert's fight, Mike can't stand Robert, Brett sleeps with three different guys
9. Brett and Jake—the status of their relationship?

10. Mike is bankrupt

11. Jake is a journalist

12. Jake goes to church but can't focus

13. Brett says she can't pray

14. Loss of faith

15. Bill seems less messed up than the rest

16. Romero's innocence and youth

17. Montoya—aficionado, wants to protect Romero

18. The loud music and fireworks

19. The ending—what will happen now?

Jake's wound; everyone's wounds

Loss of faith and hope

More general—is the novel optimistic or not?

Essay 1 Working Thesis and Basic Outline:

Working thesis: The novel is not optimistic because Hemingway is emphasizing how badly war can damage our world, as it has for these characters. Focus on certain metaphors to prove that this is the novel's message.

    I. Jake's wound

        a.   What it reveals about Jake

            i.   Physical effects

           ii.   Psychological effects

        b.   What it says as a metaphor for the other characters' "injuries"

            i.   They avoid really talking

            i.   They stay drunk all the time

    II. Bull fight—One of the last "sacred" things for Jake before it gets sullied

        a.   Montoya

        b.   Romero

        c.   Like loss of faith in everything else

In Chapter 5, we saw Bill's final draft of the essay. He did much work between composing the tentative outline, above, and completing the full, revised essay. With his task-list broken down and carefully scheduled, he was able to give each phase the attention and time necessary to produce a well-argued final essay.

8.3 Determining an Effective Essay Structure

One common misconception students entertain when they approach literary analysis essays is the idea that the structure of the essay should follow the structure of the literary work. The events of short stories, novels, and plays are often related chronologically, in linear order from the moment when the first event occurs to the moment of the last. Yet, it can be awkward to write a literary analysis using the story's chronology as a basic structure for your own essay. Often, this approach leads to an essay that simply summarizes the literary work. Since a literary analysis paper should avoid summary for summary's sake, the writer should avoid an essay structure that results in that pattern: *And then Brett goes to San Sebastian with Robert Cohn, and then she returns in time to meet her fiancé Mike Campbell, and then....*

Note that in Bill's essay on *The Sun Also Rises*, he decided to focus on two significant metaphors and to dedicate a major section of his paper to each. He does not mention Brett's trip to San Sebastian at all since it does not pertain directly to the paper's discussion of the metaphors. How *does* he determine the paper's arrangement? Why does he discuss the metaphor of Jake's wound before that of the tainted bull fights? In the novel, we do learn of Jake's wound first, and according to Bill, this metaphor helps establish the theme of psychological wounds caused by the war. So, chronology does influence the arrangement of the paper to some extent, but it is not the primary factor in the paper's structure. Rather than beginning his paper with a description of Jake's wound and then moving on to relate Brett's trip to San Sebastian with Robert, the ensuing antics of the group in Paris, their journey to Spain, etc., on through the list of the novel's plot events, Bill only includes the plot details supportive to his point, first illustrating the irreversible wounds of the group, represented by Jake's war-wound, and second examining the spoiled bull fights representing the group's irreparable loss of faith and hope. The arrangement of the paper does not *reject* chronological order simply for the sake of doing so—Bill relates the events in the sequence of their occurrence when it is reasonable. However, it is his focus on the two metaphors that provides the basic structure for his paper.

Similarly, in Katherine Jones's essay arguing that Brett Ashley is not a monster but a woman caught between two ideologies, she structures the paper this way:

I. Brett Ashley as sympathetic character in spite of some readers' disapproval of her behavior

    a.   Description of Brett's unconventional ways

    b.   Signs that her rebellion takes its toll on her

        i.   Alcohol

        ii.   Promiscuity

        iii.   Alienation and despair

II. Conclusion: Her behavior is understandable given her challenging circumstances

Like Bill, Katherine structures her paper by arranging the major points logically: The description of Brett's nontraditional behavior comes first in the essay's body because it helps set up the points that follow, points supporting Katherine's argument that Brett's struggles illuminate her very human, and thus understandable, reactions to her challenges.

If chronology is not the primary structural factor in setting up a literary analysis paper, what is? You might consider the following hints in arranging the points of your own essay:

1.   What *are* your major points? In Bill's essay, he explores *two important metaphors*; in Katherine's she examines (a) *Brett's unconventionality* and then (b) *evidence* that her nontraditional behavior is *more than simple pleasure-seeking*, seen in (i) her *alcoholism*, (ii) her *promiscuity*, and (iii) her *expressions of despair*. In Marion Velis's essay "Clinging to Love: Theodore Roethke's 'My Papa's Waltz'," printed in Chapter 2, her major points focus on Roethke's use of *rhythm*, the poem's *point of view*, and its *controlling metaphor*. These major points should form the main organizing components of the essay.

2.   What order will *most effectively lead the reader* to your perspective on this subject? In each of the essays mentioned above, the first point of discussion helps to set up the paper. These writers work to *draw in* and *orient* the reader, first with the introduction and then, further, in the second body paragraph. Conversely, the *final*

point of the paper's body should be one that helps to "clinch" the paper's argument or end it "with a bang" just before the conclusion reiterates the overarching argument in the essay's final lines.

3. Paragraph breaks should (a) cue the reader regarding shifts in focus (hence Bill begins a new paragraph when he finishes discussion of Jake's wound and starts his exploration of the spoiled bull fights) and (b) break down ideas into small enough chunks that the reader does not lose sight of the currently emphasized point (thus Katherine breaks her discussion of Brett's *need to cope* into separate paragraphs on *alcohol abuse, promiscuity,* and *expressions of Brett's despair*). On the other hand, in an academic essay, the paragraphs should not seem "choppy." Rather each should be long enough to develop its point thoroughly before shifting to the next.

The literary analysis paper can be written with examination of only the primary source, or, as we will discuss in the next chapter, you may integrate into your argument the perspectives of other scholars (secondary sources). Regardless, *your own findings* from your analysis of the primary text should be a priority in your interpretation of the work. Analytical skills are invaluable as you explore any subject, investigating the subject by breaking it down and looking closely at how it functions. Finding patterns in your observations, then, helps you to interpret your analysis and communicate to others how you came to your conclusions about the subject's meaning and/or effect. As you make your case to the readers, it is crucial that you make it clear how your perspective is relevant to them. Ideally, they will come away from your argument intrigued by the new insights you have revealed about the subject.

The Research Paper

Although analysis is a crucial phase in writing about any subject, the next step of contributing to society's knowledge and understanding is to participate in the *scholarly dialogue* on the subject. This point can be clarified by comparing a biology lab report with a scholarly scientific article. During the lab experiment, the scientist might examine a cancer cell, for example, after it has been treated with a particular substance. This first-hand (or primary) research is necessary to discovering whether the substance will have the desired effect on the cell. However, what if other scientists have tested this same substance on cancer cells previously? The results of your experiment do not exist in a vacuum. Chances are that you chose this substance for testing because, in your reading of existing scholarship, you learned which other substances have already been tried and what the outcomes of those experiments were. In testing this substance, you and your team may have altered the conditions of the experiment a bit to see if, under slightly different circumstances, the substance will act differently than it has in previous experiments. As the research is refined, and scientists continue to communicate their discoveries to each other and to the world, the body of knowledge on the subject grows and deepens. As a result of this "team" effort, human understanding expands. The dialogue among scholars, conveyed through academic articles and books, is a crucial resource for any researcher.

While it might be a bit intimidating to enter this dialogue as a college freshman, one must start somewhere! Certainly, you may feel strange disagreeing with something an expert in the field has said about your subject, but participating in this dialogue becomes easier with practice. One can disagree with a scholar while maintaining a tone respectful of that scholar's credentials and experience. After all, we are grateful for the groundwork our predecessors have laid for our own studies. However, things change, and with the benefit of hindsight, as well as of new technologies and new discoveries, your generation will undoubtedly further human understanding. You are encouraged to take up the mantle with curiosity and determination.

9.1 Getting a Handle on Academic Research

Likely born in the Information Age, you are probably quite adept at researching on the internet for information you use in your daily life. From finding a replacement screen for your broken cell phone to determining who wrote the terrific song you heard yesterday on the radio, you probably find it fairly easy to track down certain kinds of information. However, most students find it challenging to navigate university library search tools to find an academic article for a class project. Why the difference?

First, because academic search engines do not turn a profit as Google and Yahoo do, refinement of these systems happens at a much slower pace. If you type "tamixifen" into the Google search bar, you will be asked if you meant to search for "tamoxifen," and you'll be presented with a list of sources on that correctly spelled topic. Conversely, if you type "tamixifen" into your college library's science index search bar, you'll get a message that there are "no matches" for your search—a dead end. This is an example of the sophistication of commercial search engines as compared with academic ones. It may seem odd that scholars of today use substandard tools, but this is an effect of the differing economic models used by the for-profit and not-for-profit realms. In doing your research, you might be tempted just to revert to the Google search instead of struggling with Academic Search Complete. However, if you do so, you will find that publications on the most cutting edge research in your field cannot be accessed through Google. Academic journals usually require a paid subscription for anyone seeking to read their articles. Scholarly books recently published will not be distributed free of charge on the internet. The authors and publishers of these works function with a production model that requires funding but, for important ideological reasons, does not depend on advertising for that support, and thus access to these academic sources is limited. The chart in Chapter 3 will help you distinguish between **popular sources**, like those most often found on Google, and **scholarly sources** like those found in your college library.

Perhaps the most distinctive factor of the scholarly article or book is the peer-review process it must undergo before being accepted for publication. Through this process, the professionals of each discipline uphold its standards to ensure that the body of research in that field is truly expanding and is maintained at a high quality.

With these points in mind, let's consider the best ways for finding up-to-date scholarly resources for your academic research paper. As a student enrolled in a college or university, you have likely paid fees that give you access to your library's holdings. These include the many books (both physical and digital) that your library has purchased as well as subscriptions to academic journals in a multitude of fields. Consider the example of Rebekah Fish's poetry research paper assignment. She has chosen for her topic the poem "The Hunting of the Hare" by Margaret Cavendish.

On the advice of her instructor, Rebekah goes to her college library's web page and clicks on MLA International Bibliography. In looking at the other indexes available, she can see that there are indexes dedicated to research in biology, art, education, business, the medical fields, and many other disciplines. She makes a mental note in case she needs to use one of these for an assignment in another class.

In MLA, she types "The Hunting of the Hare" into the search bar, and under "Select a Field" she clicks on "subjects." She clicks on "Search," and soon the tool yields a list of article and book titles. Not all of these titles indicate a focus specifically on the poem she has chosen to write about—it appears that some articles simply include a paragraph or two on the poem. But Rebekah does not rule out these sources. Her professor has advised the class to *start narrow* and *then broaden* their search as necessary. Since Rebekah has found only a few sources written specifically on this poem, she does a new search on the poet, and again selects "subjects" as the field since she is not currently interested in finding works written *by* this poet. After printing the resulting list of articles, to go just a bit broader, Rebekah finds the web page listing the library's book holdings. Rebekah types "seventeenth century women poets" into the search bar, and finds two helpful book titles: *Margaret Cavendish: Gender, Genre, Exile,* by Emma L.E. Rees, and *Reading Early Modern Women's Writing,* by Paul Salzman.

Now that Rebekah has a good list of possible resources, she begins tracking them down and reading them. She makes notes about the focus of each work in case she needs to consider any of them again later. As she reviews her list, she puts a star next to the most promising articles and books. She needs five secondary sources for this project, and there is no use trying to force into her essay sources that do not match her focus. She picks those that will be most helpful to her as she defines and develops her argument.

9.2 Thesis Revisited

Although Rebekah has had in mind a working thesis shaping the argument for this paper, she now revisits this thesis. Having read several intriguing interpretations of the poem during her research, she works to refine her own thesis to reflect its unique angle on the subject. Now that she has a better sense of what her own argument will contribute to the general dialogue on "The Hunting of the Hare," she works on her paper outline, considering where her discussion of each selected secondary source will fit best.

9.3 Integrating Research into Your Own Arguments

Striving to establish her own perspective on the poem, to say something original rather than simply reporting what other scholars have said, Rebekah works to keep her own voice dominant in the essay. While she incorporates paraphrase, summary, and quotes from her secondary sources, she is careful that the majority of the essay's words are her own and that she does not allow the critics to speak *for* her. To clarify whose ideas are whose, she employs **tag words and phrases**, such as "according to," "Smith argues," "Smith claims," and "contrary to Smith's position on this point, Jones argues…." These tag words guide Rebekah's readers through the variety of perspectives to a clear view of *Rebekah's* argument. Further, she is careful to cite all references within the paper and to include a bibliography at the end of the essay listing every source she has mentioned in the paper.

It is important to note that because Rebekah's subject is the poem, she must draw from the poem itself for her primary evidence. Thus, *quoting* from the primary text is not only helpful, but necessary. While she works to control the discussion with her own voice, she enriches the texture of the essay by pulling in important lines of the poem at key moments in her argument. Not only do they serve to support her major points, but they also generate a poetic quality in the essay itself, bringing the poem to life for readers.

9.4 Documentation

Several major *documentation styles* can be employed for academic projects, each style common to certain disciplines. In the past, you may have employed MLA style in your own English papers. MLA, maintained by the Modern Language Association, is generally used for writing in the humanities, particularly on language and literature topics. However, it is important to be aware of the other major styles for use in projects in other areas. APA (established and maintained by the American Psychological Association) is usually used for writing in the social sciences. Chicago

Manual Style (or CMS) is often used in the field of history, though it is employed by various publications across the humanities. CSE, established and maintained by the Council of Science Editors, is employed in biology and other sciences. As a student moving among the disciplines, keep in mind that *conventions vary among fields*. You can find guidelines for each of these documentation styles online at the Purdue Online Writing Lab (OWL) website: https://owl.english.purdue.edu/owl/. Below is a list of the basic rules for MLA documentation style to guide you as you compose your literary research paper.

9.4.1 In-Text Citations

A common way to cite your in-text sources is *parenthetically*, as in the following example:

> Jake participates in "gossip" about his peers' activities (Adair 114) perhaps as a means to get revenge for their engagement in intimacy, which he cannot enjoy.

Here, the writer includes the last name of the article's author and the page number from which the information or concept comes. The writer might alternatively *mention* the author and then in parenthesis include only the page number:

> Jake participates in "gossip" about his peers' activities, as Adair notes, perhaps as a means to get revenge for their engagement in intimacy which he cannot enjoy (114).

MLA emphasizes the avoidance of footnotes and endnotes unless absolutely necessary. Consequently, we have omitted footnote and endnote formating information. Please refer to the latest MLA guide for futher information regarding proper formatting: https://style.mla.org/2016/02/29/using-notes-in-mla-style/.

Subsequent References:

After you provide a full "note" on a source in your paper, if you refer to that source again, you do not need to provide the full "note" again. Instead, include just the author's name (or the work's title, if there is no author) and the page number(s) being referenced, as demonstrated below:

Adair 116.

9.4.2 Work Cited Page

You will likely need to provide a Bibliography, or Works Cited page, in addition to footnotes or endnotes; such a list will certainly be required if you have employed parenthetical notes. These entries require a somewhat different format than the footnotes/endnotes, so pay close attention to the differences. For the Works Cited Page, arrange the entries for your sources *in alphabetical order* according to the *authors' last names*, or if there is no author listed, by the article title's first word. List authors by last name first. Also, note that unlike in a paragraph or a footnote, which indents the first line and brings the rest of the text back to the margin, a bibliography entry does exactly the opposite!

Print Journal Article:

Author's last name, first name. "Article Title." *Journal Title,* vol. number, issue number, Date of Publication, page numbers of entire article.

William, Adair. "Ernest Hemingway's The Sun Also Rises: The Novel as Gossip." *The Hemingway Review*, vol. 3, no.1, Spring 2012, pp. 114-118.

Journal Article from an Electronic Database:

Author's last name, first name. "Article Title." *Journal Title*, vol. number, issue number, Date of Publication, page numbers if available. *Database from which the article was retrieved (such as JSTOR)*. DOI or URL. Date on which it was retrieved.

Adair, William. "Ernest Hemingway's The Sun Also Rises: The Novel as Gossip." *The Hemingway Review*, vol. 3, no. 1, Spring 2012, pp. 114-118. *ProQu*est. http://search.proquest.com/docview/1022331888/abstract/D8BB688BB6264584PQ/2?accountid=159965. Accessed 28 Feb. 2013.

Book:

Author's last name, first name. *Title of the Book*. Publisher, Date of Publication, page numbers used if applicable.

Boehrer, Bruce Thomas. *Animal Characters: Nonhuman Beings in Early Modern Literature*. U of Pennsylvania P, 2010, pp. 32-3.

A Work in an Anthology:

Author's Last Name, and First Name. "Work Title." *Anthology Title*, Editor's Name, Publisher, Date of Publication, Page numbers on which the work appears.

Locke, Alain. "The New Negro." *The Norton Anthology of African American Literature*, edited by Henry Louis Gates, Jr. and Nellie Y. McKay, W.W. Norton, 1997, pp. 961-970.

Article from Online Reference Book (no author):

"Article Title." Publication title. *Website*, Date posted, URL address. Date accessed.

"The Nobel Prize in Literature 1954." *Nobelprize.org*, 2014, https://www. nobelprize.org/nobel_prizes/literature/laureates/1954/. Accessed 30 July 2014.

9.5 Sample Student Paper

Rebekah's research essay on Margaret Cavendish's poem "The Hunting of the Hare" illustrates several of the principles discussed in this chapter:

- How to integrate scholarly secondary sources without relinquishing control of the argument
- How to make it clear whose ideas are whose through use of tag words and phrases
- How to employ parenthetical in-text citations according to MLA guidelines
- How to construct a Works Cited page according to MLA guidelines

Rebekah Fish
English 3460

Human Nature in Margaret Cavendish's
"The Hunting of the Hare"

Margaret Cavendish's 1653 poem "The Hunting of the Hare" relates the cruel fate of a hare that has fallen prey to a group of hunters. A study of this poem suggests that Cavendish can be viewed as one of the first supporters for animal rights as she criticizes the cruelty of men who kill animals for sport. On a more personal level, Cavendish could have closely identified with the hare, which is ostensibly humanlike, and also with its fear. She might have even intended to parallel her critics to the dogs and the hunters within the poem. On a grander scale, Cavendish might be making the critical judgment that humankind seeks enjoyment through violent competition with others. Through a study of the many different thematic levels of the poem, Margaret Cavendish's "The Hunting of the Hare" seems to have an overarching theme of humanity's destructive attraction to violence in order to achieve supremacy.

It is evident through the poet's portrayal of the hare that it is meant to be seen as a significant and even a symbolic figure, beginning in the first line of the poem where the hare is granted the name "Wat." He is humanlike, "glaring" across the landscape as his "Haires blew up behind" him in the wind instead of his fur (4 and 6). The hare is also described as "wise" instead of merely being a sentient creature, and Cavendish makes its humanlike features even more evident as the hare "walks about" rather than hopping or crawling (Cavendish 7 and 11). Another way the rabbit is seemingly anthropomorphized is through the continual use of the personal pronoun "him" in the poem, which is used instead of "it." To indicate her disapproval of the unethical treatment of all animals, near the very end of the poem Cavendish grants all creatures the same humanlike quality as the hare by saying that creatures are being "murdered" (100) by men instead of "killed."

The word "murder" connotes unlawfulness and makes a connection between that illicitness and the killing of animals, indicating that all sentient life, that of humans and animals, is important and worthy of being preserved. Some may even argue that Cavendish was trying to make a point that humankind should not express dominant authority over other creatures through use of violence, because within the last lines of the poem, man is portrayed not only as murderous, but also as an oppressive tyrant that rules over all other living creatures.

Cavendish's humanlike portrayal of the hare might raise concerns for some readers. Bruce Thomas Boehrer discusses some critics' objection to an author's anthropomorphizing nonhuman characters. To anthropomorphize is to project one's own tendencies and traits onto another species. Some critics argue that this act ignores a nonhuman species' real behaviors and traits and illustrates humans' feeling of dominance over nature. However, as Boehrer explains, many animal characters in literature "challenge the human-animal divide" (5) and force people to examine their values, especially those related to nature. Donna Landry supports the view that "The Hunting of the Hare" raises these issues. She argues that in Cavendish's work, she promotes the "democratizing of relations between humans and other species" (471). Rather than emphasizing the superiority of human emotions by anthropomorphizing the hare, Cavendish humanizes him in order to bridge the gap between the reader and the hare. Paul Salzman states that Cavendish's main goal as a writer was "to enter into an empathetic relationship with the world around her" (142). In "The Hunting of the Hare," Cavendish portrays the hare with empathy in order to persuade the reader that committing unnecessary violence on animals is cruel and terrible.

In addition, the description of the hare is used to form and emphasize the strong connection between the hare and Cavendish, who was similarly being pursued by her critics as a female writer. This criticism is clearly shown through the description of Cavendish by Mary Evelyn, who portrayed her as extravagant and vain and said that her discourse was "as airy, empty, whimsical, and rambling as her books" (Qtd. in Damrosch and Dettmar 2058-9). Many people of Cavendish's time viewed her as outrageous, partly because publicly recognized women writers were rare during the seventeenth century. Although scholars seriously study Cavendish's work now, Emma L.E. Rees says that because of the harsh critics of her time, "The impression which lasted for many years was of an eccentric, disturbed and arrogant woman" (11). "The Hunting of the Hare" could be interpreted as a response to this criticism. Her critics, paralleled by both the "cruel dogs" (16) and the men in the poem, are often referred to as merciless. The critics are described as nosy through common references to the dogs and how they always "thrust [their] snuffling nose[s]" into things (64). They are also described as loudmouths through the image of the dogs who cry out with their "wide mouths" (19). While at times Cavendish seems to be uncaring as to what the critics say about her, at other times she seems terrified of the public's opinion of her life and writing, much like the hare's terror of being pursued. She suggests that in public, she hides her fear of the critics, similarly to the hare when, "Licking his feet, he wiped his ears so clean / That none could tell that Wat had hunted been" (41-2). Although the critics continued to pursue her, Cavendish emphasizes through the poem that she will continue to maintain her composure until the very end, like the hare does until his death. Yet, this continual pursuing and killing of hares, which parallels Cavendish's experience, critiques human nature's desire for supremacy over all living things—even each other.

Not only can Cavendish's poem be seen as a response to the cruelty to animals and the cruelty of the critics, but it can also be seen as an assessment of how humankind treats its brethren. In the poem, the men are portrayed as bloodthirsty monsters that thrive off cruelty to others. The men in Cavendish's poem, who "destroy those lives that God did make" (98) solely for "sport or recreation's sake" (97), seek to kill the rabbit, the symbol, through heavy personification, of a fellow human (Cavendish 2062).

To conclude, Margaret Cavendish's "The Hunting of the Hare" is a comment on human nature and the desire for obtaining dominion over others by any means necessary. Through her extensive use of pathos throughout the poem, her audience was meant to feel a sense of culpability and a desire to change. Despite her portrayal of human nature as inherently evil, the guilt the audience is supposed to feel offers a sense of hope, as it indicates that human nature is capable of being altered and even changed.

Works Cited

Boehrer, Bruce Thomas. *Animal Characters: Nonhuman Beings in Early Modern Literature*, U of Pennsylvania P, 2010.

Cavendish, Margaret. "The Hunting of the Hare." 1653. *UC Press E-books Collection*, http://publishing.cdlib. org/ucpressebooks/view?docId=kt7q2nc9xn&chunk. id=ss1.55&toc.depth=100&toc.id=ch09&brand=eschol. Accessed 3 October 2013.

Damrosch, David and Kevin J. H. Dettmar. "Margaret Cavendish, Duchess of Newcastle." *The Longman Anthology: British Literature*, edited by David Damrosch and Kevin J. H. Dettmar, Longman, 2010, pp. 2060-63.

Landry, Donna. "Green Languages? Women Poets as Naturalists in 1653 and 1807." *Huntington Library Quarterly*, vol. 63, no.4, 2000, pp. 467-89. *JSTOR*. www.jstor.org/stable/3817613. Accessed 2 Oct. 2013.

Rees, Emma L.E. *Margaret Cavendish: Gender, Genre, Exile*. Manchester UP, 2003. *EBSCOHost*, libproxy. ung.edu/login?url=http://search.ebscohost.com/login. aspx?direct=true&db=mzh&AN=2004581244&site=e ds-live&scope=site. Accessed 8 Nov. 2013.

Salzman, Paul. *Reading Early Modern Women's Writing*. Oxford UP, 2006.

9.6 Research Paper Checklist

When you write an academic research paper, there are so many factors to keep in mind that it can become overwhelming. Often, students finish an assignment like this having overlooked an important requirement or two. This chapter closes with The Research Paper Checklist below, intended to help you double-check your paper before you make the final submission.

Criterion	Check if Completed
Asserts a clear and interesting thesis that controls the entire essay	
Opens with an engaging and effective introduction, which provides background on the topic and writer's position	
Is clearly and effectively organized	
Employs clear and engaging prose (prose that is not riddled with grammatical errors or awkward constructions)	
Provides transitions and explanations that help reveal relationships between ideas (develops coherence)	
Provides adequate evidence to prove the writer's point (asserted by thesis)	
Effectively integrates outside sources, providing internal documentation according to appropriate documentation style	
Uses tag phrases (such as "according to Smith," "Smith argues," etc.) to indicate whose ideas are whose	
Incorporates minimal number of scholarly sources in the essay according to the professor's instructions	
Avoids plagiarism by __indicating all quoted material (even short bits) with quotation marks and in-text source information and __providing in-text source information for all paraphrased and summarized material	
Wraps up with a conclusion that effectively reiterates the point and/or urges the reader to action or change of perspective	
In Works Cited section, lists only sources that are mentioned in the essay	
In Works Cited section, lists all sources that are mentioned in the essay	
Follows field-appropriate documentation guidelines for Works Cited entries	

Glossary

Aesthetic: Pertaining to art and/or beauty

Alliteration: The placement of same or similar sounds near each other to draw our attention, sometimes to the sound, sometimes to meanings of the words being linked to each other by the sounds, and sometimes both

Allusion: A work's reference, sometimes subtle, to another work in order to "plug into" the meaning the reader associates with the other work

Analysis: Breaking down a thing or idea to its smaller parts in order to better understand the whole

Annotate: Adding explanation or comment; to annotate a work is to make notes on it for increased understanding; annotation can also refer to the summary of a source in an annotated bibliography

Archetype: A character-figure that is seen often in stories (such as "the hero" or "the devil"); some attribute the archetype's symbolic power to the idea that these patterns are etched in the human psyche

Ballad: Associated with common songs and poetry; the ballad stanza is a quatrain (a four-line stanza), and the rhythm alternates iambic tetrameter lines (featuring four iambs) with iambic trimeter lines (containing three iambs each). While there may be no rhyme with line one or line three of the stanza, line two rhymes with line four, giving the poem a "sing-song" quality. A ballad is a song/story that uses this form

Blank Verse: An iambic pentameter line (five two-foot syllables with the stress on each second syllable) but without rhyme

Catalog: A list; often used by writers for poetic effect to produce a "panoramic view" of a scene or experience

Central Argument: See thesis

Cite: To mention or refer to a source

Climax of Plot: The point in the plot where the conflict is "brought to a head," to its most intense moment

Comedy: Associated with Greek drama, maintains a farcical tone and usually ends in marriage

Conflict: The struggle between two opposing forces

Controlling or Extended Metaphor: A metaphor developed all the way through a work and which, through its structural role, conveys the poem's meaning

Conventions: Rules that govern genres, such as visual appearance, line length, subject, and plot patterns

Couplet: Two rhyming lines of poetry in iambic pentameter

Creative Nonfiction: Written in prose form, the creative nonfiction essay generally strives for a poetic effect, employing a kind of compressed, distilled language so that most words carry more meaning than their simple denotation (or literal meaning). Generally, this kind of essay is not heavy with researched information or formal argument; its priority, instead, is to generate a powerful emotional and aesthetic effect

Critical Perspective: An interpretation based on evidence gathered from a text combined with the values of the critic

Deductive Reasoning: Conclusion based on logical equation; see syllogism and enthymeme

Denouement: The resolution of a story where "loose ends are tied up" (in French, "the knot is untied")

Description: Revelation of a thing's or person's state, usually through sensory detail or exposition

Dialogue: Conversation related as if it were actually occurring

Diction: Word choice

Drama: A play in which characters "dramatize," or act out the story

Enjambment: Carries one poetic line into the following one, yielding two meanings—one generated by the first line alone, and the other produced by taking the finished phrase or clause as it is completed in the next line

Enthymeme: A logical statement missing the major premise; for example,

261

"Cynthia is mortal because she is a woman." That she is a woman is the minor premise, and the conclusion is that she is mortal. What is missing is the major premise, that "All women are mortal." See syllogism

Ethos: The appeal to ethics, or a reader's trust in the author/speaker

Exposition: Direct explanation rather than illumination by narrative or dialogue

Fiction: Non-historical story

Figurative Language: As opposed to literal language, suggests meaning beyond a word's denotation

Form: Refers to the category and/or conventions of a work; for example, detective fiction or sonnet

Formalism: An approach to literary criticism that came about in the 1920s and remains well-regarded by many today; holds that the art work (including literature) should be considered as an object separate from the author. Formalists feel that a text means on its own and that its meaning can be derived by analyzing its elements and their function

Free Verse: Poetry not governed by common rules

Genre: Refers to types or categories of literature

Inductive Reasoning: Forming conclusions based on samples

Irony: An idea turned back upon itself; in an ironic passage, the words mean something different than the literal meanings would suggest

Logos: The appeal to intellect or logic

Lyric Poem: Originated in classical poetry, following specific rhythms and rhyme schemes; these poems were often accompanied by music

Metaphor: A comparison of two generally unlike things in order to emphasize a particular quality that they do share

Narrative: A story, composed of a sequence of events, often associated in a cause-effect relationship

One-Act Play: A drama that can usually be performed in an hour or less and in which the entire story is performed in one act as opposed to several

Paraphrase: Restatement of a passage in one's own words; the retelling is roughly the same length as the original

Pathos: The appeal to a reader's emotions

Peer-Reviewed Source: A researched article or book that has been reviewed and evaluated by experts in the same field before being approved for publication

Persona: Term for the main "character" in a poem, spoken of in third person, "he" or "she"

Plot: The sequence of events that develops the conflict and shapes a story

Poetry: Literary genre by which the author expresses a story and/or ideas in verse, employing rhythm and other aesthetic qualities of language to achieve the desired effect

Point of View: Perspective on the events or ideas of a work; common points of view are first person limited (an "I" in the story or poem who only knows what he or she thinks, experiences and observes), third person limited omniscient (speaks in third person about the characters, using "he" and "she," but only knows the thoughts and feelings of the protagonist), and third person omniscient (is not a character in the story, thus speaks of all characters using "he" and "she"; knows what all characters think and feel as well as information the characters don't know sometimes)

Popular Source: An article, book, newspaper, blog, website, or other source written for and marketed to the common reader, rather than to experts on the subject

Primary Source or Primary Evidence: The thing being studied; for example, a lab report recording direct observations of an experience or a poem

Prose: Non-poetic writing; that is, writing not broken up into distinct lines

Protagonist: The main character of a work, generally expected to learn and mature

Rhetoric: The art of persuasion

Rhyme: The effect that occurs when two words ending in the same vowel sound are juxtaposed with one another

Rhythm: Sound created by patterns of language; often based on numbers of syllables in the words of a line; sometimes based on number of stressed sounds (beats) in a line

Scholarly Source: See peer reviewed source

Script: The written version of a play, including dialogue designated for each character

Secondary Source: A source analyzing and interpreting a primary source; for example, a scholarly article about *The Sun Also Rises*

Sensory Detail: Detail that can be observed by the senses: taste, smell, hearing, touch, sight

Set: The backdrop and props in a play that recreate the setting for an audience

Setting: The place that provides the context for a story or poem

Simile: A comparison—using "like" or "as"—of two generally unlike things in order to emphasize a particular quality that they do share

Slant Rhyme: An "almost rhyme" with words that look like they should rhyme but don't (like "be" and "fly") or with words that sound alike but not exactly the same (like "room" and "storm")

Sonnet: A fourteen line poem usually following recognized rules for rhythm, line-length, and rhyme scheme. In the fourteen-line Shakespearean sonnet, each line is written in iambic pentameter, and the rhyme scheme of the poem follows this pattern: ABAB CDCD EFEF GG. Concluding with a couplet, the Shakespearean sonnet resolves the conflict or problem in the final two lines, and the GG rhyme enhances this feeling of completion

Speaker: A consciousness (or person) constructed by the author to provide point of view for the work

Stage Direction: Directions in a play's script regarding where and how actors should stand and move, instructions regarding props, and sometimes recommendations regarding tone and speech delivery

Stanza: Unit of text in a poem (paralleled by the paragraph in prose); many poetic forms dictate a certain number of lines in each stanza

Summary: A condensed reiteration in one's own words of a passage from another source

Syllogism: A three part logical statement including

A general statement, or major premise: All women are mortal.

A minor premise: Cynthia is a woman.

And a conclusion: Cynthia is a mortal.

Symbol: Represents something else, usually because of long-term association with that thing (For example, for many people, an American flag symbolizes freedom and a red rose symbolizes love)

Tag words and phrases: Words and phrases attributing credit to an author for an idea or original wording ("according to," "claims," "asserts," "argues," etc.)

Tension: Intensity generated by two conflicting forces

Textual evidence: Examples from a text (conveyed through direct quote, paraphrase, or summary) that can be used to interpret the work as a whole

Theme: Emphasis regarding the topic or meaning of a text; for example, fear of death or the dangers of pride

Thesis: The central argument of a text which controls the text as a whole

Tone: The feeling, atmosphere, or mood of a work

Tragedy: Associated with Greek drama, maintains a gloomy tone and usually ends in death

Working thesis: A tentative thesis for use while composing an essay; refined and crafted over time into its final form

Villanelle: Poetic form requiring nineteen lines, distributed into five tercets and a quatrain, and also requiring that the first and third line of the first stanza be repeated alternately in the last lines of the stanzas that follow it. In the final quatrain, the two repeated lines conclude the poem

Resources for Instructors

1.0 Suggested Themes for the Course:
*Texts not included in this book. For links to these texts, see 2.0
Additional Readings, below.

Negotiating Personal Relationships
    *The Sun Also Rises** or *The Awakening**
    Trifles
    The Tempest
    "My Papa's Waltz"
    Shakespeare's Sonnet 130
    "Do Not Go Gentle into That Good Night"*
    "Those Winter Sundays"*
    "Annabel Lee"
    "The Story of an Hour"
    "Old Lady Down the Hall"*

The Individual vs. Society
    *The Adventures of Huckleberry Finn**
    *A Room with a View** or *The Awakening**
    Trifles
    Shakespeare's Sonnet 130
    "The Weary Blues"*
    "Still I Rise"*
    "Frederick Douglass"
    "The Story of an Hour"
    "The Passing of Grandison"
    "How to Tame a Wild Tongue"*
    "Why I Write"*

Determining an Ethical Code
  The Sea-Wolf*
  The Adventures of Huckleberry Finn*
  The Scarlet Letter*
  The Sun Also Rises*
  A Room with a View* or *Frankenstein**
  Trifles
  The Tempest
  "The Gettysburg Address"
  "Dover Beach"
  "Annabel Lee"
  "Frederick Douglass"
  "Those Winter Sundays"*
  "The Hunting of the Hare"
  "Young Goodman Brown"*
  "The Open Boat"
  "The Passing of Grandison"
  "The Value of Science"*
  "Why I Write"*
  "Design"*
  "Of Luddites, Learning, and Life"*
  "How I Got My D.I.Y. Degree"*

Science: Friend or Foe?
  Frankenstein*
  "Dover Beach"
  "The Value of Science"*
  "Of Luddites, Learning, and Life"*

From the Margins
  The House Behind the Cedars*
  The Scarlet Letter*
  Frankenstein* or *The Awakening**
  "The Weary Blues"*
  "Still I Rise"*
  "Frederick Douglass"
  "Those Winter Sundays"*
  "The Story of an Hour"
  "The Passing of Grandison"
  Trifles
  The Tempest
  "How to Tame a Wild Tongue"*

The Power of Nature
    *Frankenstein** or *The Sea-Wolf**
    "I Heard a Fly Buzz—When I Died"
    "The Open Boat"
    "The Death of the Moth"*
    "The Value of Science"*
    "Design"*

The Function of Art
    *The Awakening**
    The Tempest
    "Ode on a Grecian Urn"
    "The Weary Blues"*
    "Poetry"*
    "Do Not Go Gentle into That Good Night"*
    "Blackberry Eating"*
    "Annabel Lee"
    "Frederick Douglass"
    "The Open Boat"
    "Why I Write"*
    "Design"*
    "How to Tame a Wild Tongue"*

From Naïveté to Experience
    *The Adventures of Huckleberry Finn**
    *The House Behind the Cedars**
    *The Awakening** or *Frankenstein**
    Trifles
    "My Papa's Waltz"
    "Those Winter Sundays"*
    "The Story of an Hour"
    "The Death of the Moth"*
    "Goodbye to All That"*
    "Why I Write"*
    "Young Goodman Brown"*
    "Design"*
    "How I Got My D.I.Y. Degree"*

2.0 Additional Readings

The Adventures of Huckleberry Finn　　　　Mark Twain　　　　　　　novel
Project Gutenberg
http://www.gutenberg.org/files/76/76-h/76-h.htm

The Awakening　　　　　　　　　　Kate Chopin　　　　　　novel
Project Gutenberg
http://www.gutenberg.org/ebooks/160?msg=welcome_stranger

"Design"　　　　　　　　　　　　Robert Frost　　　　　　poem
Poets.org
http://www.poets.org/poetsorg/poem/design

"The Five Orange Pips"　　　　　　Arthur Conan Doyle　　　short story
Project Gutenberg
http://www.gutenberg.org/files/1661/1661-h/1661-h.htm#5

Frankenstein　　　　　　　　Mary Wollstonecraft Shelley　　　novel
Project Gutenberg
http://www.gutenberg.org/ebooks/84

The House Behind the Cedars　　　　Charles W. Chesnutt　　　　novel
Project Gutenberg
http://www.gutenberg.org/ebooks/472

"How I Got My D.I.Y. Degree"　　　William Upski Wimsatt　　　　essay
Self Education Foundation. Originally published in *Utne Reader* (May/June 1998).
http://selfeducationfoundation.wordpress.com/sef-history/diy-degree/

"How to Tame a Wild Tongue"　　　　Gloria Anzaldua　　　　essay
Borderlands/La Frontera
https://www.sfu.ca/iirp/documents/Anzaldua%201999.pdf

"Of Luddites, Learning, and Life"	Neil Postman	essay

Technos Quarterly 2.4 (1993).
http://www.faculty.rsu.edu/users/f/felwell/www/Theorists/Postman/Articles/
TECHNOS_NET.htm

"Old Lady Down the Hall"	David Sedaris	essay

Esquire.com. 1 October, 2000.
http://www.esquire.com/news-politics/a498/old-lady-hall-sedaris-1000/

A Room with a View	E.M. Forster	novel

Project Gutenberg
http://www.gutenberg.org/ebooks/2641

The Scarlet Letter	Nathaniel Hawthorne	novel

Project Gutenberg
http://www.gutenberg.org/ebooks/33

The Sea-Wolf	Jack London	novel

Project Gutenberg
http://www.gutenberg.org/ebooks/1074

The Sun Also Rises	Ernest Hemingway	novel

Internet Archive
https://archive.org/details/sunalsorises030276mbp

"Young Goodman Brown"	Nathaniel Hawthorne	short story

Project Gutenberg
http://www.gutenberg.org/files/512/512-h/512-h.htm#goodman

3.0 Assignment Ideas
Article Critique Assignment
This assignment offers students experience in reading and evaluating a scholarly article, requiring them to practice their rhetorical analysis skills. It can be an effective scaffolding exercise as you build toward the research paper. Please, feel free to modify this assignment to address a peer-reviewed article more pertinent to your class's theme or focus.

Jacob Michael Leland. "'Yes, That is a Roll of Bills in My Pocket': The Economy of Masculinity in *The Sun Also Rises*." *The Hemingway Review* 23.2 (2004): 37.

In this 600-800 word essay, you will offer an evaluation of the article cited above. Your introduction should convey in your own words Leland's central argument, or thesis, as well as your judgment regarding the article's persuasiveness. Does Leland convince you that his interpretation of *The Sun Also Rises* is valid?

The body of the essay should develop support for your answer to the question above. If you are not convinced of Leland's perspective on the novel, what are your reasons? What aspects of Leland's article weaken his case and keep him from achieving his purpose effectively? If you find Leland's case convincing, on the other hand, which rhetorical strategies persuaded you? Remember to organize the essay according to the major points you have selected to support your position.

Annotated Bibliography Assignment

Another effective building block, this assignment not only requires students to practice finding, reading, and understanding peer-reviewed sources, but it also helps them achieve substantial progress toward the research paper if that final assignment focuses on the same literary text.

For this assignment, you will gather, cite, and annotate (summarize) five secondary, scholarly sources on a text from our reading assignments (these are not the type of sources you normally find by doing a Google search). Your bibliography will need to cite both articles and books, if possible. Citations must follow current MLA guidelines. Each annotation will provide a summary (between 90 and 110 words) of the source, stating the author's main argument and key points/evidence supporting that argument.

The entries for your bibliography should be alphabetized by the authors' last names (or first word of each entry). They should not be numbered.

Be careful that your annotations are summarized and not quoted. The challenge of writing these short annotations

271

is in capturing the gist of each text in a summary using your own words. To summarize something, one must understand it! If you have trouble understanding some of the sources you find, you can email me for an appointment to discuss the article or book.

Sample Literary Analysis Paper Topics

1. In "Ode on a Grecian Urn," how does Keats employ nature imagery? What is the role of nature, as represented here, in the poem's assertion about art?

2. In "The Weary Blues," how does Langston Hughes incorporate features of blues music into the poem itself? How does this device contribute to the poem's meaning? (What is the poem's meaning?)

3. In "Dover Beach," how does Matthew Arnold contrast positive images and diction with negative images and diction? What point does the poem make through this contrast?

4. Is the speaker of Edgar Allan Poe's "Annabel Lee" reliable? What is the effect of our learning about Annabel Lee only from him?

5. Compare and contrast Kate Chopin's *The Awakening* with Susan Glaspell's *Trifles*. What can we learn from this comparison? For your thesis, focus on an important insight that comes from the comparison.

6. What does Shakespeare's *The Tempest* reveal about the potential dangers of power?

7. Compare and contrast Matthew Arnold's "Dover Beach" with Richard P. Feynman's "The Value of Science." Does Feynman address the problem raised by Arnold?

8. How does death shape our daily lives? Choose from the following works and explore how the text addresses this question: *The Sea-Wolf*, "Do Not Go Gentle into That Good Night," "Annabel Lee," "Ode on a Grecian Urn," "I Heard a Fly Buzz—When I Died," "The Open Boat," and "The Death of the Moth."

9. How does economic class shape people's everyday lives? Choose from the following works and explore how the text addresses this question: *A Room with a View, The Awakening, Trifles*, "My Papa's Waltz," "Those Winter Sundays," "Annabel Lee," "The Passing of Grandison," "How to Tame a Wild Tongue," "Still I Rise," and "How I Got My D.I.Y. Degree."

10. Revise #9 to focus on race/ethnicity, gender, or "difference." The latter topic could include *Frankenstein*, in which the monster suffers and is hardened by the mistreatment he experiences simply because he is different.

Research Paper Assignment(s)

Any of the topics listed for the Literary Analysis Paper could, of course, be modified to require integration of scholarly research. The comparison/contrast topics might be a bit challenging for first year composition students to transfer into the research context, since formulating an effective thesis for a comparison/contrast paper is sometimes a challenge in itself. However, if used flexibly, any of the topics listed above could open doors to fruitful research projects.

Another possibility for expanding the scope of the research paper is to allow students to take one of the themes generated by their literary readings and transfer it into another discipline of their greater interest. Below is an example of such an assignment:

> For this research paper, you will investigate a question associated with *The Sun Also Rises.* Your topic should be one that will deepen our understanding of Hemingway's novel, although there is no need to mention the novel in your paper. Remember that a good research paper, in the area of history or sociology, for example, does not just tell facts; it interprets those facts in a logical way that suggests a *meaningful perspective* on the information (a thesis). If you choose to focus on a literary topic for this paper, you will use MLA style for documentation; if history, Chicago Manual style (CMS); if sociology or psychology, APA style. You will use footnotes to cite your in-text references, and a bibliography page at the end, listing all sources referenced throughout the paper. In addition to the MLA guidelines included in Chapter 9 of this book, you can find helpful information on MLA, CMS, and APA styles at Purdue Owl: https://owl.english. purdue.edu/owl/.
>
> This essay should be 1500-2000 words in length (approximately 5 to 7 pages) and must be typed, double-spaced. You should integrate 6-7 scholarly sources into the discussion.

Sample topics:

1. How did warfare change during World War I, and how did these changes impact military personnel psychologically?

2. Why did many feel that World War I did not resolve the world's political issues satisfactorily?

3. How did World War I impact the field of medicine?

4. How did World War I serve as catalyst to evolving women's roles?

5. What is PTSD and how has our understanding of this condition improved? What are the most effective treatments for those who suffer from PTSD?

6. What is the common relationship between alcoholism and personal trauma? What steps can be taken to treat alcoholism in these circumstances?

7. How are notions of manhood and virility commonly intertwined? What does this relationship tell us about social definitions of masculinity?

Bibliography

Angelou, Maya. "Still I Rise." *And Still I Rise*, Random House, Inc., 1978. *Poets.org*, http://www.poets.org/poetsorg/poem/still-i-rise. Accessed 22 July 2014.

Anzaldua, Gloria. "How to Tame a Wild Tongue." *Borderlands / La Frontera*, 2nd ed., Aunt Lute Books, 1987. *Simon Fraser University*, https://www.sfu.ca/iirp/documents/Anzaldua%201999.pdf. Accessed 21 Dec. 2014.

Aristotle. *Rhetoric*. Translated W. Rhys Roberts. 1954, *Eserver*. Hypertext resource compiled by Lee Honeycutt, 27 Sept. 2011, http://rhetoric.eserver.org/aristotle/. Accessed 21 July 2014.

Arnold, Matthew. "Dover Beach." 1867. *Poetry Foundation*, http://www.poetryfoundation.org/poem/172844. Accessed 22 July 2014.

Cavendish, Margaret. "The Hunting of the Hare." 1653. *UC Press E-books Collection*, http://publishing.cdlib.org/ucpressebooks/view?docId=kt7q2nc9x-n&chunk.id=ss1.55&toc.depth=100&brand=ucpress. Accessed 3 August 2014.

Chesnutt, Charles W. *The House Behind the Cedars*. Project Gutenberg, 9 Oct. 2008, http://www.gutenberg.org/files/472/472-h/472-h.htm. Accessed 25 Jan. 2014.

——. "The Passing of Grandison." 1899. *AmericanLiterature.com*, https://americanliterature.com/author/charles-w-chesnutt/short-story/the-passing-of-grandison. Accessed 22 July 2014.

Chopin, Kate. "The Awakening." *The Awakening and Selected Short Stories*, 1899. *Project Gutenberg*, 11 Mar. 2006, http://www.gutenberg.org/files/160/160-h/160-h.htm. Accessed 9 Mar. 2014.

——. "The Story of an Hour." Version 2, *St. Louis Life*, 5 Jan. 1895. *The Kate Chopin International Society*, http://www.katechopin.org/the-story-of-an-hour/. Accessed 22 July 2014.

Crane, Stephen. "The Open Boat." *The Open Boat and Other Stories*, William Heinemann, 1898. *Project Gutenberg*, http://www.gutenberg.org/files/45524/45524-h/45524-h.htm. Accessed 21 July 2014.

Dickinson, Emily. "I Heard a Fly Buzz—When I Died." *The Poems of Emily Dickinson*, edited by R.W. Franklin, Harvard UP, 1999. *Poetry Foundation*, http://www.poetryfoundation.org/poem/174972. Accessed 22 July 2014.

Didion, Joan. "Goodbye to All That." 1967. *Julia Allison*, http://juliaallison.com/goodbye-to-all-that-by-joan-didion/. Accessed 27 July 2014.

Doyle, Arthur Conan. "The Five Orange Pips." *The Adventures of Sherlock Holmes*, George Newnes, 1892. *Project Gutenberg*, http://www.gutenberg.org/files/1661/1661-h/1661-h.htm. Accessed 21 July 2014.

Dunbar, Paul Laurence. "Frederick Douglass." *Poets.org*, http://www.poets.org/poetsorg/poem/frederick-douglass. Accessed 22 July 2014.

Feynman, Richard P. "The Value of Science." Address to the National Academy of Science, November 1955. *Engineering and Science*, vol. 19, no. 3, pp. 13-15, http://calteches.library.caltech.edu/40/2/Science.htm. Accessed 2 May 2014.

Forster, E. M. *A Room With a View*. 1908. *Project Gutenberg*, 31 Dec. 2008, http://www.gutenberg.org/files/2641/2641-h/2641-h.htm. Accessed 4 January 2014.

Frost, Robert. "Design." *The Poetry of Robert Frost*, edited by Edward Connery, *Poets.org*, http://www.poets.org/poetsorg/poem/design. Accessed 21 Dec. 2014.

Glaspell, Susan. *Trifles*. *Plays*, 1916. *Project Gutenberg*, 7 Jan. 2004, http://www.gutenberg.org/files/10623/10623-h/10623-h.htm. Accessed 24 July 2014.

Hawthorne, Nathaniel. *The Scarlet Letter*. *Project Gutenberg*, 15 May 2005, http://www.gutenberg.org/cache/epub/33/pg33-images.html. Accessed 12 Mar. 2014.

——. "Young Goodman Brown." *Mosses from an Old Manse and Other Stories*, Wiley, Putnam, and Waterloo Place, 1846. *Project Gutenberg*, 13 Sept. 2008, http://www.gutenberg.org/files/512/512-h/512-h.htm. Accessed 7 Mar. 2014.

Hayden, Robert. "Those Winter Sundays." *Collected Poems of Robert Hayden*, edited by Frederick Glaysher, 1985. *Poetry Foundation*, http://www.poetryfoundation.org/learning/guide/177415#poem. Accessed 22 July 2014.

Hemingway, Ernest. *The Sun Also Rises*. Scribner, 2006. *Internet Archive*, http://www.archive.org/stream/sunalsorises030276mbp/ sunalsorises030276mbp_djvu.txt. Accessed 10 June 2014.

Hughes, Langston. "The Weary Blues." *Collected Poems*, 1926. *Poetry Foundation*, http://www.poetryfoundation.org/poem/176785. Accessed 21 July 2014.

Keats, John. "Ode on a Grecian Urn." 1819. *Poetry Foundation*, http://www.poetryfoundation.org/poem/173742. Accessed 5 Aug. 2014.

Kinnell, Galway. "Blackberry Eating." *Mortal Acts, Mortal Words*, 1980. *Poetry Society of America*, https://www.poetrysociety.org/psa/poetry/ poetry_in_motion/atlas/chicago/blackberry_eating/. Accessed 22 July 2014.

Leland, Jacob Michael. "'Yes, That is a Roll of Bills in My Pocket': The Economy of Masculinity in The Sun Also Rises." *The Hemingway Review*, vol. 23, no. 2, 2nd edition, 2004, p. 37. *EBSCOhost*, libproxy.ung.edu/login?url=http://search.ebscohost.com/login.as px?direct=true&db=edsglr&AN=edsgcl.116861879&site=eds-live&scope=site. Accessed 12 Apr. 2014.

Lincoln, Abraham. "The Gettysburg Address." 19 Nov. 1863. "Bliss Copy." *Braham Lincoln Online*, http://abrahamlincolnonline.org/ lincoln/speeches/gettysburg.htm. Accessed 21 July 2014.

London, Jack. *The Sea-Wolf*. William Heinemann, transcribed from the 1917 William Heinemann edition by David Price, 1904. *Project Gutenberg*, 24 Dec. 2010, http://www.gutenberg.org/files/1074/1074-h/1074-h.htm. Accessed 4 Nov. 2013.

Moore, Marianne. "Poetry." *Others for 1919: An Anthology of the New Verse*, edited by Alfred Kreymborg, 1919. *Poets.org*, http://www. poets.org/poetsorg/poem/poetry. Accessed 21 July 2014.

Orwell, George. "Why I Write." *Fifty Orwell Essays*, 1946. *Project Gutenberg Australia*, Jan. 2003, http://gutenberg.net.au/ ebooks03/0300011.txt. Accessed 6 May 2014.

Poe, Edgar Allan. "Annabel Lee." *Poetry Foundation*, http://www. poetryfoundation.org/poem/174151. Accessed 22 July 2014.

Postman, Neil. "Of Luddites, Learning, and Life." *Technos Quarterly*, vol. 2, no. 4, Winter 1993, http://www.faculty.rsu.edu/users/f/felwell/www/Theorists/Postman/Articles/TECHNOS_NET.htm. Accessed 3 June 2014.

Roethke, Theodore. "My Papa's Waltz." *Collected Poems of Theodore Roethke*, 1942. *Poetry Foundation*, http://www.poetryfoundation.org/poem/172103. Accessed 22 July 2014.

Sedaris, David. "Old Lady Down the Hall." *Esquire*, 29 Jan. 2007, http://www.esquire.com/news-politics/a498/old-lady-hall-sedaris-1000/. Accessed 5 Feb. 2014.

Shakespeare, William. "Sonnet 130: My Mistress' Eyes Are Nothing Like the Sun." *The Norton Anthology of English Literature*, vol. 1, 7th edition, 2000. *Poetry Foundation*, http://www.poetryfoundation.org/poem/174375. Accessed 22 July 2014.

——. *The Tempest*. 1611. *Open Source Shakespeare*, http://www.opensourceshakespeare.org/views/plays/playmenu.php?WorkID=tempest. Accessed 25 July 2014.

Shelley, Mary Wollstonecraft. *Frankenstein; or The Modern Prometheus*. 1818. *Project Gutenberg*, 17 June 2008, http://www.gutenberg.org/files/84/84-h/84-h.htm. Accessed 22 Feb. 2014.

Thomas, Dylan. "Do Not Go Gentle into That Good Night." *The Poems of Dylan Thomas*, 1952. *Poets.org*, https://www.poets.org/poetsorg/poem/do-not-go-gentle-good-night. Accessed 22 July 2014.

Twain, Mark. *The Adventures of Huckleberry Finn*. Webster, 1885. *Project Gutenberg*, 20 Aug. 2006, http://www.gutenberg.org/files/76/76-h/76-h.htm. Accessed 4 Apr. 2014.

Woolf, Virginia. "The Death of the Moth." *The Death of the Moth and Other Essays*, Hogarth, 1942. *Project Gutenberg Australia*, Oct. 2012, http://gutenberg.net.au/ebooks12/1203811h.html. Accessed 14 Apr. 2014.

Wimsatt, William Upski. "How I Got My D.I.Y Degree." *Unte Reader*, May/June 1998. *Self Education Foundation*, http://selfeducationfoundation.wordpress.com/sef-history/diy-degree/. Accessed 7 Feb. 2014.